**REPORT
FROM
PRACTICALLY
NOWHERE**

OTHER BOOKS BY JOHN SACK:

The Butcher

From Here to Shimbashi

ILLUSTRATED BY SHEL SILVERSTEIN

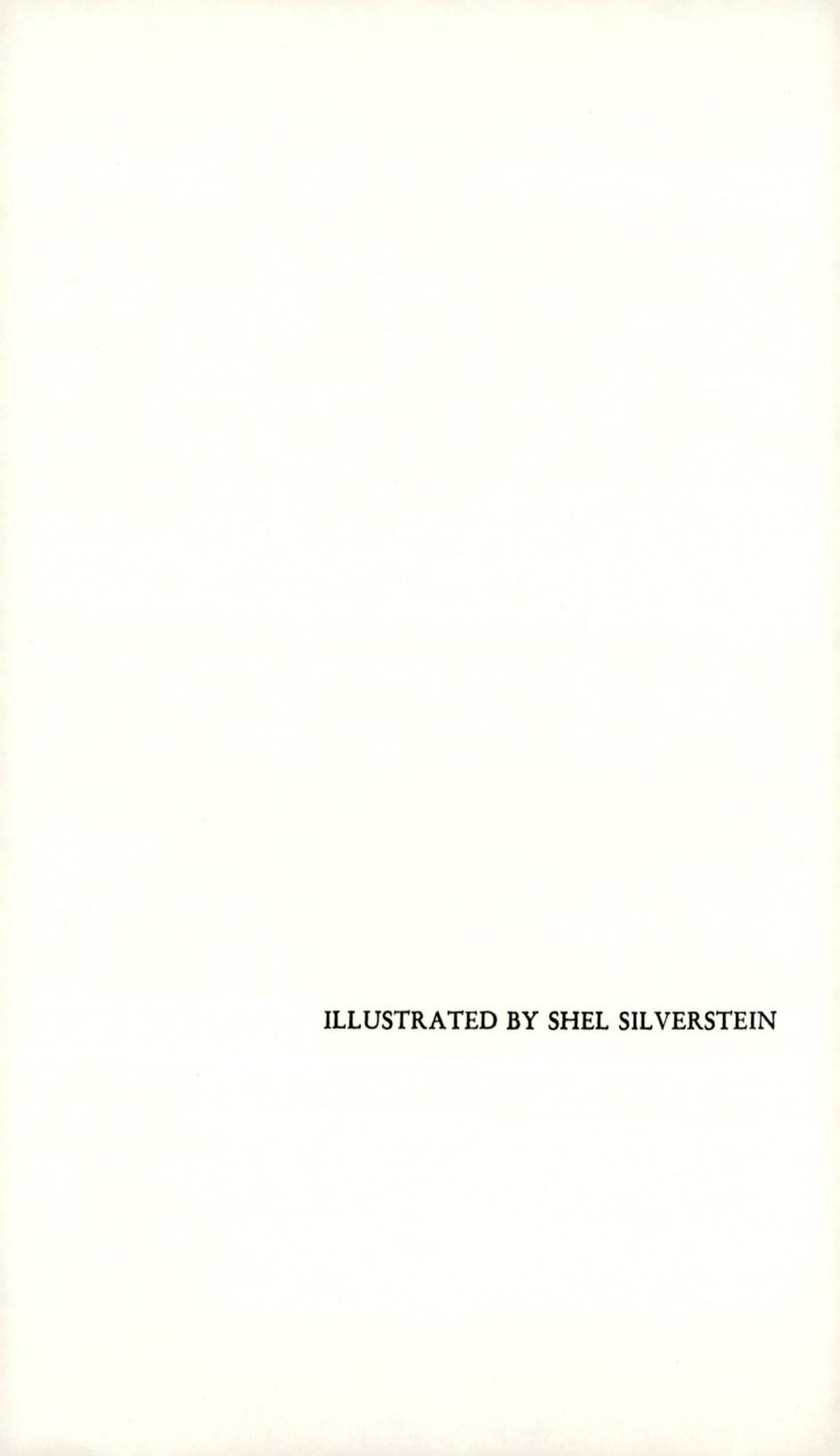

REPORT FROM PRACTICALLY NOWHERE

BY JOHN SACK

AN AUTHORS GUILD BACKINPRINT.COM EDITION

Report From Practically Nowhere
All Rights Reserved © 1955, 1956, 1957, 1958, 2000 by John Sack

No part of this book may be reproduced or transmitted in any form
or by any means, graphic, electronic, or mechanical, including photocopying,
recording, taping, or by any information storage or retrieval system,
without the permission in writing from the publisher.

AN AUTHORS GUILD BACKINPRINT.COM EDITION
Published by iUniverse.com, Inc.

For information address:
iUniverse.com, Inc.
620 North 48th Street, Suite 201
Lincoln, NE 68504-3467
www.iuniverse.com

Originally published by Harper & Brothers

All of the material in this book except for the chapter
entitled "Athos" has been previously published in shorter, somewhat
different forms. "Lundy" and "Swat" appeared in *Harper's Magazine*,
"Liechtenstein" in *Town and Country*, and "Punial" in *Holiday*.
All of the others originally appeared in *Playboy*.

ISBN: 0-595-08918-6

Printed in the United States of America

For Joan Rubinstein Urdan

CONTENTS

LUNDY 4

SARK 26

ANDORRA 43

ix

MONACO	69
LIECHTENSTEIN	84
SAN MARINO	114
THE S.M.O.M.	132
ATHOS	148
SHARJA	164
SWAT	182
AMB	193
PUNIAL	202
SIKKIM	217

REPORT

FROM

PRACTICALLY

NOWHERE

Lundy . . . Sark . . . Andorra . . . Monaco . . .

Looking back on it, I can't remember any countries further from my mind as I started around the world on that so long-anticipated summer's evening in 1955. To tell the truth, I hadn't heard of most of them. I was going abroad, or so I thought, to see the sights of England, Italy, Egypt, India; to see the sights everybody sees; to see the world before it's all gone. I'd managed to save enough money for this, and I'd started east on Pan American World Airways. The very next day, though, something happened. ". . . the Bristol Channel," our stewardess was saying as I woke up, "and, sir, if you'll look over there it's England, and over there is Wales, and over *there*"—I rubbed my eyes open, and she pointed from the airplane to a faraway, foggy island—"is Lundy."

"Lundy?" I said; and that was the end of my well-laid plans. For Lundy, the stewardess explained, is a little country —a little gray, windswept country inhabited by untold thousands of rabbits and birds, notably puffins, and by a dozen or so gray, windswept human beings who stoutly maintain that its sovereign is a king by the name of Mr. Harman. Great Britain, she continued, a larger and more heavily populated country twelve miles away, stoutly and antithetically maintains that its sovereign is a queen by the name of Elizabeth II. "And I," the stewardess said. "*I* would have hoped that something as vital as this would have been settled *ages* ago, but the terrible fact, I'm afraid, is Lundy's status still is up in the air after eight hundred years of yeses and noes. In fact, it was still using its own postage stamps the last I heard." So saying, the stewardess buzzed off and, like a mother octopus, began to wake up the sleepy, feed the hungry, play with the kids, and minister to the lame and halt, and I was left to look in wonder at that faraway implausibility of Lundy. A little country? A king by the name of Mr. Harman? What the Sam Hill, I wondered, is coming off in Lundy? And then the plane landed in London, and I hurried to Lundy to find out.

That was the start of a glad, somewhat mad, and quite out-of-the-ordinary trip around the world. In Lundy, I happened to hear of Sark—the only feudal state surviving in Europe, according to the feudal old lady running it—and I couldn't help hurrying to Sark, and I couldn't help hurrying to Andorra, and I couldn't help finding myself, soon, on a trip to practically nowhere, to the countries nobody hears of. Well, it's years later, and I still haven't seen the London Bridge, the Eiffel Tower, the Pyramids, or the Black Hole of Calcutta—but I've seen the Wali of Swat, and I've played a little "seven-and-a-half" in Andorra with a bullfighter, a dozen smugglers, and a blonde; I've suffered from an explosion in a salami-skin factory in Liechtenstein; I've caroused with a fellow who thought he was a monkey in Athos; I've eaten an eyeball lying on the floor in Sharja; I've watched a man choking a polo player in Punial; and I've stumbled on the smallest country there is, next door to a haberdashery shop. And this is a book about them—an account of thirteen no-account countries.

The importance of these places can hardly be underestimated. Each of them has ambassadors, passports, visas, or customs —but nobody knows it. Each of them is autonomous—but nobody cares. For me, however, each of them was a wonderful and a not-at-all wasted stop. As Captain Lemuel Gulliver found out in 1699, and as I found out in 1955, 1956, and 1957, the microcosm is just the macrocosm seen up close. We shouldn't ever laugh too easily at Lilliput: we may be laughing at ourselves.

"Lundy is a vest-pocket-size, self-governing dominion."

—THE KING OF LUNDY.

LUNDY

In Lundy's case, I also found out that it's very, very confusing to happen to live in Lundy. Not the least of this confusion was in 1929, I learned, when Mr. Harman, the King, or Non-king, depending on whose side you're on, started issuing his own coins as well as his own postage stamps and, shortly after, was hauled into court on the neighboring island for allegedly violat-

4

LUNDY

ing its Coinage Act of 1870. The trial was held on January 13, 1931, at the King's Bench Division of the High Court of Justice, in London, and, it was hoped at the time, would settle the status of Lundy once and for all. It didn't—but it did show how utterly confused the situation was. In his defense, Mr. Harman said he had every right to mint money, for Lundy, in his words, was "a vest-pocket-size, self-governing dominion," out of the realm for every practical purpose. The Lundy residents, he pointed out, never had paid any taxes to England and were liable to customs when they went there, for Lundy itself was a free port. The Attorney General, who was prosecuting Mr. Harman, said that Lundy was surely a Utopia but that its inhabitants would be just as happy if the face of King George V, rather than of Mr. Harman, were depicted on the place's currency. (Mr. Harman's face was on the front of the coins, and that of a puffin on the back. There were two denominations, a one-puffin coin and a half-puffin coin, neatly convertible to a penny and a ha'penny at the legal rate of exchange. The postage stamps were in several denominations, the twelve-puffin stamp portraying twelve puffins, the nine-puffin stamp nine puffins, the six-puffin stamp six puffins, etc., and the half-puffin stamp half a puffin—the upper half.) The Attorney General also noted that Lundy was specifically listed in the Wild Birds Protection Order of 1930 as part of England, but Mr. Harman replied, in effect, that the Wild Birds Protection Order could specifically list China, too, and it wouldn't mean a thing—"It wouldn't cut any ice" were his exact words. Furthermore, Mr. Harman said, there weren't any policemen in Lundy, and the laws of England weren't enforced there, but the Attorney General rebutted that a policeman went there as recently as December 18, 1871, to arrest a murderer, to which Mr. Harman surrebutted that the Attorney General's rebutter was all wrong. All this, and more of the same, was heard by the Lord Chief Justice, Mr. Justice Avory, and Mr. Justice MacKinnon with an attitude of intense mirth, and anyone studying a transcript of the trial soon real-

A little country inhabited by untold thousands of rabbits
and birds, notably puffins, and by a dozen or so human beings.

izes that Mr. Harman, the defendant, was the only person there who took it at all seriously. The following excerpt is typical:

MR. HARMAN: The mainland did not interfere when Lundy was reasonably well governed. And it repudiated all responsibility when anything really called for investigation, like the murder of the whole population.
THE LORD CHIEF JUSTICE: Does that often happen? [*Laughter.*]
MR. HARMAN: It happened two or three times in the past.
MR. JUSTICE AVORY: The population of what? Rabbits? [*Laughter.*]
MR. HARMAN: There are about one thousand rabbits to every human being, but the residents number about forty-five, apart from visitors.

Such arguments as these having been heard, the justices deliberated and then handed down the opinion that it had been a very entertaining case—it was to *them*—which had been lost by Mr. Harman. They ordered Mr. Harman to take his puffins out of circulation and to pay a fine of twenty-five dollars, which Mr. Harman did.

That was 1931. Today, a quarter of a century later, the residents of Lundy *still* aren't paying any taxes, and still are liable to customs when they go to England. There aren't any policemen in Lundy, and the laws of England aren't enforced. Lundy is still using its own postage stamps, and a letter cannot be gotten off it without one, and Mr. Harman's coins, which he priced at a penny and a ha'penny when they were legal tender, are considered, nowadays, to be historical relics, and are sold in Lundy to tourists and numismatists for forty-eight times as much. Mr. Harman is dead, but his son, Mr. Albion Harman, has succeeded him, and he stoutly maintains that Lundy is "a vest-pocket-size, self-governing dominion," out of the realm for every practical purpose.

Unfortunately, I wasn't able to attend the trial in 1931 (I was ten months old), but in 1955, as soon as I'd landed by Pan American World Airways in London, I was able to attend to

Mr. Harman, and I decided to look him up and learn how Lundy finds itself in such a curious position. Mr. Harman is a healthy middle-aged man with a quiet smile and a spray of unkempt white hair and, when I met him at Soho Square, he was himself in a curious position—sitting amidst a pile of junk in his old, weather-beaten auto. He told me that he worked, in London, as a mining engineer for the Maschaba Rhodesian Company and the Balakhany Black Sea Oil Company and that he used the car on geological field trips, which accounted for its condition. Presently, we decided to continue our chat at a nearby pub, and we drove to one of Mr. Harman's favorites, the Horse and Groom, ordering a Worthington apiece. Worthington, Mr. Harman said, is the only beer or ale aging right in the bottle, and he started to explain how this singular chemical process occurs, when I steered the conversation to Lundy; at this, he revealed that he visits the place once or twice a month, that he enjoys it hugely, and that its sovereign status arises from the English penchant for keeping things just as they always were. In 1135, Mr. Harman said, Lundy belonged to the King of England, but in that year he gave it to the Marisco family, one of England's foremost. Since then, it has belonged, essentially, to whoever was there at the time, a heterogeneous group that includes not only the Mariscos and the Mr. Harmans, father and son, but also a Reverend Mr. Heaven and *his* son; a smuggler named Benson; a pirate named Salkeld; a pirate named Nutt, who still haunts the place; and other pirates of Turkey, Spain, France, and Holland, the last of whom murdered the whole population in the 1700's to the immense amusement of the Lord Chief Justice in 1931.

Continuing his story, Mr. Harman said the Mariscos had no sooner gotten hold of Lundy, in 1135, than they began to assert its independence, getting up an army and navy and raiding the English coast off and on for ninety-nine years. Eventually they went too far, though, when they got somebody to try assassinating the king. (Holinshed describes it this way: "A learned Esquire, or rather a Clearke, of the Universiti of Oxford, bearing some

LUNDY

malice towar the King, fained himsel madde and espying thereby the secrete places of his house at Woodstocke, where he then lay, upon a night by a windowe, he gote into the King's bedchamber and coming to the bed's side threw off the coverings, and with a knife strake divers times into a pillowe, supposing the King had been there but, as God would, that night the King lay in another chamber with ye Queene.") The King, Henry III, having been woken up and apprised of this, sent a few soldiers to scale Lundy at night. Sir William de Marisco was taken prisoner, dragged by a horse's tail to the Tower of London, hanged, drawn, and quartered, the pieces being sent to England's four leading cities as a warning to other potential evil-doers, and Lundy was given to some other Mariscos, of all people, who began raiding England themselves. By the 1600's, Lundy was a sovereign den of pirates, Mr. Harman told me, and by 1748 it was the den of Mr. Thomas Benson, a smuggler, gambler, and member of Parliament who fired on any ship that didn't dip its colors. Benson also contracted with England to ship some of its convicts "over the sea," presumably to Maryland or Virginia; instead, he shipped them to Lundy, and the island's sovereign, transoceanic status was upheld in an English court. (Some years later, Benson was caught in the act of barratry and fled.) In all these years, Parliament never butted into Lundy's affairs or tried to tax it, feeling, apparently, it was too far away to bother with, and so setting a precedent that still obtains.

Next, Mr. Harman recalled that the pirates of Lundy had enacted a total of two laws, and said that nowadays its body of legislation still is admirably brief. The laws of the pirates were these: "The man who shall snap his arms or smoke tobacco in the hold or carry a lighted candle without lanthorn shall receive Moses' law [forty lashes]. If any man meet with a prudent woman that offers to meddle with her, without her consent, he shall suffer death." The laws of contemporary Lundy, Mr. Harman said, are a few letters and scribbled notes that he and his father left about. The first time they were codified was today, by me, and as follows:

THE LAWS OF LUNDY

ARTICLE I. Nobody can come here if Mr. Harman doesn't want him to.
ARTICLE II. Anybody with a gun must give it to Mr. Gade before it gets dark.
ARTICLE III. Nobody can shoot any birds, especially puffins.
ARTICLE IV. Everybody's dog must be of the same sex, and visitors can't have any dogs at all.
ARTICLE V. Anything else, ask Mr. Harman.

A few explanatory notes and judicial interpretations on this body of law seem to be called for at this point. Article I, Mr. Harman told me, has resulted in a blacklist of a dozen-odd people who are forever barred from Lundy—for example, a trawlerman who used naughty language there, an alcoholic, a homosexual. Article IV, the anti-dog statute, is to stop their proliferating about the island, and the sex that everybody's dog currently must be is female. Article II, firearms, was enacted when two of the islanders were feuding over a lady friend: but that was 1927, and Mr. Gade doesn't enforce it any more. Mr. Gade, I learned, is Mr. Harman's viceroy and the King of Lundy *pro tem*, as well as the postmaster, innkeeper, grocer, bartender, Lloyd's of London agent, Volunteer-in-Charge of the Rocket Life Saving Apparatus, and official representative of the Shipwrecked Fishermen and Mariners Society or the Shipwrecked Mariners and Fishermen Society—no one can remember which, including Mr. Gade. Also, Mr. Gade is judge and jury at Lundy's trials, of which, historically, there have been two, a civil one and a criminal one. In the civil action, he handed down a writ of mandamus directing everyone at the dock to divvy up their tips, and in the criminal one he fined a visitor five dollars for bringing a dog in, in contravention of Article IV. The corpus delicti, incidentally, a chowchow, got lost in Lundy soon afterwards. It was discovered in a cleft of rock, dead, thereby demonstrating to the satisfaction of everyone resident in Lundy the simple, laconic wisdom of their country's legislation.

LUNDY

Having familiarized myself with the laws of the realm, and having thanked Mr. Harman for the interview, and for the Worthington, I went to Lundy itself. Once, a three-seater plane had gone there—at various times it was called the Lundy and Atlantic Airlines, the North Devon Flying Club, and Devon Air Ltd.—but a bit earlier it had fallen into the Atlantic, and the only way to Lundy was now a boat, a big white paddle-wheeler that made the trip every two or three days from Ilfracombe, the British equivalent of Atlantic City, if one can imagine such a thing. The journey took one and a half hours. Ilfracombe was sun-drenched as I left it, a hill of pretty cottages above a gaudy, honky-tonk beach, but the sky was cloudier as I neared Lundy, and a cold drizzle was falling when, finally, I saw it. Lundy was like an immense aircraft carrier seen in the mist. It is three miles long, roughly half a mile wide, and its granite sides are like the Palisades: and yet, I learned, the sea spray goes over the top in the heavy gales. At such times, hundreds of ships have gone aground there, including a battleship on its maiden voyage, but thousands of others have hidden from the storms on the leeward, eastern side of the island. It was here that our paddle-wheeler laid anchor, a little way from the shore; gray motorboats came out to meet us, bobbing on the waves like some of the one-shilling rides at Ilfracombe; and the passengers disembarked.

There were seven hundred passengers. Except for me, they were excursionists who would pass the afternoon in Lundy and return to Ilfracombe on the paddle-wheeler. I am utterly unable to account for such an extravagant number of them, and, after studying their behavior at close range in Lundy itself—they looked at one or two pigs there, had a beer, and that's all—I find it even more mysterious. A tourist's lot is a hard one almost anywhere, but in Lundy his adversities are of epic proportions. Many of the seven hundred were seasick; the drizzle fell on them, and the ocean slapped over the flimsy wooden pier, soaking their skirts and trousers. A man fell into the water, and a middle-aged lady who had endured some unknown misfortune on shore was carried back to the paddle-wheeler all bloody, as the rest of us were getting off it. Most of these tourists, I gathered, had been enticed to Lundy by a small yellow handbill, circulated in Ilfracombe by the paddle-wheeler company, which said, in no uncertain terms, that a voyage to the island is something "which every holiday-maker should make . . . an excursion which is unrivalled anywhere." Lundy itself does not advertise, although it did once, sticking the signs RECOVER YOUR POISE ON LUNDY all over the London Tube. That was in 1939, when very few people in London had any poise left; scarcely two of them had recovered it on Lundy, when the war broke out.

The seven hundred tourists bore their crosses stoically. Huffing and hawing, they climbed the palisades by a steep, switchback trail and hurried to the island's only gay spot, the Marisco Tavern; they pressed inside like subway riders, and they were given beer furiously by a gaunt, eminently harried man whom I took to be Mr. Gade. Mr. Gade was afforded no quarter by the tourists: as postmaster he was being called on for postage stamps, as grocer for fig newtons and crumpets, as bartender for beer, and all the while his assistant, Audrey, was being hectored for puffin bookends, puffin ash trays, and plaster puffins of no apparent utilitarian value. The tiny tavern was full of smoke and noise: of men calling for beer, of plaster puffins falling to the floor, of a boy crying, "Buy a pennant, Mommy, so they'll know we've been to Lundy." ("Hush, dear, we already have a puffin.") I surveyed the Doré-like scene for a minute or two, and then I pushed outside for a breath of air. The drizzle had stopped, and the sunlight was falling in party streamers; the island of Lundy dried beneath it, a desolate plain of scrub, stones, and faraway gray sheep. The color of everything was gray—the stones, the gray abandoned lighthouse, the Marisco Tavern and the ashen houses near it, the church—an island that was built of rain clouds. I strolled to the edge of the cliff and saw the sunlight's glare on the water, a hundred yards below. And then I returned to the Marisco

LUNDY

Tavern; the tourists had left, and Mr. Gade, Audrey, and two or three islanders were sitting quietly in the darkness, desperately trying to recover their poise.

Now the Marisco Tavern was a friendly, easygoing place, and these people made it so. Mr. Gade, using all the slow deliberation of a bartender pouring a pousse-café, had filled his pipe, and he was leaning against the gray stone wall, cheerily smoking it; the others were sitting with beer mugs in their laps and talking idly of the unimportant, important things of life. They were dressed in plaid shirts and disintegrating pin-stripe suits; their faces were stubbled, weather-beaten. The Captain and Charlie, who ran the boats at the waterfront, came from there in black turtleneck sweaters, nodded for a beer apiece, and started throwing darts at a raggedy bull's-eye, beginning each of their games with an esoteric cry of "Middle for diddle!" or "Muggs away!" A few others drifted in, and every now and then the gathering raised its glasses, toasting itself with enthusiasm: *"All* the very *best!"*

"All the *very* best," cried Charlie, at the dart board, "and muggs away!"

It was a friendly crowd, and I saw that everyone was liked by everyone else. Afterwards, I learned these dozen or so full-time residents work at the tavern, like Mr. Gade and Audrey, or at the waterfront, like the Captain and Charlie, or at the new north and south lighthouses; or they are retired and never work at all. They call themselves the "islanders," as distinguished from the seven hundred "trippers," or "bluebottles," who just had left. (A bluebottle, my dictionary explains, is a *Calliphora erythrocephala,* a pesky insect that flies about in circles, going buzz.) A third category, halfway between the "islanders" and the "bluebottles," are the members of the Lundy Field Society, who migrate there when the birds do, and of the Lundy Lodgers, who vacation there for several weeks at a time and whose rites of initiation into the L. L. are a dreadful secret that wild horses couldn't drag from them. These people—islanders, ornithologists, Lundy Lodgers, and

13

occasional bluebottles who missed the boat—gather every night at the Marisco Tavern. Saturday night is an especially gala one; the tavern is open until all hours, something unheard-of on the neighboring island, and the rules of admittance are "sing, story, or shake"—sing a song, tell a story, or shake your pockets empty.

It was such a Saturday night a few days later. By eight o'clock, the Marisco Tavern was full of every variety of person: dart players, bird watchers, Lundy Lodgers, lighthouse keepers, small fry, old salts, brothers-in-law of Mr. Harman, authors, all of us drinking beer and getting along fine. Audrey, the girl who sold puffinware, sat herself at a piano, and we all sang "Home on the Range" and "The Whiffenpoof Song"; then, "What d'ya say you jive it, Audrey, up a bit?" cried Charlie, and we all sang "Tavern in the Town," "Oh Landlord, Fill the Flowing Bowl," and two choruses of "The Halls of Montezuma." It was sing, story, or shake time at ten o'clock; a retired sea dog with a vivid, animated face began it, singing the ballad of Alfonso Spugoni, a bullfighter who had behaved in the same caddish fashion as the man on the flying trapeze:

> *When I catch Alfonso Spugoni, the toreador,*
> *With one mighty swipe I will dislocate his bally jaw,*
> *I'll fight the bullfighter, I will,*
> *When I catch the bounder, the blighter I'll kill,*
> *He shall die. . . .*

Whenever the old sailor came to this particular point, he swiped himself on the jaw. Next, Mr. Gade was called upon, and he maintained the toreador theme by singing "Flow Gently, Sweet Afton" in a voice that occasionally is heard in Spain, emanating from mortally wounded bulls. I, being an American, was asked to get a fiddle somewhere and call a square dance, and after many remonstrances on my part, all unsuccessful, I agreed to do a Charleston instead, with Mr. Harman's sister. *She* ducked out of the room and reappeared soon as a flapper, and she

LUNDY

stood at the bar, kicking her heels. The children took part, too. Dressed in bed sheets and hideous masks cut from the back of Corn Flakes boxes, they swooped down on the tavern, said "Whooo! Whooo!" and then, in a precise, English accent, "Have we managed to frighten you?" A birthday cake for Mrs. Gade was brought in, a happy birthday was sung, a good time was had by all, and there were cries until early in the morning of *"All* the very *best!"*

Lundy seemed like such a delightful place to be that I wondered, naturally, how the Harman family had managed to come by it. I asked about this the next day, and I learned that the late Mr. Harman—Mr. Harman I, or "M.C.H.," as his subjects knew him—had set his heart on Lundy when only a bluebottle, aged eighteen, and finally had bought it in 1925 for eighty thousand dollars, a thousand times what it went for in the Mariscos' days. Until then, Lundy had been owned and operated by the Reverend Mr. Heaven, and it was known as the Kingdom of Heaven, of course, while the voyage to Lundy was known as Purgatory. The island, I also learned, has gone by many other names historically, but all of them sound decidedly like Lundy—Landy, Londi, Londey, Londay, Lounday, Lunday, Lundeia, Londia, and Londai—and scholars have just as many explanations of the word, one of the more extravagant being that of Westcote, who suggested, in 1646, that it was "island" backwards. Other scholars say it's the Norse for "grove," although there is scarcely a tree in sight; the truth, apparently, about the word "Lundy" is that it's from the Icelandic *lundi,* meaning puffin, and *ey,* meaning island, and so it means Puffin Island. Etymologically, then, we must note that "Lundy Island" is a tautology, and that a resident is properly a Lundyskeggi, two or more of them being Lundyskeggjar. The late Mr. M. C. Harman was in the forefront of the battle against the ungrammatical use of "Lundy Island," and, a few years before his death, he wrote an impassioned letter to the Lundy Field Society about it, saying, "The uninitiated often refer to

Lundy as Lundy Island, forgetting that *lundi* means puffin and *y* or *ey* means island. I hope members will help me to combat this practice. As the British Post Office insist on perpetuating the error we shall never quite succeed, but we can at least do our best." It is not recorded, however, that Mr. Harman ever called himself a Lundyskeggi.

Another battle in whose forefront Mr. Harman invariably was, was that for Lundy's continued independence. He wrote to the Lundy Field Society about that, too; the British, it seems, had put some of the Lundyskeggjar on their voting rolls, and he furiously penned the following: "They just don't want the vote. They want to be left alone. I ask for the support of the members of the society in the resistance I propose to offer to having these unwanted votes forced down our necks." In other years, Mr. Harman had ordered the British coast guard off his island, ordered the British postmaster off, ordered three officers of the British army, navy, and air force off and demanded, and was given, a formal apology from the War Office for their having been there, and, of course, issued his own, non-British money and postage stamps. Mr. Harman's stamps are still the tangible sign of Lundy's independence. The original ones, whose value could be determined by adding up the puffins, or partial puffins, thereon, have been succeeded by four more imaginative sets portraying such eminent non-puffins as Eric Bloodaxe, Mrs. Graham in her aerial balloon, and Betty Brown, a horse; a complete set is worth about one hundred and twenty dollars in philatelic circles. The stamps will get a letter from Lundy to the dock at Ilfracombe, and anyone who hopes to see them gotten farther must stick on British ones, too. The British stamps, or "postage," are put on the front, and the Lundy ones, or "puffinage," are put in back, something that would relegate them to the status of tuberculosis seals if they weren't dutifully canceled by Mr. Gade, the country's concurrent postmaster and puffinmaster.

So much has been said, on these pages, of non-puffins, half-puffins, puffinage, puffinware, and puffinmasters that a word or two about the puffin itself seems to be called for. Puffins, in Lundy, are there in the spring and early summer, and as I was there in the late summer we missed one another; I was told, though, by the islanders that they are a small, black-and-white sea bird with an unbelievable beak of every color, a singing voice that somewhat resembles Mr. Gade's, and a gait like a rolling ship. Further research turned up the news that puffins were eaten in the Middle Ages; that they themselves eat animals 98.22 percent of the time and algae 1.78 percent of the time, that they are popularly known as sea parrots, Lundy parrots, tommie noddies, tammy nories, and bottlenoses, and taxonomically as *Fratercula arctica*—"little arctic brother." A great deal of what is known about puffins, and Lundy's puffins especially, was learned there in 1939 by Mr. Richard Perry, a naturalist who went about it with the same patience and self-abnegation that characterized the Curies. For eighteen weeks, Mr. Perry did little else but sit on a rock, looking at puffins, and eventually he developed as intimate a fellowship with them as could be expected in two beings of such widely disparate species. At first, the puffins were quite embarrassed by his attentions—Mr. Perry confesses how they would frequently break off their love-making "for a moment's reflection or a sheepish look around"—but finally, when they realized that Mr. Perry could not be shamed into withdrawal and had become, indeed, a rather permanent fixture in their lives, they began "to ring me round . . . conducting their various little intimacies, indifferent to my presence, so suspect to most wild birds; so that I was conscious of what was, perhaps, man's true relationship with beasts and birds. Here was tranquillity."

Once this true relationship had been established between Mr. Perry and puffin, the former observed that the latter like to kiss one another rapturously with their extraordinary bills, and he remarked, "This most vigorous and prolonged performance was an abiding joy, and remains my most vivid memory of puffins." It should be stressed, of course, that Mr. Perry merely observed this activity and didn't participate in it; however, he was joined in his spectator capacity by a good number of leisured puffins, who, presently, were not only kissing each other but were kissing the initial kisser's wife or being themselves kissed by *him*—as idyllic a scene as one could wish. Theorizing, Mr. Perry said the bills of puffins exude a kind of nectar pleasurable to other puffins. After several days of this behavior, the birds "were approaching their zenith of emotional excitement," and Mr. Perry was also approaching his— but then the puffins flew bashfully to sea to mate, and Mr. Perry ruefully concedes that "I only saw one attempt, and that unsuccessful, at a mating on a boulder: the hen puffin running around it, with the cock balancing precariously on her stern with wildly fanning wings. This was evidently an abnormal procedure." Mr. Perry doesn't cast any judgments on his *own* procedure at the time, but he does say that the puffins' procedure results in a little egg and, subsequently, a baby puffin.

In biological circles, Lundy is noted not only for the puffin but for a kind of cabbage, supposedly the ancestor of every cabbage; Dr. F. R. Elliston Wright, a botanist, came upon it several years ago while walking to the Marisco Tavern, subsequently naming it *Brasicella wrightii* in his own honor. Some Welsh ponies, Norwegian rats, and Japanese deer are also at large in Lundy; two kangaroos were tried there with Mr. Harman's permission (see Article V), but they hopped, respectively, into a well and into the Atlantic; snakes, lizards, frogs, toads, and salamanders don't exist, and the *National Geographic* of May, 1947, says there aren't any bacteria, either. Besides puffins, one hundred and forty-five species of birds inhabit Lundy, and many others visit it from time to time, including such transoceanic rarities as the Sardinian warbler and the American robin. Personally I'm not a practicing bird watcher, and none of this stuff especially fascinates me, but, I realize, there are readers of mine whom it does, who are anxious to hear even more, and, for their benefit, I have studied some of the voluminous ornithological logs that were kept in Lundy for many centuries, and I have recorded in the next paragraph, and in no particular order, a few of the sightings that seem of

LUNDY

more than routine interest. It is a paragraph that people, like me, who aren't markedly fond of birds are well advised to ignore.

Lundy, anyhow, I learned from my readings, has been visited by such exotic feathered creatures as the great auk, the great tit, the twite, knot, teal, stint, snipe, shag, rook, wigeon, and wood pigeon, as well as by two apparently distinct species, the chaffinch and the chiffchaff. The chaffinches were seen in great profusion at lunchtime, September 3, 1880, and a year later one was caught by a fellow named Ward, who gave it to Annie. The chiffchaff, for its part, was duly noted, but escaped captivity, from March 12 to October 23, 1954, and a fate worse than a chaffinch's was meted to a gray phalarope on December 9, 1881, when it was shot by W.B.; Cecilia Harriet Heaven called it "an evil deed," and so do I. Mr. Norman H. Joy saw an arctic skua on August 22, 1905. "A lady visitor," writes Loyd, in a memorandum on the reed warbler, "insisted she saw birds of this species daily in a certain spot. . . . A very careful search on many occasions failed to reveal the bird, and the assertion of its presence must be accepted with great reserve." Mr. Norman H. Joy saw a cirl bunting on an unspecified day in April, 1906, and Mr. Perry looked up from his puffins on May 20, 1939, to observe a plover of some sort; he hadn't decided *what* sort when he was at his puffins again. A peregrine falcon was recorded in 1274 A.D. and an albatross on June 13, 1874, but, I think, the assertion of its presence must be accepted with great reserve. Crespi saw a goshawk, but Loyd says he is "obviously in error," and Hendy saw a tree pipit, but Davenport says, "As may be imagined, we saw no tree pipits"; the consensus on yellow wagtails is three to four, with Perry, Davenport, and an unnamed bluebottle maintaining the affirmative; Crespi, Rousham, Ross, and Cummings upholding the negative; and Loyd keeping his own counsel on the matter. On September 23, 1954, a spotted flycatcher caught a butterfly and hit its head against a tree, and in October, 1874, a yellow-billed cuckoo hit *its* head against a tree and dropped

19

dead, after flying non-stop from the United States. Jack snipes, by way of contrast, have been hitting their heads against a lighthouse, while the foghorn there has frightened away the choughs, which were "as common as crows" in 1860, and the gannets, which were as common as choughs in 1321 A.D. A nightjar sang at 10:30 in the evening, May 30, 1922. Bluebottles in Lundy have reported nightingales, white-tailed eagles, and lesser gray shrikes, but nobody ever believed them, and in 1953 a cook at the Lundy Field Society reported a pelican, and everybody laughed and laughed. Well, it *was* a pelican; it had just escaped from the Bristol zoo.

While W.B., the lighthouse, and the foghorn have played, of course, an unparalleled role in the lives, respectively, of the gray phalarope, the jack snipe, and the gannet, there surely hasn't been anything of such profound consequence to the average bird of Lundy as the founding of the Lundy Field Society there, in 1946. Since then, the birds have scarcely known a moment to call their own. Not only are they kept under a constant surveillance that would be reserved anywhere else for suspected criminals, but a full blotter is being maintained on their comings and goings, their associations with other birds, their sexual indiscretions, and such intimate details of personal hygiene as even Mr. Perry would blush at, such as the name, number, and whereabouts of their body lice. Many of these birds, after a dozen years of such scant privacy, are beginning to betray the same signs of nervous collapse that

LUNDY

might be expected in a human being. A case in point is the Manx shearwater, a shy, rather introverted bird whose mental state became so desperate that the elder Mr. Harman had to memorialize the Lundy Field Society on its behalf. "This particular colony," he wrote, "has suffered from rats, but has also suffered a bit from being over-birdwatched. I don't take any exception to this, for it is all in the cause of science, but I understand that not a single bird hatched."

Mr. Harman's charitable attitude toward the Lundy Field Society seems to have been tempered, at the start, with an uneasy suspicion of its real motives. When the idea of the society was broached to him, in 1946, by its moving spirit, Professor L. A. Harvey of University College, Exeter, his reply "was only mildly encouraging, as well it might be," the professor said. "But it was not actively *dis*couraging." Later, though, Mr. Harman had braver second thoughts, and he not only invited the Lundy Field Society to Lundy but gave it two hundred and fifty dollars, its first subscription, and the abandoned lighthouse to live in. Today, the lighthouse is still the society's roost, being inhabited in the migrating season by a half-dozen earnest bird watchers and in every season by Miss Barbara K. Whittaker, its warden, a young, personable, studious woman whose tireless devotion to the birds is regarded by the present Mr. Harman with the same uneasy suspicion that his father once had.

The first I'd seen of Miss Whittaker was from the paddle-wheeler the day I came: she was sitting on the beach beneath a rotted, upturned rowboat and peering into the drizzle with grim intensity, swallow-watching. A little later, I visited her native habitat, the lighthouse, and I met Miss Whittaker more formally, and she, in turn, introduced me to several other bird watchers there and to Mr. Oliver Hook, a lively old Englishman who watches seals but hasn't anything in particular against birds. The lighthouse itself was a perfect chaos: of tables and rickety orange crates, of dirty dishes, of unwrapped butter, marmalade tins, Spam cans, and dismembered bits of liverwurst and baloney, of shaggy, gray-green books in topless heaps, of bulletin boards, broadsides, and ornithological pinups, and, in the interstices of all this, moving guardedly, of Miss Whittaker and the bird watchers, all of them wearing baggy woolen sweaters and looking absolutely in the pink of health. The bird watchers, for the most part, were eating liverwurst, and Miss Whittaker was writing assiduously in the daily log. I saw that her entry was a curious one, this:

WEDNESDAY, SEPT. 7. Oliver Hook arrived. O.H. entered straight way into L.F.S. activities and visited Seal Hole with B.K.W., where a calf about 24 hours old was found. The spirited young lady left her imprint on O.H.

Puzzled by this, I asked O.H. for a fuller explanation, and hastily was told that the spirited young lady referred to wasn't Miss Whittaker but the seal, and that the imprint was of its teeth —by now, a terrifying purple welt on his forearm. Mr. Hook assured me it wasn't malignant and, when I inquired about the seal, observed it had been shooed away by splashing water in its face, apparently, in Lundy, the accepted procedure for shooing away seals. Later, Mr. Hook said, he managed to get the seal again, weigh it, measure it, and tag it for future reference with a small aluminum band. Both parties to the operation had set a record for Lundy, the seal being the first of its species to be tagged by a human being, and Mr. Hook being the first of his to be bitten by a seal.

For the time being, Mr. Hook said, he proposed leaving the seals to their own devices and investigating the birds, instead, and, if possible, even catching some for more particularized study. The idea of catching a bird rather fascinated me, and, although I confessed I wouldn't know how to begin, he invited me along, and Miss Whittaker came too. When we left the lighthouse, it was late afternoon, and the setting sunlight swept across the island like a wind. Below us, the beach already was in twilight; sea gulls circled in the warmth above it, and

LUNDY

black cormorants stood on rocks, spreading their wings like Prussian eagles. Miss Whittaker, Mr. Hook, and I walked silently for ten minutes and came, presently, to a heavy thicket of bramble and stones, rising like a dinosaur out of which was an extraordinary contrivance of wire fences, wood, and ropes, of doors and pulleys moaning in the breeze. This, Miss Whittaker said cheerfully, was a Heligoland bird trap, the most serviceable kind there is. I stared astonishedly at the Heligoland bird trap, estimating it one hundred feet long, thirty feet wide, and eight feet high—roughly one million times as large as the average bird.

Presently, Miss Whittaker saw my dismay, and observed that a Heligoland bird trap—although such elemental devices as dead herrings, balls of wool, and W.B.'s rifle had been used instead—is superior to any of these because of the sheer intricacy of its mechanism, which only the most erudite of birds could hope to grasp. Its proper utilization begins, she continued, when she thrashes about in the bramble and frightens a bird into the trap, shutting a screen door behind it. The bird flies about in consternation, and more and more screen doors are closed by Miss Whittaker, who—did I say?—is also inside the Heligoland bird trap; the woebegone bird finds itself in smaller and smaller quarters, and finally, when the last door closes, in a small, accessible, wooden box. As she explained this, Miss Whittaker scurried about the trap, thrashing her arms, yanking ropes, and closing doors by way of demonstration, and when she had finished, she put her hand demonstratively into the wooden box and discovered, to her astonishment, there *was* a bird inside. It was a female redstart, which apparently had been there all along, and Miss Whittaker drew it forth in triumph.

Until now, I hadn't considered what Miss Whittaker would do with a bird-in-the-hand once she had it there, so she explained that the customary procedure is to weigh it, measure its wing, bill, and leg bone, observe the color of its eye, put all this in a notebook, appropriate its body lice, put all *that* in a bottle, assign the bird a serial number, put this serial number—a tiny aluminum band—on its leg, and finally let the bird, band, and serial number fly blithely away. So saying, Miss Whittaker carried the redstart to a little shack and began to perform these operations, and, as she did so, commented, "The Lundy Field Society ringed more than a thousand birds last year—one thousand and ninety-eight, I believe, of forty-six different species. The late Mr. Harman discovered that we are relatively very active in the bird ringing business, since the neighboring island is forty thousand times as large but rings only twenty times as many birds. Birds that were ringed in Lundy have turned up, later, in such places as Chaves, Portugal; Alicante, Spain; and Izmozen, Spanish Morocco; and, of course, that helps us to understand how they migrate, as do the ectoparasites. In Lundy, the birds are lousy, and as you can see—they have a lot of lice, that is—and as you can see, this redstart has two or three of them in the scruff of her neck. I don't care for ectoparasites myself, but Mr. Gordon B. Thompson does, and he's asked us to save them. Mr. Thompson has discovered that the most common ectoparasite here, in Lundy, is a tick, *Ixodes reduvius*." Mr. Hook and I listened to this attentively, but the redstart seemed to have heard it all before. It didn't look frightened, it looked bored, and after being released it flew to the bramble and sat on a juniper twig as if nothing out-of-the-way had happened. It didn't even make its experiences known to the other redstarts, to whom, I gathered, the whole bird ringing business was old hat.

Presently, Mr. Hook observed something to the effect that two birds in the hand are worth one in the bush, and proposed that the three of us try to capture, measure, and ring another one, having had such notable success with the redstart. This struck Miss Whittaker as an excellent idea, so she, Mr. Hook, and I equipped ourselves with branches and began thrashing about in the bramble by the Heligoland bird trap. We managed to rouse a single bird—another redstart, which popped from the underbrush like a champagne cork and flew over my

LUNDY

shoulder to distant, unknown parts. Miss Whittaker and Mr. Hook watched it go, and turned to me with disappointment.

"I'm awfully sorry," I said.

"That's all right," Miss Whittaker said, but I knew that her heart wasn't in it.

A few days later, before departing from Lundy on the paddle-wheeler and going, out of a growing curiosity, to Sark, I visited the old lighthouse again to see what mention had been made of our activities in the Lundy Field Society's daily log. I knew, of course, that these logs had been around for centuries and would be, inevitably, for centuries more, so I was delighted to see the following:

THURSDAY, SEPT. 8. B.K.W. swallow-watched all day, but in the evening she, an American author (or journalist) Mr. Fach (?) and O.H. worked the Heligoland Trap on the terrace and caught and ringed a ♀ redstart.

The hesitant nature of this entry doesn't bother me at all. The bird was the first and only ♀ redstart whose capture and enringing I have been to any degree responsible for, and I'm proud as a peacock, happy as a ♀ lark, to have been granted this unsolicited measure of immortality.

*"I don't think
that's funny at all!"*

—THE DAME OF SARK.

SARK

Sark, as I have said, is the only feudal state surviving in Europe. It is a fief; it was given, as such, to a feudal lord by Queen Elizabeth I in 1565, and it passed from hand to hand for almost four hundred years until, in 1959, it occupies those of Mrs. Sibyl Hathaway, a very proper, elderly, sensible British lady who lives in a venerable manor house there and chooses to be known as the Dame of Sark. Mrs. Hathaway, as Dame, is

SARK

not only lord and mistress of Sark and its five hundred or so inhabitants but also, in the words of Queen Elizabeth, owns "all of its rights, members, liberties and appurtenances, and all and singular castles, fortresses, houses, buildings, structures ruined with their fragments, lands, meadows, pastures, commons, wastes, woods, waters, watercourses, ponds, fees, rents, reversions, services, advowsons, presentations, rights of patronage, of rectories, vicarages, chapels or churches, and also all manner of tithes, oblations, fruits, obventions, mines, quarries, ports, shores, rocks, wrecks of the sea, shipwrecks, farms, feefarms, knights' fees, wards, marriages, escheates, reliefs, heriots, goods and chattels waived, goods and chattels of felons, fugitives or pirates, or felons *de se*, out-laws, of persons put in exigent, and the forfeited or confiscated goods of persons condemned or convicted any other way whatsoever; also all forfeitures, paunages, free warrens, courts leet, views of frank pledge, assize and assay of bread, wine and beer; all fairs, markets, customs, rights of tolls, jurisdictions, liberties, immunities, exemptions, franchises, privileges, commodities, profits, emoluments, and all the Queen's heredits whatsoever with every of their appurts, situate within the seas or seacoast contiguous or appertaining to the island, or within its shores, limits or precincts, and whatsoever were held, known, or accepted as members or parts of the Island of Sark."

It's clear that Mrs. Hathaway is a power to be reckoned with in Sark. (Incidentally, the place is one of the Channel Islands—the smallest one.) There are other powers in Sark, but almost all of them are chosen by Mrs. Hathaway and are known collectively, by many of the people there, as "Mrs. Hathaway's gang"—the Seneschal, who can be thought of as a president; the Prevot, who can be thought of as a sheriff; the Treasurer; and the Greffier, who can be thought of only as a greffier—and there is a legislature, the Chief Pleas, but Mrs. Hathaway has the veto power. She herself is supported, in high style, by an intolerable lot of feudal taxes exacted from the five hundred citizens of Sark, who can be thought of as vassals and serfs: a

Mrs. Hathaway's attitude toward this unparalleled deal of feudal power is that it's terribly quaint.

SARK

tithe on wheat, on cider, on lambs, and on wool, a royalty on minerals, a *rente* on property, a *tresième* on property sales, and a tax on chimneys to be paid every year in live chickens. She has been called a dictator by the Chief Pleas.

Mrs. Hathaway's attitude toward this unparalleled deal of feudal power is a rather curious one, and can best be described by saying that she thinks it's terribly quaint. She is, as I have said, a very proper, typical suburban lady of the sort that sponsors musical evenings and literary teas in the United States, and when she is asked by students of medieval history or by other proper, typical suburban ladies to acquaint them with some of the feudal laws under which she administers Sark, she invariably replies, firstly, that the Dame of Sark is the only one on the island permitted to keep a female dog, and, secondly, that the Dame of Sark is the only one permitted to keep a pigeon. No one will deny, of course, that these particular laws are awfully quaint, even accruing to the well-being of the community, but, which is also true, a country can't hope to be adequately governed nowadays by these two principles alone. They are, if anything, the beginning and not the end of a body of laws; and yet whoever inquires further of Mrs. Hathaway as to the Sarkese legal processes, or who looks into them himself, finds that everything else is chaos. The laws of Sark are three and four hundred years old; they are written by hand, and often illegibly, in English, French, and Anglo-French, the language of Medieval Normandy; and the Seneschal, who is not only Sark's president but its only judge, is kept in such a fine sweat trying to understand them that he is known to blench and get visibly agitated when a lawyer is brought into his court. The Seneschal, it would appear, must generally cite the law off the top of his head, trying to bluff it out, a judicial procedure that leads to such interesting courtroom exchanges as this, in a tax case:

THE SENESCHAL: Do you know on what your tax is based?
MR. SUTCLIFFE: No.

THE SENESCHAL: On one thousand two hundred pounds. Can you prove to the court that you haven't one thousand two hundred pounds?
MR. SUTCLIFFE: The onus is on you, sir. Is it money in the bank, plant, or equipment?
THE SENESCHAL: On capital.
MR. SUTCLIFFE: Will you define capital?
THE SENESCHAL: Only capital.
MR. SUTCLIFFE: What capital do you refer to? This is quite absurd.
THE SENESCHAL: I presume I can do as I please. I have every authority to sue you for contempt.

The prospect of a man trying to prove how much money he doesn't have and of a judge suing the defendent for contempt of court, does not, apparently, strike Mrs. Hathaway as an undesirable one, and at her lectures at women's clubs in the United States, where she is introduced as "Mrs. Sibyl Hathaway, the Dame of Sark," she is always delighted to say that the laws of Sark haven't changed since 1565, but that "we wouldn't have it otherwise, for we believe that they serve our purpose and meet our needs." Meanwhile, at home, the laws of Sark have reached such a hopeless state that it's debatable if Mrs. Hathaway *is* the Dame of Sark; a great many Sarkese are sure that Mr. Michael Beaumont, of 5 Whitepost Hill, Redhill, Surrey, England, is really supposed to be their feudal lord.

Thus encumbered with a body of law that only makes sense when applied to the disposition of dogs and pigeons, Sark is staggering through the twentieth century like a man in medieval armor, and, like him, it is causing a rather terrifying din and shower of sparks as it runs into the revolving doors and high-tension wires of this modern age. Sark's collision with the electrical power lines of the twentieth century is more than a metaphor; it really happened, in 1949, and it shows the rather slapdash mechanism of the Sarkese legal process. Sark was without electricity until 1949, when Mr. Henry Head, a wry, stocky, enterprising member of the Chief Pleas, proposed in that deliberative body to have the country electrified. Mrs. Hathaway said yes, the Seneschal said no, and the Greffier was so deaf that he didn't hear the vote, which consequently isn't known to this day; at this, Mrs. Hathaway ordered the electric company to put the poles up, the Seneschal ordered it to take them down ("They make a heck of a noise when it blows," said the Seneschal), and the Greffier promised to get a hearing aid by the next legislative session. By now, as can well be imagined, the electric company was fit to be tied, and all was pandemonium when the Chief Pleas sat again. Mrs. Hathaway spoke first, and was fast interrupted by a loud whistle.

"I don't think that's funny at all!" said Mrs. Hathaway, bristling, but the Greffier hurriedly explained that he just hadn't gotten the hang of his hearing aid. This experience with the manifestations of electricity was enough, apparently, to convince Mrs. Hathaway that the stuff couldn't be trusted, for soon she was speaking against it. The Seneschal helped matters not at all by recommending a vote of censure against Mr. Henry Head, who, it will be remembered, had started the whole trouble, and the meeting ended amid unanimous catcalls, directed, for the most part, at Mr. Head. Well, the electric company realized that it's every man for himself in Sark; it put up the poles, electrified such theretofore inviolable places as Mrs. Hathaway's house and the Chief Pleas' deliberative halls, and has been making a healthy, illegitimate profit ever since. Meanwhile, Mr. Head went angrily the next day to the Greffier's office, the Greff, and began acquainting himself there with Sarkese law, an unprecedented and absolutely perilous thing to do in Sark, and, when the Chief Pleas sat again, he triumphantly told that astonished body that *it* was illegitimate and that all its laws for the past quarter century were null and void. For almost a year after that, the Chief Pleas was thoroughly in a stew trying to legitimize itself—amending its constitution, carrying on elections, and writing desperate letters to King George VI, in his capacity as Queen Elizabeth I's successor, all the time keeping Mr. Head at bay by charging him the equivalent of one dollar and five cents an hour to do any

31

further research into the Sarkese law books. (Even today, the members of the Chief Pleas have to pay thirty-five cents an hour to read the law.) When everything had been set aright, the Chief Pleas turned its attention furiously to Mr. Head, elected him the Constable and Colorado beetle inspector, and told him that under the provisions of feudal law a constable (and by extension, presumably, a Colorado beetle inspector) is required to serve for two years—and without pay—as police chief, jail warden, district attorney, tax collector, harbor master, truant officer, impounder of unauthorized bitches, and superintendent of public works, roads, and sanitation. At that, Mr. Head turned purple again, and swore that his first act as Constable would be to jail every member of the Chief Pleas, but the unchartable ways of Sark are shown by the fact that the only such to be jailed, subsequently, was Mr. Henry Head himself, the Constable.

All of this had blown over by the time I got to Sark. The gorse on the hillsides was quietly in flower, and two or three cows walked unambitiously among it, and a soft Atlantic wind sent yellow tremors through the wheat fields. Mr. Head was clipping his hedges idly; he was no longer the constable, he told me, but on pleasant days he liked to stroll along the beach to look for Colorado beetles on the incoming tide. It was a relatively peaceful Sark while I was there, and Mr. Head expressed the hope it would last. A few months later, therefore, I was rather dismayed to come across an issue of the *Guernsey Star* and learn that Mr. Head had set off still another wave of hysteria in the Chief Pleas by making what would be, in any other legislature, a not especially inflammatory proposal—that taxpayers should be given receipts. The *Guernsey Star* records the following exchange:

MR. HEAD: I have received no receipt from the Constable for the pound I sent him last November.

THE CONSTABLE: [*his color rising*] I have Mr. Head's receipt at home. What does he think—I've kept the money?

SARK

MR. HEAD: [*likewise*] I am asking again for my receipt.
THE CONSTABLE: I'll *send* you your receipt.
MR. HEAD: I am not the only person who has not had a receipt. Will receipts be sent to everybody?
THE CONSTABLE: They will all have receipts!
MR. A. G. FALLE: I can't understand why Mr. Head is asking all these questions; we will be here all day.

By now, however, a number of other questions had occurred to Mr. Head, having to do with land reform, contracts, sea gulls, and a feudal officer identified as the Proctor of the Poor; he also pointed out that a law requiring the registration of .22 and .303 rifles had been passed five years earlier and straightway thought no more of ("The fact remains," said Mr. Head, "that we gladly pass new laws and then forget all about them"); and he complained that his Personal Tax Bill had been called twelve pages of trash by the Seneschal, whereupon:

THE SENESCHAL: Well, it *was* twelve pages of trash.
MR. HEAD: And I thought it was such a brilliant piece of work!

Presently, it would appear, everybody in the Chief Pleas was shouting at once, some of them in English and some in Norman Patois, the very peculiar dialect of Sark; "Let them learn our language!" shouted Mr. A. G. Falle in Norman Patois; "Can you teach it? You can't even write it!" shouted Mr. Harold de Carteret in English; "I have a wolf in the stomach and a sponge in the gullet!" yelled Mr. Head, metaphorically; and the meeting was boisterously adjourned. It was no doubt resumed the following day, but I've been unable to get hold of that day's *Guernsey Star*.

In Sark, one of the laws vigorously enforced by Mrs. Hathaway is there can't be any cars there; Mrs. Hathaway is very proud of it, and she regularly tells the women's clubs, in America, that this is one of Sark's most delightful virtues. The result is that everyone uses, instead of cars, tractors to get about. These are ever to be seen on the Sarkese landscape—great, ungainly, rusty spiders that thunder along the roads and kick up the dust with their man-sized, rubber wheels; at night, they are really a caution. When I came to Sark, a tractor was in readiness at the pier; my baggage and that of the other people was put in back, and we ourselves sat uncomfortably among it, and a bony, uncommunicative fellow got into the saddle, did a number of things there, caused the tractor to emit a splendid amount of blue-black gases, did a number of other indescribable things, and took a course uphill; five minutes of this and he was altogether spent, brought the tractor to a stop, discontinued the blue-black gases, and hurried into a tavern. We, the excursionists, were none too steady ourselves, and followed him in.

The tavern was an oaken and quietly *gemütlich* one, and it was frequented, at this hour, by what I learned was a cross-section of the Sarkese community—some farm hands, some hired men, and some propertied folk whose ancestors had lived in Sark since 1565, some old-timers with tired, yellowing, porous mustaches and the faces of Norman fishermen, some Englishmen and women who made their homes there, some tourists. The old-timers were in a brown study and hadn't much to say, but the others had enthusiastically given themselves over to gossip, and within an hour had told me of a dozen indecorums, dating to the 1800's, on the part of people who weren't there, including the Hathaway family itself. (Mrs. Hathaway's father, they assured me, was given to kicking her mother downstairs, and her late husband, a Yale man by the name of Robert Hathaway, was trying to make a living selling tennis balls when he stumbled fortunately on Mrs. Hathaway.) This sort of gossip is always to be heard in Sark; it is not only made by the highly unreliable sources I met in the tavern but is reciprocated by the impeachable authorities in the Hathaway family itself; there is so much of it, and so much of it said in malice, that, I'm afraid, it would be difficult to find a less delightful place than the country of Sark to live. The general ill feeling is bound to rub onto the tourists, who never seem to be especially happy, and who develop a wary, conspiratorial look after too long a vacation there. It's really a far cry from Lundy.

It took a bit of doing to get past all of this gossip and learn something about Sark itself, but, after making inquiries of the most persistent sort, I am pleased to report some of the native customs that have been peculiar to Sark as long as anyone can remember—namely, that wine and cake are given to everyone on wedding days, that apples and oranges are given to children on New Year's Day, that rabbits are shot on Christmas Day, that clay pipes are shot on Christmas and New Year's Day, that model boats are built at home and floated on Good Friday in the Petit Beauregard Pond, that *all* boats are built at home and taken overland to the ocean, and that the lady who launches them is put on the deck with a champagne bottle and is simultaneously launched herself. The *Sark Guide*, which is sold there for a shilling, informs me that at certain times "almost the whole population of Sark, armed with hooks and baskets, may be found in the most inaccessible places on the shore, frantically turning over boulders, often being rewarded with as many as two hundred ormers," a native custom that, I trust, will be clarified in future editions, and the Reverend Mr. J. L. V. Cachemaille, writing in the 1800's, reports that a common entertainment was to dress a man as a donkey. "Many an evening was passed in this way, particularly in winter," says the Reverend Mr. Cachemaille, "and the result was that much time was wasted, bad habits were contracted, and were followed by immorality." A man as a donkey is very frightening to Sarkese children, but even the grownups are given a nasty turn when they run into Tchico, the dog of the dead, a ghost. Naturally, you expect to hear of a reasonable number of disembodied spirits at a tourist resort, but Sark has more than its share, I think, being haunted in season by a headless rider, a riderless coach, an amphibious manner of spook at the bottom of wells, and some as yet unidentified apparitions in the village jail, as well as others; indeed, the atmosphere there is so thick with ectoplasm that everybody must needs take practical measures against it, notably by fixing a few stones to their chimneys to keep the witches out. Mrs. Hathaway herself, speaking of the manor house she lives in, has written that it "has no less than four of these stones, and so effective are they that not a single witch has come down the chimneys within living memory." I take it that Mrs. Hathaway is being merry with us here, but I also note she resorted to the black magic of Albertus Magnus when one of her daughters, Douce Alianore Daphne Beaumont Brisco, had warts, and that she had some white knitting wool tied to one of her cows when it was, allegedly, bewitched. "I have no comment to make upon this," Mrs. Hathaway has written since, "except the important one that I still have the cow."

Not only is Sark so possessed by witches and spooks as to be almost uninhabitable by human beings, but, I learned, its most prominent and reigning family, the Hathaways, is cursed —not a very pleasant curse, even as curses go, but one that ought to be told of, nevertheless. It began in the early 1800's, I learned, when somebody struck silver in a desolate part of Sark. I have seen the place: there is a sinkhole there, and you can go fifty yards down into it, and then to the ocean inside a cave; the ground is soft with cinnamon-brown seaweed, and the only sounds are the slapping waves. A certain Mr. Peter Le Pelley was feudal lord when the silver was found there; the assay specified muriate of silver, sulphuret of silver, sulphuret of silver and copper, sulphuret of silver and antimony, black surphuret of silver, ruby silver, antimonial silver, and silver-bearing iron pyrites, and Le Pelley's eyes must have bulged as he read all this. He put $170,000 in the silver mine, but it ran dry.

What happened next is that Mr. Le Pelley hurried to Guernsey to pay his creditor, the boat sank, Mr. Le Pelley drowned, the creditor foreclosed, and there was such consternation in Sark that Mr. Le Pelley's valet tried to jump off a cliff, being restrained by none other than the Reverend Mr. J. L. V. Cachemaille. The creditor—a Mrs. T. G. Collings—now became the Dame of Sark, and she was straightway cursed for having done so by the ghost of Mr. Le Pelley, or by some other ghost, this part of the story being not especially clear, and she died the same year without ever going to Sark. Mrs. Collings's son and the next feudal lord, the Reverend Mr. W. T. Collings, was not conspicuously cursed, but he very nearly died the same way Mr. Le Pelley had and *his* son, Mr. William F. Collings, was the man who kicked his wife downstairs. (Besides, he was arrested on Guernsey for shooting a navy officer, on Jersey for raising cain at a brothel, and on Sark for knocking the constable's hat off.) One of his children was cursed with a cleft palate, and the other—Mrs. Hathaway—with one leg shorter than the other, and in the present century the children of Mrs. Hathaway have been so awfully cursed that half of them —Basil Ian Beaumont, Bridget Amice Beaumont, and Francis William Lionel Collings "Buster" Beaumont—are already dead. It isn't a very pretty story at all, and it's carried considerably further by the gossips.

I have mentioned that one of the accursed lords of Sark was very nearly drowned at sea, and this, too, is something to be told of, not because it's an especially good story but because we hear entirely too much of the bravery of sea captains these days and, I think, it's worth while to see the other side of the coin. The story is told by the feudal lord in question, the Reverend Mr. W. T. Collings, who wrote that his ship ran against a beacon on a rainy afternoon in 1872, whereupon: "The captain threw up his arms, and uttered one awful despairing cry, 'All's lost! All's lost!' As long as we live this cry will haunt us." Everybody asked the captain what had happened, and he just replied, "All's lost." The Reverend Mr. Collings, though, pointed out that the ship was well aground and the tide was falling ("No, sir, she is filling fast, we are lost"), and his son pointed out that after all, there was a lifeboat; the captain jumped into it first, followed by women and children and, last of all, by the Reverend Mr. Collings. Mr. Collings tried to be cheery, but the captain said, "We're drifting, we are going up the Russell, we are lost." Two hours later, the boat reached shore.

Sark's predicament as the only feudal state in Europe is so awfully huggermugger that I hesitate to pursue it further, but I haven't pointed out that Mrs. Sibyl Hathaway, in her capacity as a feudal lord, continues to owe allegiance to a feudal *over*lord, the Duchess of Normandy. Sark was part and parcel of Normandy in medieval days, and its overlord for more than a thousand years has been the duke or duchess—at present a young, handsome, blue-eyed Englishwoman, who once a year is given a check for the equivalent of seven dollars as a token of Mrs. Hathaway's allegiance. The Duchess of Normandy, of course, has also been the Queen of England since 1066, and so the English generally think of Sark not as a country in its own right but as an insignificant part of their queen's domain. The Sarkese, on the other hand, think of England as an insignificant part of their duchess's domain. After all, they point out, who conquered whom?

Duchess Elizabeth II of Normandy and her predecessors have paid precious little heed to their vassalage of Sark and, historically, have given Mrs. Hathaway and her predecessors a free hand there. (None of the dukes and duchesses so much as visited the place. Duchess Victoria circumnavigated it in 1859 and was given a twenty-one-gun salute in gratitude—"which no doubt she distinctly heard," says the Reverend Mr. Cachemaille. It's lucky she didn't land, I think; some peacocks had gotten into the manor house earlier in the day and raised the devil there, and one knows how the Duchess would have felt. Elizabeth II spent an afternoon in Sark in 1949, before becoming a duchess, and thereby gave a wealth of material to the gossips that's yet to be exhausted, one of the juicier items being that her husband got to Sark with so bloody a hangover that his first words to Mrs. Hathaway were, "Have you an aspirin, please?") Elizabeth II can countermand the doings of Mrs. Hathaway and the Chief Pleas, but never has. It goes without saying that English law doesn't apply in Sark; English postage stamps are used, but the passports are those of the States of Guernsey and the money is that of England and/or Guernsey; and Englishmen who visit Sark must go through customs, paying twenty-one cents as a landing fee. After six hundred days there, they are exempt from the draft and English taxes. Sark has the power to try and punish its criminals by its own, un-English laws, but now it lets Guernsey handle the big ones, like murderers.

I haven't made a study of the judicial processes of Guernsey, though I'm told they're a peculiar thing, really—the jury is chosen for life—but I've watched a criminal trial in Sark, and I think it was *very* peculiar. The trial was that of Mr. Edmund Falle, who was accused of closing his tavern one morning at 12:40 instead of the legal hour, 12:30. The complaint, such as it was, had been lodged a week or two earlier by Mr. Phillip Perrée, the Constable, who was out to make trouble for Mr. Falle because Mr. Falle's son, Mr. Stanley Falle, Mr. Perrée's assistant, was due to become constable the next month and was out to make trouble for *him*. The prosecuting attorney was the Constable, Mr. Perrée, and the trial judge was the nephew of the defendant, as well as the first cousin of the assistant prosecuting attorney—Mr. Willie Baker, the Seneschal, who would also function as a jury. All of this was explained to me by Mr. Henry Head, who sat alongside me in court, and I'm pretty sure I've got it straight. Mr. Head explained, further, that he himself was in court as a correspondent for the *Guernsey Star*, the *Guernsey Evening Press*, and the *Jersey Evening Post;* he said it was Sark's first trial in several weeks and that he intended to whoop it up a bit, being paid on space rates. As we waited for the proceedings to begin, I read a few of his clippings and discovered, from them, that so little of any importance happens in Sark that Mr. Head must usually write about Mr. Head, notably by resigning in high dudgeon from the Chief Pleas, the constabulary, or the Colorado beetle inspectorship and hurrying to himself for an interview. "Mr. Henry

Head, Sark's go-ahead constable, may startle the island this week by giving his resignation," wrote Mr. Henry Head, the *Guernsey Star*'s go-ahead correspondent, in 1951. "This is the second time he has made this threat within two months. In an exclusive interview yesterday . . ." The doings of Mr. Head were warmly applauded by Mr. Head in many of the clippings ("The existent law is too terrible to think about. Mr. Henry Head's proposal deserves support."), and, on one memorable occasion when the outlook for news was especially desperate, he accorded himself a three-thousand-word eulogy in the columns of the *Guernsey Evening Press,* some of the more cordial passages being, "Mr. Head, who several years ago earned from me [i.e., Mr. Head] the pseudonym of the 'stormy petrel of Sark,' has over the past two years more than qualified for the title. . . . The fact remains that none will dispute the fact that Mr. Henry Head has made history with a capital 'H' during the past two years of his reign as constable and in doing so has gained for Sark more publicity than it ever before received. Mr. Head has made few friends but many enemies in Sark, but no one will begrudge him his due in the fact that he has done his honorary job with rare conscientiousness, even if, at times, in the opinion of some, without tact."

The courtroom where I was reading all this, and where the trial of Mr. Falle would begin momentarily, was a small, unpretentious room in the elementary boys' school. Its desks were sandy-colored, with several oases of blue-black ink; chalk was everywhere, and the blackboard at the front was full of arithmetic, like "How many 1½d stamps can be bought for £2-11s-7½d?" Presently there was a call for silence, and the room was entered by Mr. Willie Baker, the Seneschal, a trim, careful, bespectacled man who was wearing a brown suit with leather hems, and by Mr. Hilary Carré, the Greffier, who looked as I had imagined a greffier would—rather like a gopher, with a jolly face, two buck teeth, and a potbelly. The two men sat down in front of the blackboard, and the Seneschal opened the trial by observing that the matter in dispute was whether Mr.

Edmund Falle did, or didn't, serve any drinks between the hours of 12:30 and 12:40 A.M.; that Mr. Falle said he didn't; and that the Constable said he did—a point the Constable clarified at once by springing to his feet and saying, "I couldn't of said for whom customer it was—but it was." The Constable, I took it, was accustomed to Norman Patois, not English. His lips were tight and bitter.

The Seneschal now called upon the Constable to produce his witnesses, and the Constable answered, in what was very close to astonishment, "I'ven't *got* any witnesses." This disclosure was followed by a great deal of silence, which lasted till Mr. Falle's lawyer harrumphed a bit and observed, "It is customary, I believe, for the prosecution to have witnesses when they call a case." The Seneschal said something to the effect that customs differ in different lands, and suggested that while the prosecution hadn't any witnesses, perhaps the defense *had*, and Mr. Edmund Falle took the stand in his own behalf.

"It was 12:30 o'clock, and I called out, 'Time!'" said Mr. Falle, "and nobody got any drinks after. I tried to get them, everybody, out, and if the Constable hadn't of been there, I would of gotten 'em out. The Constable was—"

"What did you do to get them out?" said Mr. Falle's lawyer.

"I called out, 'Time!' I turned the lights on and out. The Constable was taking names, like I said, and everybody was waiting to see what'd happen." By now, it was clear to everyone but the Seneschal that the Constable had nothing but a grudge against Mr. Falle. "I asked the Constable to help," said Mr. Falle, "but he's busy taking names, he said."

"Yes," said the Constable, interrupting again, "but there'd been no nothin' there, and Mr. Falle called out time and showed no head to pushin' 'em out, and they're still servin' drinks at the other end."

"When?" said the Seneschal, who was fast going into a quandary.

"It was 12:40, you can test m' watch," said the Constable.

"It was 12:30," said Mr. Falle.

"You, Mr. Falle, are you absolutely sure of that?" said the Seneschal.

"I am absolutely sure of that," said Mr. Falle.

"Abso*lutely*?"

"Absolutely."

"Well," said the Seneschal brightly, "one of the watches must have been wrong!"

"There was money circulatin' after the bell had rang, half past twelve," said the Constable.

"There's something wrong somewhere," said the Seneschal.

The Seneschal adjourned the court to deliberate, the Constable shooed everyone outside, Mr. Henry Head hurried to a telephone, and the Greffier slapped a beret onto his head and rode furiously off on a bicycle. I ran into the Seneschal a few days later. "It's quite a problem," he told me, "quite a problem." I sailed away from Sark before he had solved it.

"... *now that smuggling
is a thing of the past.*"

—THE PRESIDENT OF ANDORRA.

ANDORRA

By now, I had realized that my trip wasn't to be any ordinary one. After I left Sark, I spent a few days in France and another few days in Spain, and then I got to wondering about the little country *between* France and Spain—Andorra—so I went there. It was November now; there wasn't any snow on the Pyrenees, but the air was gray and crisp, and little rivers of ice hung to the mountainsides like tinsel. The road from Seo de Urgel, Spain, went along a valley in gentle meanders, and into Andorra unobtrusively: I saw, at first, a couple of haciendas sewn to the mountainside like pant patches, and then a couple of barns along the road, with brown tobacco leaves hanging in rank and file on the southern wall to dry in the scanty hours of sunshine, and then, presently, the Andorran village of Sant Julià de Lòria, clean, chic, and full of the things that tourists want. A few miles further was Andorra the Old, the country's capital; a few *yards* further was Les Escaldes, a tourist spot; and to drive still further was to leave Andorra. I stayed in Les Escaldes in a room overlooking the village square—it is a triangle, really, and so little that only one thing at a time can happen in it. Watching the square was like watching the click-clicking of Kodak slides. At first, Andorra would be serene; and then click! and it's full of a thousand rams, pushing and bleating, their horns curling like quoits around their ears; another click, and it is serene again. And then a bus arrives from France, and click! Andorra is seething with tourists who yell in French and whistle at the girls and swagger about the square as the bullfighters swagger about the ring in Barcelona, to the south. And then, the slide changes again; Andorra is serene again.

The road to Andorra from Seo de Urgel, Spain, is free of snow and open the year round, but the road from France is over the Pyrenees' highest pass, at eight thousand feet, and is just about hopeless in the winter and early spring; at those seasons, it is attempted only by smugglers, and by American journalists who wish to convey to their readers the impression that Andorra is out of this world. Andorra *isn't* out of this world if one arrives from Spain, and coming this way, as I did, a traveler is sure to wonder why in the world the place is independent. The answer I was given, in Andorra, is that it was proclaimed so by Charlemagne in 784, after the Andorranos had helped him to fight the Moors (or maybe it was the Basques): "He who helps Charlemagne doesn't rue the day,"

ANDORRA

Charlemagne is said to have said, at any rate, and created Andorra in a trice. Today, the Andorranos call themselves the sons of Charlemagne, and the Andorran national anthem, which loses almost everything in translation, has it that

> *My father, Charles the Great, the Great,*
> *Rescued me from the Moors*
> *And . . . I am the only remaining daughter*
> *Of the Carolingian Empire.*

A footprint of Charlemagne's is still pointed out in Andorra, more than a thousand years later, and a house in Sant Julià de Lòria is still advertising that Charlemagne slept there, and the story is also authenticated by an old document, kept in Andorra behind a half-dozen locks and keys: it is written in Latin, is dated 784, is signed and sealed by Charlemagne, and says, in part, "By the grace of God the Omnipotent King and of Jesus Christ our Saviour, Emperor Charles [the Great] and his son, King Louis [the Debonair, or the Pious], expelled, by divine mercy, the pagan populace of the region of Spain known by the name of Barcelona. . . . We have found a small valley by the name of Andorra, not far from the lands of Toulouse, which also had been sacked and ravaged by the accursed infidels. We decided to send peasants or farmers there to establish themselves, to build houses, to work the land and live of their work, [and] we ceded to them for the future all the lands incorporated within the limits of the small valley of Andorra." This document is the Charter of Andorra, which is not only treasured by the Andorranos themselves but which has been examined, with much interest, by the scholars of other nations, who are virtually unanimous in calling it a shameless forgery. Its language, they say, is that of the eleventh century.

The story of Charlemagne, then, doesn't give us much of an inkling why Andorra is where it is; but there it is, nevertheless, and nothing can be done about it at this late date. Andorra is roughly eighteen miles wide and sixteen miles from north to south, and roughly seven thousand people live there; they talk in Catalan, a language that's also heard in neighboring France and Spain and parts of Sardinia, Cuba, and Argentina, but isn't official anywhere but Andorra. "Andorra" is not a Catalan word (it's from the Arabic, meaning "woods," though Charlemagne is supposed to have taken one look at the place and cried, "Wild valleys of hell, I christen thee Endor!"), but the word *Andorrano* has been taken into the Catalan language: it means a man of silence, a clam. I myself didn't find them so, but that's what people say. Andorranos, for the most part, are tight, rugged people of the mountains; their usual occupation is said to be smuggling, but I was quickly assured in Andorra that smuggling is a thing of the past, having been supplanted in recent times, and in that order, by the cultivation of tobacco and tourists. Andorra's tobacco is sold in tins, usually for people who roll their own, but it's also made into two-foot cigars for the tourists and into eight popular brands of cigarettes—Charlemagnes; Carmelas; New Havanas; Imperials; Ysers; Reig Gresas; Duxes, which can easily be mistaken for the German Luxes; and Golden Suns, which can easily be mistaken for Lucky Strikes by those who aren't aware that Lucky Strike green has gone to war, and which bear the inscriptions, on the packs, MADE IN U.S.A. and A BLEND OF THE FINEST TURKISH AND DOMEST TOBACCOS GOLDEN SUN FORMULA AN ENTIRELY PRINCIPLE IN CIGARETTE MANUFACTURE. The first four of these brands are manufactured in Sant Julià de Lòria by Mr. Julian Reig, who made his fortune as a smuggler and turned his hand to tobacco when smuggling became a thing of the past; the Golden Suns and the Duxes, not to mention the Reig Gresas, are manufactured a few doors away by Mr. Reig Gresa. Mr. Gresa—it's Senyor Gresa in Catalan, incidentally—is a big, friendly, ill-shaven man who can easily be mistaken for a neighborhood grocer, and, when I asked him to tell me something of the cigarette business, he replied it was going badly of late: France and Spain were not letting any cigarettes in, he said, and now that smuggling was out of the question, all of

ANDORRA

*I computed that everybody in the country would be
smoking eighteen cigarettes at a time
morning, afternoon, and night.*

Andorra's tobacco had to be consumed domestically. To be sure, Mr. Gresa continued, a number of shady characters in Sant Julià de Lòria came to his factory every week and bought two or three hundred cartons, but, in the absence of any evidence to the contrary, he had to presume they smoked them. I asked Mr. Gresa how much tobacco had been grown in Andorra that year; he said it was nine hundred metric tons, and I computed that everybody in the country would be smoking eighteen cigarettes at a time morning, afternoon, and night if this were consumed domestically. Mr. Gresa allowed that the rate didn't appear to be anywhere near so high, and, confronted with this evidence, said it wasn't unthinkable that some of the tobacco crop manages to find its way to foreign markets.

The tobacco industry in Andorra is old as the hills, but the tourist industry is something new, and, I think, the Andorranos aren't really up to it. Clearly, it isn't easy to change the mentality of a smuggler to that of a shopkeeper—to change the underhand to the gladhand—and the older Andorranos haven't fully done so; they seem to be ill at ease whenever a customer is browsing about their shop, as if the jig nearly were up. (An Austrian who's living in Andorra told me of his troubles getting a radio there. At every radio store, he was taken for a competitor's spy and was told there weren't any; eventually, he took out an import license and had a radio shipped from Germany.) The outside world is making itself felt, though, on the younger Andorranos; so many have emigrated to France and Spain that today more Andorranos are outside the country than in it, while the younger folk who remain can generally be found in the caffè espresso shops, tapping their feet to such current Andorran favorites as "Papa Loves Mambo" and "Rock Around the Clock," which emanated constantly from Radio Andorra while I was there. The traditional folk dance of Andorra, the sardana, is rarely to be seen there any more; I saw it only once myself. That was on a Sunday evening, when thirteen of the younger Andorranos made a circle beneath my window, in Les Escaldes, and went through the motions of the sardana—a sort of jiggle that somebody might do to keep his toes warm, without any of the boisterousness of the Basque dances, at the other end of the Pyrenees. None of the dancers had any enthusiasm for the thing, and finally, at the end of the sardana, they threw their arms at the center of the circle in what could be taken as a gesture of despair.

ANDORRA

Later in the evening, however, I saw these same Andorranos get into a perfect lather doing the foxtrot, the rumba, and the waltz, and attempting, with less success, the jitterbug and the rock-and-roll. The Andorranos and I had gone over to Andorra the Old, to the Brasserie Française, one of two dance halls that were built in recent years along the village's main drag, the Avenue Meritxell. ("X" is pronounced "sh" in Catalan, and *xocolate* is a favorite drink at the Brasserie Française and at the other dance hall, the Rotunda.) The Brasserie is a clean, well-lighted, but somewhat sterile place with a linoleum floor and powder-blue walls, and it was being patronized by two dozen people when I got there, all of them males. For the first half hour, a party of Andorran girls stood outside the door giggling, but then they screwed their courage to the sticking place, scurried across the room like soldiers to a foxhole, and fell headlong, and with sighs of relief, into some chairs in the corner, where they began to giggle again. The girls wore the sort of plain, unsophisticated dresses you see in Sears Roebuck catalogues, and which didn't quite fit; also they wore heavy shoes with crepe soles, and the men wore double-breasted, pin-stripe suits. The pin stripes were bold, even flamboyant, such as we in America would associate with Sicilian gangsters. At first, the men pretended not to have seen the girls, but eventually they themselves took heart and asked the prettier ones to dance; more girls arrived, and soon the floor was full. The Andorranos did a foxtrot when foxtrot music was played, and they did an uneasy compromise of the foxtrot when a rumba or tango was played; they were all knees for the paso doble, and late in the evening two or three of them tried to jitterbug, did a few steps in an aw-shucks way, realized they might be terribly wrong, and hurried back to their tables in confusion. I felt that everyone was having a high time but still was a little sheepish about it, as someone might be who finds himself in a community bath. At the end of every dance, the girls bolted from the floor without a word, and the men were studied with envy and admiration by their friends.

The music for all this came from a Victrola, and consisted of

49

some Mexican songs, some waltzes by Strauss, and such American importations as "High Noon," "In the Mood," "Vaya con Dios," and, of course, "Papa Loves Mambo" and "Rock Around the Clock." Only ten years ago, before the tourists began coming, the music was always a sardana; a dance was very decorous, a courtship was five years, and it was always the parents who chose the bride. Nowadays, you can see the awakenings of true love at the Brasserie Française. Such a case was shown to me there by Mr. Auguste Pi, a businessman who makes his home in Andorra, who had been sitting at my table this night; it befell a handsome boy of fourteen and a blonde of the same age and was called a "drama" by Mr. Pi. The boy's face was the delicate, sleepy one of a French matinee idol, and his hair was neatly mussy, and he asked the blonde for a dance early in the evening; *"Ah, sympathique,"* said Mr. Pi, twitching me at the elbow, meaning the boy and girl felt for one another. Mr. Pi was nodding his head in agreement with himself when somebody cut in; *"Jalousie!"* cried Mr. Pi; and the rest of the evening he detected all sorts of meaningful glances between the three. I could detect nothing of the sort, but Mr. Pi is a Frenchman, and I defer to his judgment in these matters. *"C'est la vie!"* he cried—he really was getting carried away by now—"There it is, life! life!" It was obvious to Mr. Pi that love, at last, has come to Andorra, on the heels of the tourist industry, and I'm willing to take his word for it.

The topography of Andorra is that of a "Y"—three valleys whose crystal, cold rivers come together in Les Escaldes, not far from where I was staying. One of the valleys goes to Seo de Urgel, Spain, along the road I came by; another goes to France, over the Pyrenees. The third valley doesn't go anywhere in particular. I drove along it one afternoon as far as I could; the road was of macadam at first, and then gravel, then dirt; then it was full of ruts and cobbles, and then it disappeared entirely. Two or three gloomy, gray stone houses stood in the area like mausoleums, and gray stone walls were like basking snakes on

ANDORRA

the hillside. On the oldest stones, I counted at least eight kinds of lichen; their colors were gray, green, gold, black, and umber, and seen at a distance they faded into a pastel green, the color of sailboat hulls at the end of summer; and there was a hint of snow, now, on the highest mountains. Eventually, a peasant came by and said I could proceed along the valley on foot, getting to a desolate part of France two or three hours later; instead, I returned to Les Escaldes.

The official name of Andorra is *Valls d'Andorra,* the Valleys of Andorra. (Even so fundamental a fact is none too clear, like so many things about Andorra. A number of state papers call it "the Valley of Andorra," and the Sentence of 1278, of which more in a minute, plays it close to the chest, always calling the place "the Valley or Valleys of Andorra.") There isn't any question, of course, that Andorra is a valley, or valleys, but there *is* a question that it's a republic, as it's often called, and a good case could be made that it isn't even a country. Such a case, an embarrassing one, naturally, for all Andorranos, was made six years ago, during one of the recurrent crises in Franco-Andorran affairs, by the French, who said that "relations between France and Andorra cannot be broken, because Andorra is not a sovereign state." What they meant is that the president of France is *ex officio* the reigning prince of Andorra, too. There is still another reigning, *ex officio* prince of Andorra, the bishop of Urgel in Seo de Urgel, Spain, and between the two of them the co-princes do so very much reigning that Andorra behaves, generally, not so much like a sovereign country as like a hundred and ninety-one square miles of land belonging simultaneously to France and Spain. The telephone, telegraph, and mails in Andorra are managed by France and Spain: there is a *Postes et Télégraphes* in Andorra the Old for mail going to France, and a *Caja Postal de Ahorros,* across the street, for mail going to Spain, and since neither of them gives a hoot about mail going to anywhere else in Andorra, it has to be carried free, at public expense. Andorra's foreign affairs are run by France, its churches are run by Spain, its law courts are run by France and/or Spain. There are French, Spanish, and Andorrano police, and when the French and Spanish police can't agree, the Andorrano police are in a pickle. There aren't any Andorran schools; all of them are French or Spanish, the former teaching in French instead of Catalan, and the latter teaching in Spanish instead of Catalan, and, since there aren't any Andorran textbooks, either, the children at the former are taught their fatherland is France, while the children at the latter are taught: "My fatherland is Spain. As good Spaniards, we ought to respect, love, and be ready to defend our fatherland. Oh Spain! I love you as a beloved mother. My glorious country! Ever and everywhere may your name be praised." And several pages further: "As good Spaniards, we ought to love our Leader. ¡Viva Franco! ¡Arriba España!"

The Andorranos would have you think that this arrangement is just ducky. "A man can have two defenders, but he cannot have two masters," they tell you, but their heart isn't always in it, and there are times Andorra has two masters and isn't happy with either. When Andorra wanted a gambling casino, the President of France said no, readying a battalion on the border; when Andorra wanted a telegraph, the Bishop of Urgel said no, cutting it down; when Andorra first wanted to grow tobacco, the President *and* the Bishop said no, pulling it up by the roots. When Andorra wanted to be in the Brussels Fair, the President said no and the Bishop said yes. Naturally, this sort of business has kept the Andorranos in a constant dither, and their only solution is to lean to one of the co-princes to get more favors out of the other. Unhappily, it isn't always apparent which way to lean: in the 1860's, half of the Andorranos wanted to lean north and the other half wanted to lean south, and the upshot was a civil war—the Revolution, as it's called in Andorra. The Revolution was two years long, was ended by the Treaty of Pont dels Escalls, and was credited with only one fatality, an old woman who was hit by a ricochet bullet as she watched the war from a balcony; her last words are said to have

ANDORRA

been, "Well, just *look* at those silly people." At the Revolution's end, the silly people were still leaning north and south.

The incumbent co-princes of Andorra, M. de Gaulle and Mgr. Ramón Iglesias Navarri, to my knowledge have never yet been introduced to one another. It's all an awfully inconvenient arrangement, I think. When I tried to learn the historical reason for it, I kept getting snagged in the tangled yarn of Charlemagne, but what apparently happened is that Andorra was something of a hot potato then: to protect it, Charlemagne gave it to his son, Louis the Debonair (the Pious), who gave it to *his* son, Charles the Bald, not to be confused with the Duke of Burgundy, Charles the Bold, who gave it to the Count of Urgel, who gave it to the Bishop of Urgel, who—anyhow, by 1203 it belonged to the Count of Foix. At this point, the Bishop decided he wanted it back, and everything was in a how-de-do for most of the century. War was declared, but, through the good offices of King Pedro III, the Bishop and the Count made up, signed the aforementioned Sentence of 1278, and agreed in it to make Andorra a co-principality, to be its co-princes, and to receive from it an annual co-tribute. The Sentence of 1278 is still in effect, but, what with the fluctuations of the franc and peseta, the tribute to be paid by Andorra is $2.75 to the French and $10.82, six hams, six cheeses, and a dozen hens to the Bishop, who gives them to the Old People's Home in Seo de Urgel, Spain. The Bishop of Urgel is still the Bishop of Urgel, but the Count of Foix became, in the course of time, the King of France, whose successor today is the President, M. de Gaulle. In another sense, of course, the successor to the King of France is the great-great-grandson of the last one, Louis Philippe—M. Henri D'Orléans, the Count of Paris, who is not only the pretender today to the throne of France but, with notably less enthusiasm, to that of Andorra. M. D'Orléans' pretensions were more or less passive until the summer of 1934, when he sent a courtier of his to Andorra to reign as co-prince in his stead. The man, whose name is remembered there as either Escassirev or Skossyref, came to Andorra in a taxi, checked into the Modern Hotel, wore a monocle, proclaimed himself as Prince Boris I, proclaimed some other things, beat his wife, broke her arm on one memorable occasion, and was amiably tolerated by the Andorranos for roughly a year, when he was told to beat it, which he did.

What with French presidents, Spanish bishops, and occasional envoys of M. D'Orléans trying to govern Andorra, there is precious little governing left for the Andorranos to do. What there is of it is done by the Very Illustrious Seignoir Francisco Caerat, the President (or First Síndic) of Andorra, a small, fleshy, venerable, white-haired man who manifests the courtly air of a Spanish don, being one of the very few Andorranos to wear a coat and tie—usually a black one with a red-and-white regimental stripe. His fellow citizens have been electing Mr. Caerat as president every three years as long as they can remember. Generally, he discharges the functions of his office from ten o'clock to one on weekdays in a dusty, sunless room at Andorra the Old, but after trying, and failing, to find him there for seven days running, I eventually sought him in Sant Julià de Lòria, his home town. I drove to Sant Julià and asked at the first tobacco shop if Mr. Caerat was about, and the clerk replied that he certainly was—*he* was Mr. Caerat.

For the next several minutes, the President of Andorra and I chatted at his tobacco shop as customers came and went—he sold them Old Golds, Charlemagnes, two or three cans of roll-your-own, and a vial of French perfume, Shalimar, as I recall. He apologized for not having been at the office, but said he'd gone unexpectedly to Paris for the funeral of Madame Coty, the Princess of Andorra (*the* Princess, of course; there's only one). The President recalled that he had stayed, in Paris, at the Hotel Scribe, but hadn't time for any of the sights; the hotel itself is a clean, well-run place several doors from American Express, he said, and he was happy to recommend it; the tab was twenty-three hundred francs a night. A good deal of work—mostly passports and auto licenses to be signed, and letters to be answered—had piled up on his desk in the interim,

ANDORRA

I have mentioned that Mr. Pi is a businessman, but....

and he hoped to have a go at them the following morning, at ten. His wife would run the tobacco shop in the meantime.

My last question to the President of Andorra was what, if anything, had to be done for the country in the coming years; he thought about this, and finally he said the road to France ought to be fixed, seeing how Andorra is so dependent on tourists, now that smuggling is a thing of the past.

Well, smuggling *isn't* a thing of the past, and how I found out is from nobody else but Mr. Pi, the Frenchman who went into raptures over the stirrings of love at the Brasserie Française. I have mentioned that Mr. Pi is a businessman, but I haven't mentioned that Mr. Pi, telling me this, had added the qualifying phrase "in the night." Mr. Pi did a fair share of business in the night we spent at the Brasserie Française: he was beckoned to the door two or three times by a rather seedy, stand-offish Andorrano, whispered to him a while, and presently returned to the table rubbing his hands and saying, "Big deal, big deal. Lots of money."

Mr. Pi himself can be described as a seedier version of Edward R. Murrow—he's big and husky, and the lines of his face are furrows in two or three days' stubble; his coat had a Shanghai label. He said he'd been a businessman in Shanghai for twenty years, had been taken by the Japanese in World War II, had walked across Indochina a thousand miles, had been more or less everywhere else in the world, spoke English, Spanish, French, Catalan, and Chinese, and for the preceding five years had been a businessman—in the night—there in Andorra. Mr. Pi never told me what it was he smuggled, except to mention once that two million "goods" had just arrived for him from France. (The whole two million of them weighed four tons, so I guess they're radio parts.) However, Mr. Pi did say that in the past—in the *past*, mind you—he and people he knew of had smuggled watches, cameras, Cadillacs, mules, chinaware, French tulle, and even steel and aluminum I-beams, his own specialty having been Cadillacs, which he got, apparently, from rich Americans who had taken them to Europe for a year or so's vacation. Most of this was smuggled into Spain in the Civil War, and into France in World War II, and now is smuggled indiscriminately to both, the smugglers getting less of a profit, though. (In wartime France, Mr. Pi said, a kilo of dried tobacco went for seven or eight dollars; it's worth a dollar now. Presumably this is why an elder statesman of Andorra exclaimed, in 1941, "May God continue to give us wars, not on our soil but close to it.") Mr. Pi said, in conclusion, that the usual procedure of the smugglers was to put the chinaware, watches, I-beams, etc. into a truck or one of the

ANDORRA

Cadillacs, drive to the border, and give a three- or four-hundred-dollar bribe to the customs people *en passant*.

Frankly, I was rather disappointed by this. I explained to Mr. Pi that everything I'd known of smuggling in the Pyrenees had been gotten from Act III of *Carmen* and Act III of *Man and Superman;* it had been my belief, consequently, that a smuggler went by night over the dire, snow-blown passes with a pistol at his side and a swad of contraband on his back, and to discover that what a smuggler really did was to drive a Cadillac full of chinaware and French tulle to the border, tossing three or four hundred smackers to the customs people, was, naturally, a good deal of a letdown. Mr. Pi looked hurt; he assured me that the smugglers to be met in *Carmen* are also met in Andorra. They're none of them in the big time, Mr. Pi said, as they handle only tobacco and, every once in a while, a case of absinthe, but if I wished to be introduced to some, he'd gladly take me to one of their haunts. I thanked him, and said I did.

The next scene was straight out of *Carmen*, Act III. The smugglers I met were dark, weather-beaten men of all ages in clothing of blue or brown corduroy; there were a dozen of them, and they were playing cards, just like in *Carmen*. Some of them wore sneakers, some berets. The part of Carmen herself was provided by Mrs. Diana Browne, a young, blonde, American woman at my hotel who had asked to accompany Mr. Pi and me; Diana had never worked at a cigarette factory, but she had visited one that very afternoon, in Sant Julià de Lòria. Her husband, Mr. Malcolm Browne, also was with us—I suppose he corresponds to Don José—and a discordant note from Acts II and IV was sounded by the presence of a real toreador, Paco, a friend of Mr. Pi's who had fought at Madrid and Barcelona, had been badly gored, had come to Andorra to recuperate and get his *moral* back, and who spent the evening combing his hair and protesting his love to Diana—unsuccessfully, Malcolm. All of us had been assembled, for this, at the Posada Catalunya, a café that's popular with the smuggling set in Andorra the Old. The Posada Catalunya was another discordant note from Act II: it was murky, it was naked, it was full of soot and of scurfy, unwashed drinking glasses. You entered it through a curtain of milk-white beads; inside, a dozen calendars for 1955 were on the wall—they were girlie calendars for the most part, including Ava Gardner, but one was a calendar of the saints—and a few vases of wilted blue flowers and water like old formaldehyde were on the bar. At the center of the room was a black, pot-bellied stove, and around it was an eight-sided table, and around *it* were the smugglers, all of them playing cards, smoking roll-your-own-cigarettes and Charlemagnes, and dropping the ashes into white ashtrays with the advertisement BYRRH on them, or into a heap of orange skins. I gathered they were taking the night off; Mr. Pi said, later, that most of their colleagues had gone into the mountains some days earlier with several bales of something, and that the smugglers at the Posada Catalunya were waiting for a telephone call from Barcelona to hear if it got there safely. (It did.) The smugglers were friendly, and we quickly took to each other. One of them bowed to Diana gallantly, complimenting her on her long, golden hair: it was like a saint's halo, he said, and therefore he wouldn't kill us. He was smiling all the while, and I'm sure he said it in fun, but I thanked him nevertheless.

I'm sorry to keep harping on the theme of *Carmen,* but it's my recollection of Act III that Carmen is having her fortune told in the Pyrenees and draws the ace of spades, and I think it ought to be pointed out to Mr. Bing, or whoever is in charge of these matters, that in the Pyrenees there *isn't* an ace of spades. The playing cards the smugglers were using at the Posada Catalunya had an ace of clubs, an ace of swords, an ace of cups, and an ace of *oros*—no spades. The oros were golden coins of old Catalonia, I was told; there was an oro on the ace of oros, two oros on the two of oros, three oros on the three, etc., not to mention a rather intoxicating background of anchors, flags, knights, crowns, lions, and snakes. The cups also were golden, the swords were blue, and the clubs were just that —clubs, with ugly red knots and black twigs growing along

ANDORRA

the shank. (Indeed, the ace of clubs had a smear of blood on it.) All of these suits were numbered from one to ten, and there were three picture cards, too—the squire, the caballero, and the king.

It took quite a while, naturally, for Diana, Malcolm, and me to make head or tail of this, but once we had we seated ourselves at the eight-sided table and asked the smugglers to deal us in, joining the game with gusto. The stakes were low—there was never more than a dollar on the table—and I think the smugglers were happy to have us. After the first hand, we ordered them a round of wine; it came in a *porrón*, a glass carafe with a peculiar, narrow spout, the Catalan counterpart of the Basque wineskin. One holds the porrón a foot or two away, tipping it boldly, and the cool, red wine comes squirting out of the spout and into the throat if one is a smuggler, into the left eye if one is Diana, or over the shoulder if one is me—and all three circumstances were enjoyed by the smugglers hugely. Presently, Malcolm had had enough of the porrón, and suggested we avail ourselves of this rare opportunity to have some absinthe, too. Absinthe, he explained, is an alcoholic beverage made of pimpinella and wormwood oil, so heady a brew that it commonly gives rise to delirium tremens and, eventually, drives a person crazy; it isn't allowed in the United States but is always being imbibed in the best of Hemingway, he said, and we ought to give it a tumble. The barman at the Posada Catalunya poured a glass of it for Diana, Malcolm, and me after making sure that he'd heard us rightly; then he poured water in, and the color of the absinthe went from a Paris green to a cloudy green, a chemical reaction which, Malcolm said, is spoken of highly by Mr. Hemingway, and occurred, to his recollection, at least half a dozen times in *The Sun Also Rises* alone. The absinthe didn't do anything very memorable to us. Frankly, it tasted like a pernod, an alcoholic drink that's to be gotten anywhere in France and Spain, also turns to a cloudy green, and doesn't drive you crazy.

The game that Malcolm, Diana, Paco, the smugglers, and I

were playing while drinking all this was seven-and-a-half, a little like our game of twenty-one. (The squires, the caballeros, and the kings counted a half. In case you're interested, the squire, caballero, and king of swords are carrying a sword in their right hand; the squire, caballero, and king of clubs are carrying a club in their right hand; and the squire, caballero, and king of cups are giving an exemplary lesson to the commoners by keeping hands off. The caballero of cups appears to be whistling in awe, and no wonder: the cup is poised daintily on the horse's right ear.) Generally, the smugglers played seven-and-a-half in a careful, timid, colorless way, never talking. Diana was all confusion and dealt the cards face up, and Paco, the bullfighter, played seven-and-a-half like a bullfighter: he never stood pat at six-and-a-half or seven but asked to be hit again, although the odds were three to one against him. At midnight, Paco was already in the hole by several dollars when he drew the ace of oros to the seven of cups, thirty-seven pesetas in the kitty; with that, he threw his cards down in disgust and began again his wooing of Diana, and Malcolm suggested it was time to go. We did; Mr. Pi came with us; and the smugglers at the eight-sided table shouted a cheery *adiós*.

Shortly afterwards, walking back to the hotel, Mr. Pi obligingly told us about the smugglers at the Posada Catalunya, how they operate. He said they go to France or Spain once a week, sleeping by day, walking by night, a trip of several days over the mountain passes. Only one of them carries a gun, to be discharged not at the customs people but at wolves, bears, and such; contrary to *Man and Superman,* a smuggler is scared to death of the customs people, and he'll drop everything if he sees one and take to the hills like a frightened rabbit. Every smuggler has fifty or sixty pounds of tobacco, said Mr. Pi, and thirty or forty smugglers travel at once.

"How about making it thirty-three?" I asked—meaning Malcolm, Diana, and myself.

"No. Jesus was thirty-three when he died," said Mr. Pi. "The smugglers never travel in thirty-threes." I was about to suggest

ANDORRA

thirty-one or thirty-two, but Mr. Pi was already shaking his head.

Well, Mr. Pi, we did do a little smuggling, nevertheless. It wasn't much of a haul—it was sixteen packs of cigarettes, into Spain—but you've got to walk before you can run, and sixteen packs of cigarettes is a promising start. The thing is that cigarettes are seven or eight cents a pack in Andorra, so Diana and Malcolm went and bought two of Charlemagnes, two of Carmelas, and two apiece of the other brands the day before going to Spain; the boodle of swag was then hidden in the side pocket of a red tartan B-4 bag of Malcolm's, and this, in turn, was tied above a venerable taxi that makes the run to Barcelona, with six or seven passengers, every day. We had secured the confederacy of the taxi driver by buying him drinks in Sant Julià de Lòria until three o'clock the night before, and he had shown his competence at the wheel, however drunk, by returning us to Les Escaldes at seventy miles an hour, sideswiping only a single car in the process, mine.

Diana, Malcolm, the taxi man, and three or four others departed at 9 A.M. Diana and Malcolm promised to write me whether they got to Barcelona with the bacon, and also promised, at my request, to include a report on the relative merits of the eight popular brands of Andorran cigarettes, for the benefit of any of my readers who'll be going there and who, naturally, want the brands to be as nicely discriminated as they are in the United States. Malcolm is more qualified than most to attempt such an evaluation, being a professional taster of food and liquor at the Foster D. Snell chemical company, in New York City. Diana tastes food and liquor too, though not professionally.

Diana and Malcolm's letter was delivered a week later, and I pass it along without any comment, as I myself have never smuggled or smoked to any great extent and, as a result, know very little about either. It was mailed from Madrid, was sprinkled on the inside with a quantity of loose tobacco, began with the words "Dear John," and continued: "We did it! They gave us a fishy eye at the border—the taxi seats were taken out, chassis was looked at, tires were thumped and beaten, even the motor was examined but they never thought of the B-4 bag. Heh, heh. Others in the taxi were a dour, elderly Andorran man and wife, a well-dressed 'businessman' with bright, beady eyes and bulging suitcase, the taxi driver, and the taxi driver's girl friend who spent the trip draped around the taxi driver, talking in Catalan to him, and adjusting the volume of the radio (usually up). Taxi driver had a hangover and was cheery but bleary, the road was all but impassable because of a hydroelectric thing in the works, I hadn't any breakfast, and Diana was dead tired—ideal setting for the evaluation of Andorran cigarettes. We started on an Yser in the back seat. Afraid the evaluation will be fairly unilateral as Diana now refuses to touch the stuff.

"Anyhow, the one variable from brand to brand appears to be the level of tobacco staleness. (This has nothing to do with flavor in the usual sense.) The one notable exception was Golden Sun, the cigarette that is an entirely principle in cigarettes—more about Golden Sun later. Yser had the same symptomatology as ammonia fumes: running eyes, hot lungs, aftertaste of asphalt that seemed to reach into the alveoli. Diana coughed hard. Offered it to our companions—Andorran man and wife don't smoke, 'businessman' smiles knowingly and declines, girl friend laughs and offers us Pall Malls. We decline. We try a Carmela. Not too bad; a little fresher; interesting tingling in the epithelium cells. Blew our noses several times. Ate a lunch cooked in beautiful old fireplace in roadside inn; it was delicious. Tried a Golden Sun for the first time. *Entirely* principle in cigarettes, positively the absinthe of cigarettes. As a connoisseur of the worst tobacco in the world, I can say unreservedly that Golden Sun is it. Really, every visitor to Andorra should try it.

"Barcelona very attractive, please excuse the paper. [Malcolm was writing on wrapping paper now.] Diana and I got a little sleep, went to a gypsy spot—the Brindis Cave, taking along

ANDORRA

a Rhodesian girl. The gypsy singing and dancing were magnificent, just magnificent. Afterwards we offered gypsy a Golden Sun; he seemed offended. Rhodesian girl doesn't smoke. After several days, took a night train to Madrid which took only fifteen hours and tried to do a little more evaluating. Not very successful, as Diana and I had undergone sensory paralysis. Our compartment mate was a Portuguese wrestler, also three young Spaniards who were very active—tossing orange peels from the window at girls, doing hand-stands in the aisle, wine, much singing and so forth. Played seven-and-a-half with the Spaniards and asked them to do the evaluating. Results for all the brands not previously mentioned were inconclusive; field conditions very bad. Portuguese wrestler went to sleep along the entire bench, causing two of the Spaniards to sleep in baggage rack.

"Next week we'll be in Monaco—how about meeting us? As for your readers, if they have to be told *something* tell 'em to smoke a Dux. But I'd walk a mile from a Golden Sun.

"Best regards, Malcolm."

The art of smuggling tobacco from Andorra into Spain is getting a little ticklish for people who, unlike Diana, Malcolm, and myself, are more or less gainfully employed in it. A few have been killed by the customs people, who are being reinforced on their patrols by a small, insidious canine corps; others have been caught and arrested, as have some of the people in cahoots with them—the customs people. I think there's a growing awareness in Andorra that it's cheaper to pay an import duty nowadays than to smuggle. Of course, in Andorra itself there isn't any law against smuggling, as there isn't any law against driving drunk at seventy miles an hour, or hitting another car. (There *is* a law that smugglers can't wear masks, the Bishop of Urgel feeling that it's unreligious to ornament the human face.) There aren't an awful lot of laws in Andorra. The trouble is that the French police and the Spanish police, who are supposed to tell the Andorrano police what to do, disagree, so the Andorrano police, not knowing whether to lean north or south, usually *laissez faire*. Andorra, in these parts, has a reputation as sort of an anarchy, and I've heard that traffic cops in Barcelona will occasionally yell out, "Where do you think you are? Andorra?"

In the light of all this, it's good to know, anyhow, that you can't get away with murder in Andorra. It isn't often that a murder is committed, but it's dealt with summarily when it is—the most recent one having been in 1943, when a boy near the village of Ransol murdered his older brother with a hunting gun, and was executed only an hour after the trial. His motive was to get his hands on the family fortune. (It also came out in the wash that he poisoned his sister in 1928 for the same reason.) Once the wicked deed was done, the boy hurried to Ransol and told the sheriff something to the effect that his older brother was dead, let's bury him. The sheriff, though, reasoned that an investigation was called for, and began one immediately by visiting the scene of the crime and interrogating the most knowledgeable party, the corpse, saying, *"Mort, qui t'ha mort?"*—"Dead one, who has killed you?" The sheriff is an intelligent person, and, in fairness to him, it should be pointed out that such a question on such occasions has been customary in Andorra for many hundred years. The dead one didn't answer it, which also is customary, so the sheriff went on to exclaim, *"Mort, alça't! Mort, alçat! Mort, alçat! La justícia t'ho mana!"*—"Dead one, arise! Dead one, arise! Dead one, arise! The judge is ordering it!" (It didn't.) These proceedings were ended when the sheriff, addressing himself to the quick instead of the dead, said, *"Es un mort el qui no parla"*—"It is a dead one who doesn't speak"—by which time the guilty brother was so thoroughly unnerved that he confessed. He was tried by two Spaniards and a Frenchman, was sentenced to die, was taken to the square of Andorra the Old, and was tied to a stake, lest he flee to the cathedral, a sanctuary; a prayer was said by the Association of the Good Death, and he was killed. He was carried to a cemetery by the Good Death people and

ANDORRA

speedily buried. While I was in Andorra, I couldn't even learn his name.

The unwritten law of Andorra (almost all the law of Andorra is unwritten) says that a person like this is to be killed by strangulation, by the garrote, a grisly, black, cumbersome vise that was kept, for this purpose, in a cathedral hard by the village square. However, it was always a great bother for the judges to find someone who cared to apply this garrote—it took a month of cajolery, often—and in 1943, when the boy above was to be executed, they finally said the hell with it and shot him. The ugly garrote is now applied on nobody but the tourists, and in fun, and is kept no longer in the cathedral but in the House of the Valley, a hideous old moldering stone building that has been going to seed since 1580 in a gloomy corner of Andorra the Old, and which houses not only the garrote, and other such memorabilia, but also the national jail and the executive offices of the President, the Very Illustrious Seignoir Caerat.

The House of the Valley—the White House, as it were—is open to the general public from ten o'clock to one on weekdays, when the President is in, and, at other hours, to those members of the general public who have the time and inclination to ferret out the jailer. The jailer is a difficult man to ferret; it took me almost an hour. (I learned he has been ferreted also by some of his own prisoners, who had been sunning themselves on the terrace all day and wanted to get back in—a situation that also obtains in Sark.) Eventually, I found the jailer at a caffè espresso place a block and a half away: he was gnawing a toothpick and sibilating a caffè espresso, and he promised to be ready anon. Anon, he got agonizingly to his feet, chug-a-lugged what was left of the caffè espresso, walked to the House of the Valley with me, produced, from somewhere on his person, an extraordinary two-foot, four-pound iron key, and with it opened the House of the Valley's door. The door is rotten, and above it is a medieval, time-worn tablet that says in effect, and in Latin, that Andorra belongs to France and Spain simultaneously and is rather pleased about it:

> *Behold: these are the arms of a neutral valley*
> *And quarterings that nobler nations triumph in.*
> *Each, Andorra, blessed an alien people—*
> *Together they shall bless your golden age.*

While I was translating this, the most unferretable character in Andorra gave me the slip, leaving me alone in the House of the Valley.

—Not quite alone. I discovered, by and by, that two prisoners were there, to be seen through a knothole as a couple of fitful shadows in a dim, slovenly room covered with brick and bottle shards; one of them was a thief, the other a counterfeiter, I learned—no smugglers, of course, though my friend the jailer is said to indulge a bit. The jail is on the House of the Valley's first floor, just off the lobby; on the second floor, at the end of dilapidated stairs, is a big pink room full of ancient frescoes of the crucifixion; and at the end of *that*, as I learned by gadding innocently into it, is the office of the President, Mr. Caerat. I have already mentioned that the office is dusty, sunless; it is also cold, being heated by nothing but a small orange electric grill in front of Mr. Caerat's desk, and another in back. The desk is simple, and I was pleased to note that Mr. Caerat was making headway against the pile of state papers which, he told me, had accumulated there during his visit to Paris: only a passport and two or three letters were left, and the drawers were almost empty. To the right of this is an oaken cupboard where the Charter of 784 and other essential things are kept; it is secured by six locks and keys, as I've also mentioned, the keys being kept by someone important in each of the six Andorran parishes. The names of the parishes—Sant Julià de Lòria and Andorra the Old are two of them—are scratched into the cupboard, alongside the proper keyhole. There are a number of other scratchings on the cupboard,

ANDORRA

made, as usual, by the tourists, and elsewhere in the President's room are a heap of yellow archives, a dusty telephone, an autographed picture of M. Coty, an autographed picture of Mgr. Iglesias Navarri—who looks like a football coach, or did in 1943, when the picture was taken—and finally, along the walls, a set of twenty-four cane-bottom armchairs, to be used by the twenty-four members of the General Council, the legislative body of Andorra.

I'm afraid I couldn't learn just what sort of laws, if any, the General Council of Andorra legislates (it hasn't even the power to tax), but I did learn some other, alternative facts about it after my visit to the House of the Valley, and I'm happy to pass them along—viz., that it's elected every two years, that the selfsame men are elected every time, that all of them are thirty or older, that none of them are drinkers, that some of them are smugglers, that none of them are paid, and that, if the occasion demands it, they trick themselves out in silver shoes, blue stockings, red garters, gray trousers, white shirts, black coats, red collars, and black three-cornered hats. I also learned that the General Council of Andorra met, in the old days, in the big pink room where the frescoes of the crucifixion are, and that it met in the old, *old* days in a cemetery, to get a more sober appreciation of the business at hand. In the old days, when it met in the big pink room, the General Council not only legislated at the House of the Valley but also ate and slept there, and you can still behold, on the second floor, the rude, sooty kitchen where the twenty-four councilmen would cook (the garrote is under a sink), and on the third floor the twenty-four iron beds. Nowadays, the councilmen eat and sleep at the Hotel Mirador. They meet ordinarily at the House of the Valley five times a year, but an extraordinary session can be called *ad libitum* by Mr. Caerat, or, for that matter, by anybody else in the world willing to pay for food and transportation, and those of my readers who wish to do so should forward the sum of two thousand pesetas—about forty-seven dollars—and some sort of legislative proposal to

67

the Very Illustrious General Council of Andorra, House of the Valley, Andorra the Old, Andorra. The postage is fifteen cents, via either France or Spain.

I left Andorra shortly after my visit to the House of the Valley, and via France. The word in Les Escaldes was that it wasn't snowing much in the high Pyrenees, and that the pass into France, at eight thousand feet, still could be negotiated by car—but heaven knew how much longer. Slowly, and usually in low gear, I began to drive seventeen miles up past a half-dozen tidy hamlets—Encamp, Meritxell, Canillo, Soldeu—whose houses of ashen gray blended agreeably into the rocky, ashen gray mountainside, having been built of it. At forty-two hundred feet, at Encamp, is the tower of Radio Andorra, and at fifty-seven hundred feet, at Meritxell, is the white chapel of Our Lady of Meritxell, the Andorran patron saint. Almost all of Andorra, and a goodly share of neighboring France and Spain, can be found at the chapel every September 8, I'm told, and half a dozen priests are needed to spell one another at the masses; and the semiofficial guidebook to Andorra, *Andorra*, doesn't mince any words about the affair: "The vast crowd enters the sanctuary, when it is possible for them to do so, to pray for a moment before the Virgin and leave as quickly as they can. Human heat adds to that of the flames of thousands of paschal candles and of larger ones . . . making it practically unbearable." Now though, in December, there wasn't any heat of any kind as I drove by the chapel at Meritxell; snow began to fall at six thousand feet, and by seven thousand feet the road was thick in it. At eight thousand feet, I was at the pass. A homely Mobilgas station is there, and nothing else, and I began descending into France.

It rained torrentially that afternoon and night, and the next morning the roads in Southern France were a foot under floodwater. As I plashed ahead to Monaco, I surmised that the pass had closed. The smugglers and the American journalists would be arriving any day.

"Corbleu! So, madame, now you're my wife, and make no mistake— it's a great honor for you."
—THE PRINCE OF MONACO.

MONACO

Nobody seems to have mentioned that His Most Serene Highness Rainier III, the Prince of Monaco, Duke of Valentinois, Marquis of Baux, Sire of Matignon, Count of Thann, Baron of Buis, Seigneur of Saint-Rémy, etc., etc., and, of course, the husband of Grace Patricia Kelly of Philadelphia, Pennsylvania, is the only absolute monarch in the Western world. In this respect, he is like the King of Saudi Arabia, the Imam of Yemen, the Kabaka of Buganda, the Dalai Lama of Tibet, and, historically, the Pharaoh of Egypt, the Tyrant of Athens, the Mikado of Japan, Ivan the Terrible, Nero, and Nebuchadnezzar—an important consideration for any young lady of Philadelphia, Pennsylvania, who is invited to marry the fellow, but a consideration the newspapers, at any rate, curiously let by. Prince Rainier has the unqualified power of life and death in his principality, and if he should step outside of his gray-and-pink, parapeted palace some drowsy afternoon and slice the heads off ten or a dozen bystanders, it couldn't be questioned that he acted within his rights, although, I suspect, a good deal of grousing would be heard afterwards. In fact, Rainier may lawfully decapitate not only the twenty-one thousand Monégasques who are his subjects but, if she riles him sufficiently, his wife, too, be she Monégasque, American, or what-you-will. This disturbing fact was overlooked by the newspapers and, until recently, by Rainier himself, but in 1954 it was recalled to him by Father Francis Tucker, of Wilmington, Delaware, the court chaplain, who seems to consider it very funny. "Hmm," said Rainier, according to Father Tucker, and disappeared with a faraway look in his eyes, and soon afterwards he married Miss Grace Patricia Kelly of Philadelphia, Pennsylvania. His feelings at the time, I assume, were nothing but the highest, and yet a marriage to an absolute monarch is not to be entered upon lightly, and Miss Kelly, I would hope, has bethought herself of the possibilities.

So far, there hasn't been a happy marriage in all of this century for the absolute monarchs of Monaco, the family tree of Rainier. His parents, grandparents, and great-grandparents all were divorced; his great-grandmother was tortured by her husband, his grandfather was kidnaped by his mother, his mother was disinherited by her grandfather, and he himself was kidnaped by his father, and by this time, I think, it ought to be recognized that many terrible things can happen in

MONACO

marriages to absolute monarchs which, by and large, do not happen among the peasantry. The sort of pitfall to be encountered in such unions was seen in 1757, when Miss Marie Catherine di Brignole-Sala was married to Prince Honoré III. Miss di Brignole-Sala had sailed into Monaco to marry her prince exactly as Miss Kelly, two hundred years later, sailed into Monaco on the S.S. *Constitution* to marry hers. Prince Honoré, being an absolute monarch, had stood in Monaco and waited for Miss di Brignole-Sala, but Miss di Brignole-Sala,

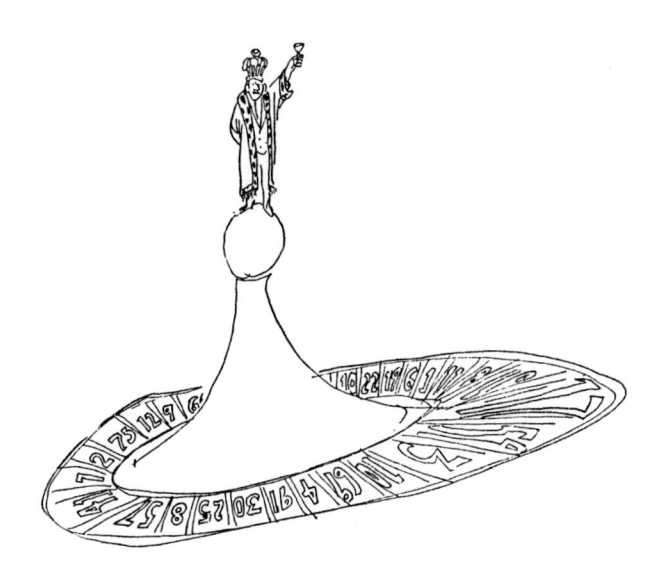

being, she explained, a niece of the Doge of Genoa, who was pretty absolute himself, had stood on the ship and waited for Honoré; so there they had stood, bride and groom, she on the ship and he on the shore, as twilight came to the quiet Mediterranean. In 1956, as the S.S. *Constitution* laid by, Rainier stood on a yacht and waited for Miss Kelly. She, fortunately, isn't the niece of the Doge of Genoa but of Mr. Walter Kelly, "The Virginia Judge," a vaudeville comic: nothing so absolute in that, of course, and Miss Kelly hurried from the S.S. *Con-*

stitution to the arms of Prince Rainier, as tens of thousands cheered.

They attempted to kiss, I see by the newspapers, but Oliver, her poodle, got in the way. Later, as the happy couple left on their honeymoon, Oliver got in the way again, and Prince Rainier was quoted as saying to "give the dog to the captain," and Miss Kelly did. Thus, another pitfall of the marriage, Oliver, was narrowly averted—but was it the last, especially? What if Miss Kelly had married an absolute monarch only to discover, on her wedding night, that he's an absolute nincompoop, too? *Then* what? In 1660, Miss Charlotte Catherine de Gramont ran against this very predicament, and what she did about it was flee to another absolute monarch, Louis XIV—a recourse no longer available to Miss Kelly. By all reports, including her own, Charlotte Catherine de Gramont had been the Grace Patricia Kelly of her century: "My teeth are dazzling," she said, "and my lips are crimson. There is something very captivating in my smile." By way of contrast, her husband, Prince Louis I of Monaco, was fat, clumsy, and dreadfully obtuse; his nose was like "a trumpet," his lips were like "blubber," and he walked "like a chair-porter with his legs far apart." On their wedding night, Louis, walking like a chair-porter and wearing a nightcap, went to the royal bedchamber with Miss de Gramont, her maid-in-waiting, his valet, two pages, and, burgeoning in the pages' arms, a portable sacristy of relics, rosaries, images, cruets, and cough drops, and, having put the sacristy on the night table and sent the domestics off, he clambered into bed with Miss de Gramont. She was certainly no virgin and was beginning to have second thoughts about the whole marriage, but rather coyly, and hoping to make the best of it, she blew the candles out. "Madame?" said Louis. "What does that mean?"

"I don't know, monsieur."

"Shall I call somebody to light them again?" Gee, how stupid can a fellow be?

"That is not necessary, monsieur."

MONACO

Here, though, I shall break off, despite the precedent of our historical novels, and visit the newlyweds at seven the next morning, when we discover Louis in bed asleep and Miss de Gramont in the next room, the maid's room, weeping hysterically. At last, she returned to the bridal chamber and waited for Prince Louis to wake up; *"Corbleu!"* he said when he did. "So, madame, now you're my wife, and make no mistake—it's a great honor for you." Really, that was too much, and Miss de Gramont gave Louis a piece of her mind—a reckless thing, as Louis had an unquestionable right to decapitate her. Amiably he didn't, but Miss de Gramont was foresighted enough to hurry to Versailles and the court of Louis XIV. "How I've laughed, and many others with me," she wrote, "the King amongst them!"—for Miss de Gramont did a book about it, which is how I found out. Prince Louis, she reminisces, got a list of her boy friends and hanged them in effigy, which also was unquestionably within his rights, and "half of the men here at court are decorating the highways of Monaco. Oh, how I've laughed!" So far, Miss Kelly hasn't written about her other boy friends, but her mother *has*—*My Daughter Grace, Her Life and Romances* it was called, and was serialized in many dozens of newspapers. It was an inauspicious idea, Mrs. Kelly, and I certainly hope that none of your daughter's friends are hanged, in effigy or otherwise.

Miss Kelly and Prince Rainier III hadn't been married when I arrived in Monaco; he hadn't even popped the question. His Most Serene Highness was sowing his wild oats, I learned, in Monaco, Paris, and a hideaway on Cap Ferrat, and, an adamantine bachelor, he was sowing with married women, who wouldn't be trying to marry *him*. Nevertheless, the names of Marilyn Monroe, Gisèle Pascal, Princess Margaret, Jo Ann Stork of Champaign, Illinois, and Princess Isabella, the daughter of M. D'Orléans, had been advanced, and Miss Kelly herself was being advocated by Father Tucker, Art Buchwald, and other influential parties; and I, contemplating a break in the situation any day, prudently tried to discover just what sort of an absolute monarch this Rainier was, and, accordingly, what sort of an existence his theretofore undetermined wife was in for. What I learned was heartening indeed. Rainier had never decapitated anybody, nor had he tortured, kidnaped, or hanged anybody in effigy; at his worst, he had fired a secretary of state and exiled a princess, but they were enjoying the best of health. Furthermore, he certainly wasn't a nincompoop, having been educated at Summerfields and Stowe, in England; at Rosey, in Switzerland; and at Montpellier and Paris, in France. He knew English, French, Italian, and Spanish; he made a tidy two hundred thousand dollars a year; he owned a very presentable gray-and-pink palace in Monaco, a hideaway on Cap Ferrat, an apartment in Paris, a fleet of royal yachts called the *Deo Juvante II*, the *Physalie IV*, and the *Raiatea*, and no fewer than four automobiles licensed as MC1, MC2, MC3, and MC4—factors, I decided, that are surely conducive to a happy marriage. Then, having learned all this about Rainier the monarch and wishing to learn about Rainier the man, I went, naturally, to the General Commissariat of Tourism and Information. There, M. Gabriel Ollivier, the Commissary, greeted me affectionately and went to his filing cabinet and withdrew a big manila envelope with the word PRINCE on it, and, having given this to his secretary and told her to acquaint me with its contents, he himself withdrew, and the secretary began to translate the insides of the manila envelope. "Hees Highness, ze Prince Rainier III, Prince of Monaco," she began, as I scribbled furiously, "ees seventy-five kilos een gravity and measures a meter seventy-five. He ees roboost, and . . . ooh, *de belle prestance*." She threw out her arms expansively.

"Good looking?" I said.

"*Oui, de belle prestance.* Everybody who has approached Hees Highness says, 'He ees charming.' He ees *un bon camarade*."

"A good fellow."

"A *good* fellow," said the secretary. "He ees passionate for ze books nautical, for ze preemitives, and for ze moosic, for

MONACO

ze horizons vast, ze silence, and for ze solitude of ze deepness. Ze soul of Hees Most Serene Highness has expressed eetself een delicate and capteevating poems. Hees body veegorous has found a relaxation eendispensable een sport, of wheech he encourages ze manifestations. He practices: ze tennis, ze golf, ze yachting, ze sweeming, ze ski, ze nautical ski, and ze submarine."

"The skin diving," I said.

"*Oui*, ze sub-marine. Ze most profound depth to wheech Hees Most Serene Highness has plunged ees forty-five meters. He recalls heemself zat, een Soomerfields, he was champion of ze boxing of ze category. Ze Prince Rainier of Monaco ees exempt of egoism: on ze contrary, he has ze altruism, and he heemself has helped ze humans of whom suffering ees ze lot. Ze Prince ees president of ze Cross-Red Monégasque, and he ees weety, seemple, gay, and *amiable*."

"Amiable."

"*Oui*."

Thus reassured, I closed my investigation into Prince Rainier and, after several more days in his principality, continued east, and I was in Punial, a kind of principality in the Himalayas, when I finally learned that he and Miss Grace Patricia Kelly of Philadelphia, Pennsylvania, had been married. One thousand six hundred journalists were at the affair, and, as I was at Punial, I don't have anything particularly to add except my very best wishes, in which the Rah of Punial, an absolute monarch himself, wishes to join me. According to the *New York Times*, Miss Kelly had looked at the prince "distraughtly" at the wedding ceremony, and considering the luck of such predecessors of hers as Miss Charlotte Catherine de Gramont, Miss Marie Catherine di Brignole-Sala, and Miss Mary Victoria Douglas-Hamilton—the one who was tortured—I think we can understand why. However, I also think an absolute monarch of Rainier's kidney can make a happy home for his covenanted wife. The Rah of Punial has no fewer than four of them, and he assures me they are happiness itself.

75

It was early December, the off season, when I visited the Principality of Monaco, but the temperature was in the sixties, and there wasn't a cloud in the blue, omnipresent sky. Monaco, of course, is on the Riviera: its average temperature for summer and winter is sixty-two, its rainfall is only two-and-a-third inches a month, its sun is shining five hours and thirty-nine minutes a day. Under this bountiful sun, palm trees grow, and the houses of Monaco simmer on the mountainside in pink, yellow, and tan pastels; the harbor below them is full of yachts, a giant canebrake of wood, wires, and ropes silhouetted against the sky.

The Principality is half a square mile in area, which is very small indeed—so small that several of its fine hotels, like the Metropole, and many of its celebrated international attractions, like the Monte Carlo Country Club, the Monte Carlo Golf Club, and Monte Carlo Beach, are really in France and not in Monaco at all. Monaco, as Saint-Simon explained, a bit indelicately, I think, "is a rock from whose center its sovereign can, so to speak, spit over his own boundaries." The boundary is never farther from the sea than seven hundred and fifty yards, and generally it's half of that; irresponsibly, irrepressibly, it scampers over the side streets of Monte Carlo, sundering a store here, a house there; and at the Boulevard de France it totters like a drunken sailor from sidewalk to sidewalk, so that any pedestrian but a drunken sailor will find himself successively in Monaco, France, Monaco, France, Monaco, and France. A situation like this is something I worry about, so I paid a visit to the Boulevard de France one morning to learn how the pedestrians were getting on. They—a very archetypical professor with a sack of oranges, a number of fat, middle-aged women in dirty raincoats, berets, and ponderous shoes, a bearded type, children—were getting on splendidly. As there weren't any customs or, indeed, any signs at any of the international boundaries, the Monégasques were gadding from Monaco to France, from France to Monaco, with utter impassivity. They didn't show the slightest grief to be leaving their fatherland nor, a minute later, the slightest joy to be returning, and eventually, when I saw that nobody else was worrying about the situation, I said the hell with it, concluding that the Monégasques just haven't any sense of national pride—alas, the truth, as I later learned.

Monaco, I'm told, was founded in 1600 B.C. by Hercules himself, who had captured the man-eating mares and was about to capture the red cattle, and who hove into Monaco's harbor and christened it "Port Hercules." Anyway, it was known as that originally, and more recently, at the time of the French Revolution, it was known as *Fort* Hercules—more of this in a moment—while the present name of "Monaco" is just another name for Hercules. Monaco has belonged to Rainier's family, the Grimaldis—one of whom, incidentally, was known as Hercules I—for six hundred years, and however you feel about absolute monarchs, you must admit the Grimaldis have a reasonable claim to it, having been given the country in 972, having conquered it again in 1297, and finally having bought it from Mr. Niccolo Spinola in 1339, at Genoa's market place. The Grimaldis have reigned with one interruption, the French Revolution. Then, Monaco proclaimed "the perpetual downfall of the House of Grimaldi," which had fled; also proclaimed the Republic of Monaco; and negotiated a treaty with the French republic, literally translated as follows:

TREATY
ARTICLE I. There shall be peace and alliance between the French Republic and the Republic of Monaco.
ARTICLE II. The French Republic is delighted to make the acquaintance of the Republic of Monaco.

Which covered the situation nicely. A month later, the Monégasque Republic was abolished, and Monaco became, at its own request, Fort Hercules, France, but these shenanigans were ended in 1814 when Talleyrand wrote on the Treaty of Paris' margin: "And the Prince of Monaco shall be restored to his state."

What happened in the next half century is proof of how

absolute, if he goes about it spiritedly, the Prince of Monaco can be. The Prince (Honoré V) returned to Monaco in his coach-and-four, running, by the way, smack into Napoleon escaping from Elba, Napoleon supposedly saying to him, "Hullo, Monaco, where are you going?" In Monaco, Honoré set an oppressive tax on bread, meat, vermicelli, playing cards, straw hats, garbage, birth, death—sixty-four thousand dollars a year, to be spent on his indulgences in Paris, where, among other things, he published a book called *Pauperism and the Best Means to Destroy It*. Soon people started to leave the country, so Honoré taxed *that*, raising considerable havoc on the Boulevard de France, I suspect. Also he cut the trees down, selling them for pocket money; the roads were allowed to go bad; the village clock had stopped; the Monégasques were starving; "and," said a delegation, "we cannot forget that formerly it wasn't so."

"I shall not listen. I came to govern you. I don't need any counsel."

Eventually, the princes were pauperized too. Charles III was living in four threadbare rooms of the gray-and-pink palace and dining on olives, anchovies, and red herrings, but at least he was open to counsel, and, when it was volunteered by a friend in 1851, he listened attentively: "Set up a gambling casino. You have already ruined your own people, so ruin other people, too." Such was the start of Monte Carlo Casino and, in time, of the Summer Casino, the International Sporting Club (Casino), the Café de Paris (Casino), the Monte Carlo Country Club, Monte Carlo Golf Club, Monte Carlo Opera House and Theater, Theater of Light, Theater of Fine Arts, Museum of Fine Arts, Museum of Oceanography, Museum of Prehistoric Anthropology, Prehistoric Grotto, Exotic Garden, and Center of Zoologic Acclimatation, and, for the further divertisement of the gamblers, the Monte Carlo Rally, Grand Prix of Monaco, Concours d'Elégance, Battle of Flowers, International Championships for tennis players, bridge players, water skiers, golfers, riflemen, and dogs, International Regattas, Galas,

MONACO

Carnivals, and Balls, Balls, *ad infinitum*. The village clock is working now; nobody is starving; and none of the citizens are paying taxes—but *are* they citizens, or are they only the ushers, underlings, and hired hands at the Circus, née Principality, of Monaco?

For a visitor, like myself, in the midst of all this gala et cetera, a week in Monaco is something like an awful, over-organized house party in which he's constantly being told to play charades or to pin the tail on the donkey. Nevertheless, as a conscientious tourist, I saw what I was expected to: stalagmites at the Prehistoric Grotto; *Homo neanderthalensis* at the Museum of Prehistoric Anthropology; *Euphorbia grandicornis*, from Ethiopia, at the Exotic Garden; live ostriches at the Center of Zoologic Acclimatation; dead whales at the Museum of Oceanography. Then, at the close of a wearying day, I sought tranquillity at the silent, cool aquarium in the Museum of Oceanography and thought about the words of Albert I, an oceanographer himself, when he dedicated it: "As beings on the earth, we are renegades who have escaped from the ocean. But are we happier in the brilliant sunshine than we were in the phosphorescences of the deep waters? Perhaps the true happiness dwells in the quiet depths." A brave opinion, that, almost heretical in sunshiny Monaco and quite contradictory to the General Commissariat of Tourism and Information, but still, I thought as I browsed about the aquarium, a very sensible opinion, too. In the quiet, phosphorescent tanks, a goldfish blew bubbles; a trigger fish, as indolent as an alley cat, rubbed its parti-colored sides against a coral; a capon, lying like a tired pancake on the olive, seaweedy floor of a tank, patiently waited for its skin to go away. Truly, here was a happy seascape—until I came to the *poisson-roi*.

The *poisson-roi* wanted out. Desperately, that poor fish was swimming hither and yon, searching the corners of its tank, trying, trying, trying to find the exit, the exit that didn't exist. Its expression was one of jaded perseverance, of desperate hope: precisely the expression that I beheld the next evening on more than a hundred poor fishes at the Society for Sea-Baths, commonly known as the Monte Carlo Casino.

The Society for Sea-Baths and Foreigners' Club of Monaco was founded in 1861, and a half century later, when it opened a hydropathic annex, it finally gave somebody a sea bath. Meanwhile, the Society had soaked the very clubbiest of foreigners—King Edward VII, King Edward VIII, a dozen other kings, queens, and emperors, the Aga Khan, the Pasha of Marrakech, Sir Winston Churchill, Charlie Chaplin, Douglas Fairbanks, Jr., J. Pierpont Morgan—and had gotten itself a reputation as the *ne plus ultra* of the fashionable world. Now, in 1959, the Society for Sea-Baths is still contending that, "from all parts of the globe, aristocrats, artists, literary men, and sportsmen rush towards Monte Carlo, the pole of attraction," but the truth is otherwise, as I discovered that evening when, after paying the admission fee, forty-two cents, and by-passing a room of slot machines, I entered the main gambling hall of Monte Carlo Casino.

The effect was that of a deadly, overheated waiting room. In its ponderous heat, waiting, as it were, for a long-delayed milk train, a hundred men and women milled insipidly: men, surely no aristocrats, with sullen, half-shaven faces; women with landlady faces, heavy, stagnant, and fat; a prostitute; a frowzy divorcee whose hair, like a colony of mud-brown worms, escaped from beneath her hat in all directions. They sat at the gambling tables like subway riders, insensible, glum, looking at life through the lower halves of their eyeballs and twisting their lips for exercise, up and down. Everywhere, a melancholy silence clung like a damp bed sheet. This was the Monte Carlo Casino, and all the while the roulette wheels turned as windmills on a torpid afternoon, and the croupiers sat with looks of exquisite boredom, and the lazy ivory ball, at last, settled in a compartment, red or black, odd or even, according to the inexorable law of averages—which is to say totally unpredict-

MONACO

ably. With pencils, papers, and arithmetical tables, the poor fishes were trying, trying, trying to predict it.

There was something magnificently mad here. Philosophically, I suppose, it was man's search for meaning in a meaningless world, his pitiful attempt to leave his little aquarium; but surely it wasn't fun, it wasn't recreation. To make the casino a little happier, less like a funeral parlor, the management, I learned, has tried such desperate innovations as double roulette, a kind that paid one thousand two hundred dollars to one, and mercury, a raceway of little tin airplanes, like at Coney Island, but always the gloom continued until, in 1950, the management went despairingly to Reno, Nevada, and returned to Monte Carlo with a craps table. For a month, the old casino was awakened by that happy hullabaloo, "Four and trey, and take it away!" "Five and two, and you're all through!" "Little Joe from Alamo!"; but then the croupiers revolted, and Little Joe, Little Phoebe, and their lighthearted friends were replaced by *"sept perdant," "le point est neuf,"* and other vapid Gallicisms which, the croupiers said, are more in keeping with Monte Carlo Casino, and the pall returned. While I was there, our happy American crap game was being played by three phlegmatic Englishmen, who, one after another, were shaking the dice rather like Captain Queeg and letting them dribble to the wardroom table. "Ah," said one of them, addressing me, "you shouldn't have come to Monte Carlo. One hour, and you're a goner."

I assured the fellow that after one hour at Monte Carlo it was everything I could do to keep awake. In fact, it was more than I could do, and as he rattled the bones, as they trickled across the table, as the croupier murmured *"Le point est neuf,"* I toddled home.

The next morning, I ran across Diana and Malcolm Browne, my smuggling and smoking acquaintances from Andorra. We had a happy reunion at their hotel: Malcolm gave me a Lucky Strike and, reaching into the side pocket of his red tartan B-4 bag, discovered a dozen bottles of Spanish amontillado there, and Diana read me a love letter she had received from Paco, the bullfighter. Paco had written,

> El valer de una mujer
> Reside, no en el tener
> Sino en el SER
> Tú ERES,

which is to say, we decided, that Diana's value didn't reside in what she had—Malcolm?—but in what she was. Diana observed that what she was, was bored silly, having been in Monaco a week and having decided the Monte Carlo Casino couldn't hold a candle to the Posada Catalunya. For another hour, we sighed for the happier, bygone days of Monte Carlo, when guns were fired, when bombs were tossed, when kings, queens, and emperors were playing; when "splendid women," I had read, "with bold eyes and golden hair and marble columns of imperial throats were there to laugh, to sing songs, to tempt"; when "sometimes, however, a person may be seized with a violent attack of hysterical screaming, in which circumstances it is convenient to have the surgery . . . close at hand"; when Mr. Charles Deville Wells, a cockney, won at least two hundred thousand dollars and caused the casino's tables to be draped in black, and so became, in 1891, the Man Who Broke the Bank at Monte Carlo, and when, in 1892, the bank at Monte Carlo broke Mr. Wells; when Lady Luck was courted not with pencils, papers, arithmetical tables, and "systems" as dreary as a dust mop, but with hambones, hangman's rope, rabbit's feet, snake skins, spiders, blonde and beautiful *mascottes*, and the withered hearts of bats; when the place was racy, electric, alive. And then, Diana, Malcolm, and I resolved to do something about it.

That evening, the three of us appeared at Monte Carlo Casino with enough paraphernalia to fission the atom. Malcolm carried a Dunlop & Jackson log-log slide rule, a pork chop, a four-leaf clover, and a periodic table of the elements; I had the *American*

MONACO

Ephemeris for 1955; and Diana had a stopwatch, a horseshoe, and a table of logarithms and trigonometric functions. With all these, and with the most intense, professorial of miens, we seated ourselves at a table, and I started to bet, often pretending to consult the trigonometric functions, the pork chop, the *American Ephemeris*, etc., and receiving from Diana and Malcolm such exotic memoranda as $AgNO_3 + HCl \rightarrow AgCl\downarrow + HNO_3$, $x = \sum_{r=-\infty}^{\infty} x_r e^{2\pi i r r_0 t}$, and $f^n(z) = \frac{n!}{2\pi i} \int_C \frac{f(t)}{(t-z)^{n+1}} dt$. From the start, we had extraordinary luck. Betting at random on red, black, odd, and even, we won continually and inside of ten minutes had doubled our capital (two dollars and seventy-five cents), at which rate, as Malcolm calculated on the slide rule, we would have realized a handsome fifty-eight billion dollars by midnight. Then, as Diana began to rub the horseshoe wildly, as Malcolm gave me the scribbled intelligence that $\cos\theta = \cos^n \frac{\theta}{n} \left\{ 1 - \frac{n(n-1)}{1 \cdot 2} \tan^2 \frac{\theta}{n} + \ldots \right\}$, I peered about, to see what kind of sensation the three of us were causing.

None at all. Nobody was watching Malcolm, nobody was watching Diana, nobody was watching me; nobody was watching the wheel, nobody was watching the ball; everybody was watching his pencil, his papers, and his meaningless arithmetical tables. So there they sat, in the Monte Carlo Casino, insensible, glum, trying, trying, trying to find the aquarium's exit.

*"It's awfully dull.
I haven't been there in ages."*

—THE PRINCESS OF LIECHTENSTEIN.

LIECHTENSTEIN

I bumped into the Princess of Liechtenstein at a cocktail party in Austria—quite literally, for I had been dancing to "Rock Around the Clock" with an American girl, Miss Alice Gray, no title, and we had come a cropper on the rice, würst'l, and snowballs all over the cocktail party's floor. The rice and würst'l had been spilled there by a pedigreed poodle belonging, I think, to

LIECHTENSTEIN

the Princess, and the snowballs had been tossed into the window by the Prince of Luxembourg. (I don't associate with royalty much, especially at times like this, but the cocktail party was being attended by just about everybody in town, highborn and low.) Alice, at any rate, was helped to her feet by a prince whose name and constituency I have forgotten, who fell to talking with her, and who made, according to Alice, some proposals for which he'd surely be hanged in effigy by Prince Louis I of Monaco. Meanwhile, I fell to talking with Princess Elisabeth of Liechtenstein. She is a girl of twenty-seven, small, chubby, but very pretty, who is democratically known at cocktail parties as Fraülein "Gucki" Liechtenstein—or as "Cookie" to people who didn't catch the name—and who was wearing the very tight, royal purple ski pants that are the coming thing in Austria, a parka of Persian lamb, and gray sealskin slippers. I was wearing gray flannels, if anyone cares, and when I had brushed the rice, würst'l, and snowballs from them, I remarked to Princess Elisabeth that I'd been to Monaco, Andorra, and some other places recently, and that I'd surely have a look-see at Liechtenstein before I called it a day. "Well, it's an awfully pretty country—trees, the mountains, snow—" the Princess said, "but I can't imagine you'll like it any. It's awfully dull. *I* haven't been there in ages." Instead, she went on, she was living in Austria, where trees, the mountains, and snow are also to be found and where it's livelier by far than the Principality of Liechtenstein. I agreed that Austria is nothing if not lively—but here our conversation was interrupted, and ended, by Alice, who seized me by the arm and said, "*Please,* John, get me another prince, this one is creepy." Alice, too, had been at the cocktails, and we left the party shortly after.

That the Princess of Liechtenstein doesn't choose to live in Liechtenstein isn't viewed with any dismay in Liechtenstein itself. At the latest census, there were no fewer than thirty-seven ladies properly called "the Princess of Liechtenstein," as well as thirty-five gentlemen "the Prince of Liechtenstein," and it's generally agreed in Liechtenstein—whose population is that of Ada, Oklahoma's—that the presence of so many highnesses there would make for overcrowding, to say the least. Tiny as it is, Liechtenstein owns to more princes and princesses than any other monarchy on earth. Not all of them are sons and daughters of the ruler, of course; Elisabeth is only a fourth cousin once removed. However, it's specified in the by-laws of the Liechtenstein family that just about everyone in the Liechtenstein family is a prince or a princess—a rather democratic practice, to be sure, at least for people in the Liechtenstein family, but a practice the other royal families of Europe have never taken exception to, so neither shall I. Indeed, after doing some research into this matter, I found only five people in the Liechtenstein family who *aren't* princes. Two of them are the children of Prince Ferdinand, who scandalized the family when he up and got married to—not a countess, not a baroness, as every good Liechtenstein had—a certain Miss Shelagh Brunner, of England, in 1925. The marriage was annulled, but alas! too late, and the Liechtenstein family found itself possessed of a prince and a princess who, by law, hadn't even been conceived. Here was a pretty mess, and what they did about it was declare them a count and a countess instead, a solution that seems to have satisfied the Liechtenstein family but doesn't satisfy *me*. Two other non-princes on the family tree are Aleene, of 4024 North Fortieth Street, Phoenix, Arizona, whose predicament is a little like Miss Brunner's was, and Wilhelm, who decided at the age of twenty-eight to be a count instead, for reasons I haven't been made a party to. Finally, we have the case of Hans, a smuggler who was caught recently, was fined $117,000, was given four months in Lindau, Germany, and was cut down a few notches by the Liechtenstein family— from "Prince Hans of Liechtenstein" to "Herr Hans of Landshut," a title not so ignominious as "Mr. Hans of Landshut" but pretty ignominious, still. The Lord of Landshut—a better translation—now is out of the clink and is living in Liechtenstein, a fat, Falstaffian man who gives rubberneck tours in the summer and draws Christmas cards in the off season. Liechten-

LIECHTENSTEIN

stein is also inhabited by six princes, three princesses, and, of course, *by the* prince, Franz Josef II Maria Aloys Alfred Karl Johannes Heinrich Michael Georg Ignatius Benediktus Gerhardus Majella von Liechtenstein, who runs the place, and it's visited at rare intervals by the other sixty-one, all of whom, though, would agree with Princess Elisabeth there are other places they'd rather be. In fact, some of them haven't been there yet.

The unenthusiastic view of Liechtenstein that is shared by all of these Liechtensteins was also shared, in the past, by the princes supposed to be reigning in it, as well as by Mr. Albert Stockvis, of Cleveland, Ohio, who has written the world's only guidebook to Liechtenstein. I came across Mr. Stockvis's book, *Andorra from A-Z: a Handbook of the Miniature Republic of Andorra in Alphabetical Order, and Liechtenstein,* in the stacks of the Harvard University Library, where some of his other scholarly works, like the *Story of My Life* and *Catalogue of the Autographs of Celebrities of All Nations of the World, Including the Far East, from A.D. 1500 to the Present Time,* are kept. What Mr. Stockvis says about Liechtenstein, under "T," for Touring, is "The principality offers the visitor NOT a variety of interesting sights. There is no atmosphere of its own and only a few picturesque costumes and customs. Relics of the past and monuments are few and what is shown is not of great artistic value. There are no attractions of fine food or the possibility of sports such as yachting, shooting, golf, etc." (Andorra doesn't fare any better, I'm afraid. "There is no question about it," says Mr. Stockvis in the Andorran part of his guidebook, "that American tourists having lived rather well will return disgruntled from Andorra, because with the exception of a few streets in Escaldas [*sic*] they found conditions terrible and also the less agreeable smells.") The reigning princes of Liechtenstein, for their part, while they'd probably hold that Mr. Stockvis has overstated his case, nevertheless chose to live until several years ago in Vienna, Austria, and did their reigning by telephone. In Vienna, they busied themselves with other properties of the Liechtenstein family, such as a lumber mill, a paper mill, a few banks, the Austrian counterpart of *Life,* an art collection—said to be the world's finest in private hands and worth $150,000,000—and some Czechoslovakian real estate, a dozen times larger than Liechtenstein and more profitable, too. Then, the Nazis came, and Prince Franz I de Paula hurried to Liechtenstein, finding to his surprise it wasn't half so bad as everyone had said. His successor, Franz Joseph II, has been living in Liechtenstein ever since, and the Liechtensteiner are pleased as Punch.

Franz Josef has taken up residence in a castle, a gray, gabled, primitive place on a cliff overlooking the Rhine—magnificent from afar, but rather cold and melancholy from up close. His Highness has been trying to spruce it up somewhat, to make it a bit more habitable, and I made certain, after I'd gotten to Liechtenstein, to stop by and see how he was getting on. Previously, I had been given a letter of introduction by one of the princes at the cocktail party, the Prince of Hohenlohe—a country I'm quite unable to locate, but a splendid chap, nevertheless. The Prince of Hohenlohe had pointed out that no sentries are on duty at the Liechtenstein castle, since the army had been demobilized ninety-one years ago; however, he said, the drawbridge is usually down, and if I went across it, continued to the outer courtyard, and rang the first doorbell on my left, I'd very likely find somebody or other at home. All of this I did on a cool spring afternoon, and the door was opened promptly by one of the retinue, a baroness, whom I told I had a letter of introduction from the Prince of Hohenlohe. *"Which* Prince of Hohenlohe?" she said, and I concluded that things are just as chaotic in the Hohenlohe family as they are in the Liechtenstein one.

"Well, he was about this tall," I said, "give or take an inch, blue eyes, brown hair, his brother married the fifteen-year-old, he—"

"Ah! Wonny. A wonderful boy," said the baroness, "and do give him my best. His Highness is out of town, I'm sorry to say. *Her* Highness is in town, at the dentist's, I think, and she ought

LIECHTENSTEIN

to be back any minute now. Can you spare a minute?" I said I certainly could, and I spent it looking out of a latticed bay window of the castle, and down at the Rhine, the Rhine valley, and the length and breadth of Liechtenstein far below—black roads where the snow had melted, and white roof-tops where it hadn't, a latticework in itself. Presently, there was a rumbling on the drawbridge, and a gray Chevrolet with the number FL2132 came into the courtyard. "Here she is!" said the baroness, the two of us ran outside, and I was presented then and there to the Princess of Liechtenstein—*the* Princess this time, the reigning one.

Her name is Gina, and she is perhaps the most gracious lady I've known. She is young, tall, soft-spoken, and very attractive, and she was wearing a wool skirt, a leather jerkin of tan, and a gray silk, abundant scarf. "His Highness has been living here since 1937," she said, "and he and I were married in March, 1943. By then, most of the interior decorating had been done, so I really haven't had to worry about it. We had a rock garden built at the bottom of the moat, as you saw, perhaps, when you came over the drawbridge, and we also had an elevator built in the castle itself. The castle is fully electrified now, and it's very livable, I think. I'd be happy to show you around it." Thereupon, the Princess took me into the small gray inner court, into the castle itself, and up the elevator to the donjon, where a number of medieval suits of armor and the muskets of the Liechtenstein army, demobilized ninety-one years ago, are kept. From there, we worked our way downward. The donjon itself was naked and rather damp, but the other rooms, where the Princess and Prince Franz Josef II live, were warm, sunny, and well decorated, and a pretty girl with a vacuum cleaner was giving them a going-over. The Princess stepped carefully over the hose. "And here is the children's room," she said, opening a paneled door, "and here are the children!" They, Prince Hans Adam and Prince Philipp Erasmus, stood up in black corduroy knickers from a Lionel toy train set, hurried to their mother, and kissed her dutifully on the cheek, and Prince Hans Adam

(Prince Johannes Adam Ferdinand Alois Josef Maria Marko D'Aviano Pius von Liechtenstein), its ruler in twenty or thirty years, looked up at me quizzically.

"*Guten Tag,*" I said, shaking his hand, and I hope it was the proper thing.

In the end, I never did meet Franz Josef II, as I never met Rainier III, but I've learned a number of things about him, as I did about Rainier, and I pass them on—that he was born in the vicinity of Graz, Austria, in 1906; that he went to high school and college in Vienna; that he, too, likes to go skiing but not to go skin diving; that he is also the Duke of Troppau, the Count of Rietberg, etc., etc.; and that he is "jovial," "regal," "uncomplicated," and "likable." He is a Hapsburg by way of his mother, and he has a Hapsburg lip, which, I'm afraid, gives him a rather sour expression in the photographs I've seen, as if he were biting a lemon. He is a second cousin seven times removed of Johann Adam (1662-1712), the first prince of Liechtenstein, and he is a half nephew, not at all removed, of Franz Ferdinand (1863-1914), the fellow who was shot at Sarajevo. He is the twelfth man to be running the country. (There weren't any women.)

While Johann Adam, as I said, was the first prince of Liechtenstein—its first sovereign, that is—he wasn't by any manner of means the first Prince of Liechtenstein, for the title had been given to his family more than five hundred years earlier, by a king, apparently to write off a bad debt. There had been, for example, a Prince Georg III of Liechtenstein, who was a cardinal, and a Prince Ulrich of Liechtenstein, a minnesinger who made a mark for himself as a crackajack lover, too. However, there wasn't any such country as Liechtenstein. A real pickle, that, and a constant source of embarrassment to the Princes of Liechtenstein, who, not knowing what to do about it, saw it perpetuated until the eve of the eighteenth century. Then, Prince Johann Adam—"Johann Adam the Rich," as he was spoken of—decided this nonsense had gone far enough, and what he did was to spend $1,200,000 of his riches, buy the

LIECHTENSTEIN

Manor of Schellenberg and the County (a country run by a count) of Vaduz, and rename it all "Liechtenstein"—a splendid idea, I think, making him a prince with a principality at last, and giving his family tree something to sink its roots into. Liechtenstein, the place, was recognized by the Holy Roman Empire on January 23, 1719—its Fourth of July—and it also became a *part* of the Holy Roman Empire, and it's the only part to have survived into 1959. Just why, nobody in Liechtenstein could tell me, but part of the reason, they decided, is that it was plumb forgotten by Bismarck when he put together the German Reich. Having gone to war with Liechtenstein (and Austria) in 1866, and having defeated it, Bismarck promptly lost track of the whole affair, and his army never occupied the place—nor has a treaty of peace ever been signed.

Of the reigning one-dozen princes of Liechtenstein, the most glorious in every way was a bachelor one, Johann II—"Johann the Good," as he was called, for he spent eighteen million dollars of *his* riches on good works for Liechtenstein. He built it schools, churches, hospitals, and other places; he put in roads, water mains, telephones, and electricity; he even financed a kind of *Oktoberfest,* in the fall. Johann had been reigning a year in this public-spirited way when, in the United States, Abraham Lincoln was elected, and he was still at it when Herbert Hoover was—seventy years in all, "perhaps the longest reign of any monarch in history," according to his biographer. (I'm afraid it wasn't. Louis XIV had him by two years, one week, six days.) In 1921, though, for all his goodness, Johann was forced by the Liechtensteiner to give them a constitution, and since then the country has been "a constitutional monarchy on a democratic and parliamentary foundation," being governed, instead, by a prime minister, a few other ministers, including a foreign minister, and a democratic, parliamentary, partisan, well-paid Landtag of fifteen men. The "constitutional monarch"—His Highness Franz Josef II, Prince of Liechtenstein, Duke of Troppau, Count of Rietberg, etc., etc., regal, likable, heir to twenty generations of Liechtensteins, a prince among thirty-five princes and thirty-seven princesses, too—has little to do nowadays but sign, sign, sign, and, whenever the Landtag convenes, to welcome it, and his welcoming speech has been paraphrased by a Liechtensteiner as "Good morning. How are you? I'm happy to be here. Good-by." Franz Josef II, like Johann the Good, is spending some of his money on Liechtenstein now, but not much. Instead, the democratic, parliamentary principality has an income tax—for some people, more than they'd pay in the United States—a property tax; a tariff; a salt monopoly; and a national debt, which, when I was visiting it, had just passed two-and-a-quarter million dollars.

I'd driven to Liechtenstein in the early spring of 1956, from Austria, and I, too, had discovered it wasn't so bad as people said. Sure, it wasn't so lively as Austria, but it was pretty lively, nevertheless—one or two movies along the main road, including *Annie Get Your Gun*; Leonardo, a hypnotist advertised as "the King of *Massensuggestion*," at a high-school gymnasium in the highlands; and even a night club, the Schlössle, with an "international floor show" at eleven o'clock (a hootchie-cootcher). Fine food, the lack of which was reported by the irascible Mr. Stockvis, was really to be had, along with a fine red wine—Vaduzer. Furthermore, there WAS a variety of interesting sights, notably a small, well-kept, well-lit art museum where some of the $150,000,000 art collection of the Liechtenstein family is hung—"Venus" and "Sons of the Artist" by Rubens, a "Portrait of a Young Man" and fourteen others by van Dyck, a few Halses, and one of the grisly extravaganzas of Pieter Brueghel, the Charles Addams of his day—"The Census in Bethlehem," full of hags, cretins, and other disagreeable persons. Almost all of these divertisements were to be found in Liechtenstein's most heavily populated and capital town of Vaduz, a flat, haphazard, not very beautiful place, I thought, rather like Andorra the Old. Like it, Vaduz is in the middle of a housing boom, and there's a good deal of untidiness—sand, gravel, cement, and similar items—there, all of it being compounded

LIECHTENSTEIN

with much ado, and much noise, at the very center of town. Otherwise, the country was lovely. The trees, mountains, and snow were east, west, and, to a lesser degree, north and south of Vaduz; the mountains were seven thousand feet, the snow beginning at two thousand. Green at the bottom, the mountains were gray-green in the middle reaches, and they were cold, quiet, and frostbite-white on top, as if they were dying there; and the clouds were the very same color, frostbite-white.

When I came to Liechtenstein, I was, of course, stopped for a few moments at the border. A customs man—a Swiss, not a Liechtensteiner—took my passport; recorded in it that I was arriving in Switzerland; took my *carnet de passages,* a sort of passport for cars; recorded in this that my car was arriving in Switzerland; said *"Auf Wiedersehen";* and waved me on—all this in spite of Switzerland's being quite another country, nine or ten miles down the road. Later, I asked for an explanation of this, and I learned that Switzerland and Liechtenstein are in a customs union and that Switzerland does all the work—a fine arrangement, of course, for the Liechtensteiner, but a very deceptive one for everyone else, who, once they get a Swiss visa in their passport, a Swiss visa in their *carnet,* and a cheery *"Auf Wiedersehen"* from the Swiss who put it there, can scarcely be blamed for thinking they're in Switzerland. Indeed, as I also learned, eighty percent of the people going across Liechtenstein in cars, ninety percent of those going across it in buses, and ninety-five percent of those going across it in trains (the Paris-to-Vienna one, for example) are blithely unaware that Liechtenstein is where they are, and of the remainder from twenty to thirty percent come to this realization only after being told—generally by a loyal, distressed Liechtensteiner. All of these hitherto unpublished figures were given me by Baron Edward von Falz-Fein, a loyal, very distressed Liechtensteiner who has done an unparalleled job, I believe, of making these travelers more widely cognizant of their whereabouts. For ten years, Baron von Falz-Fein has been the owner, manager, and most indefatigable clerk at the Quick Tourist Office in Vaduz, the largest in Liechtenstein, and at its branch on the border, a hop, skip, and a jump from the illusory Swiss customs. At these two strategic points, the Baron has sought to arrest the forward motion of as many cars, buses, and trains as one man humanly can, to inform the people inside that they are in Liechtenstein, to explain that Liechtenstein is a country and, incidentally, that he is Baron von Falz-Fein, to report some of its history, and, before any of these astonished travelers can go ahead into Switzerland or Austria, to sell them a postcard, a cheese, a cuckoo clock, or some such remembrance of their visit to Liechtenstein. Quite understandably, the Baron has hesitated actually to flag these vehicles down, but has tried to check them in other, more devious ways—specifically by assigning a number of peasants to wear *lederhosen* and *dirndls* and, when a vehicle is sighted, to throw themselves uninhibitedly into a native dance; by also retaining a band to strike up loud, picturesque, and very arresting music on such occasions; and, the most efficacious of all, by fronting the Quick Tourist Office and its suburban outlet with a wide, wide window of cuckoo clocks, cowbells, cheese, and other merchandise which, admittedly, have nothing whatsoever to do with Liechtenstein, but which are known empirically to bring the most hurried tourist to a standstill. Indeed, so many travelers are given pause by these attractions that Liechtenstein is verging on a national crisis: its traffic police have had to be reinforced by fifty percent, and the most pressing item on the Landtag's agenda is fixing the roads—not, like Andorra, to bring more tourists into the country, but to get them out. Baron von Falz-Fein is delighted, but Franz Josef II and Herr Alexander Frick, the Prime Minister, are said to feel otherwise. Herr Frick is apprehensive lest the sight of so many idlers be an unhealthy influence on the peasants, and has stated so in the *New York Times,* while His Highness, who feels that a Liechtenstein's home is his castle and a Liechtenstein's castle is his home, has taken exception to those idlers trespassing in it. Recently, he posted the place in German, English, and French—PRIVATE PROPERTY, NO CASTLE-

LIECHTENSTEIN

VISITING in German, and, simply, NO ENTRANCE in English and French.

In still another way, the Baron's irreproachable doings have backfired on him. So passionately does he go about them, so recklessly does he slow up traffic, so aggressively does he bring the people inside to their bearings, and, at last, so brilliantly does he instruct them in Liechtenstein's history that he himself is now regarded as Liechtenstein's most outstanding scenic attraction, to the detriment of its art museum, its international floor show, its fine food, and its trees, mountains, and snow. Clearly, he is considered such by Mr. Temple Fielding, the author of *Fielding's Guide to Europe*, who concluded his guide to Liechtenstein with a handy, panoramic, two-hundred-and-twenty-word guide to Baron von Falz-Fein, and also by Mr. Gordon Cooper, Mr. Fielding's counterpart in England, who, seeing Mr. Fielding and raising him one, writes that *he* regards the Baron not only "as one of the 'sights' of Liechtenstein [but] even of Europe." The Baron is one of those happy, neurotic people who cannot be motionless, a real spectacle in these unadventurous days. When he isn't working at the Quick Tourist Office or orienting aliens in its vicinity, he's off by leaps and bounds to further the good name of Liechtenstein in other, equally go-ahead ways—by an Olympic bobsled team (he's the coach), by an Olympic skiing team (he's the coach, and the Prince of Hohenlohe's the team), by a very unofficial visa, by a ski lift (for the Prince of Hohenlohe), by meeting, a few weeks ago, with representatives of Andorra, Monaco, and San Marino to draw up a "multilateral treaty of friendship" in "an otherwise weary world," by a movie, by picture postcards, and so forth, and so forth, and so forth. In the meantime, if any, Baron von Falz-Fein keeps on the *qui vive* by sweeping the sand, cement, and gravel off the streets, and that's what he was doing when I met him—on Herren Street, Vaduz, in the late afternoon, my first in Liechtenstein. The Baron was wearing a quaint gray-and-green national costume and he whistled while he worked, and, when I had introduced myself, he said "Hello!

I can't shake hands with you, and I'm sorry—dirt. Anyhow, I'm not in charge of visiting journalists. The Baroness, my wife, is in charge of visiting journalists, and she's inside. Then, if there's anything in the world she didn't tell you, there'll be a bus tomorrow—Cook's, and it'll be at the border at noon, at one if there was a puncture, at two if someone's sick, to hear me talk about Liechtenstein. So come along! and I'll give you a visa, too." Baron von Falz-Fein delivered the greater part of this rather hurriedly, never letting go of the broom, and I've surely got some of the details wrong. The *New York Times* got his name wrong, and Mr. Fielding got his nationality wrong, calling him an Englishman, and Mr. Gordon Cooper, for Pete's sake, even got oriented wrong. Mr. Cooper discusses the Baron in *Your Holiday in Switzerland*.

Anyway, I thanked the Baron for his invitation, said I'd be there, and, acting on his advice, I think, went to the Quick Tourist Office, sought out the Baroness, explained that I was a visiting journalist, and asked to be taken charge of. Imme-

LIECHTENSTEIN

diately, I was. "Liechtenstein," said the Baroness, a firm, unsmiling lady of thirty or thirty-five, raising her voice above the cuckoo clocks, "is sixty-one square miles in area. Liechtenstein has a population of eleven thousand people, plus two thousand seven hundred foreigners. Liechtenstein is ninety-three percent Catholic, and if I see another visiting journalist, I'll scream." So saying, the Baroness gave me an indescribable look, hurried away, and began addressing herself to a lady—a visiting non-journalist, I supposed, who was watching the cuckoo clocks. "*Here* is a cuckoo clock," said the Baroness, "which is very lovely, I believe, and which we are selling at thirty-eight and a half francs."

"How much is that in money?" said the lady.

"Nine dollars," said the Baroness, and as the deal was consummated, I went to the Quick Tourist Office's book corner, determined to continue my research, come what may. Here, I perceived, was every book to have been written about Liechtenstein, save Mr. Stockvis's, and every book to have been written about anything by Mr. Paul Gallico, who lives in Liechtenstein, has been doing so for half a dozen years, is a chum of the Baron's, and, like him, is recommended by Mr. Cooper as "quite fantastic"—one of the "sights" of Liechtenstein, though not of Europe. On the top shelf was a truly felicitous alliance, I thought, a book about Liechtenstein by Mr. Gallico—*Ludmila,* which I presently began to read, meanwhile keeping a wary eye on the Baroness. "Part way up the valley from Steg, in the Principality of Liechtenstein," I read, "where the torrent Malbun comes tumbling down its glacial bed from the peaks of the Ochsenkopf and Silberhorn, you will find the shrine of St. Ludmila, *die heilige Notburga.* [Nearby] are to be encountered from time to time the scattered plants of that herb not found in the lowlands, one of the rare *Garbengewächse,* of the Species *Alchemilla,* which the Liechtensteiners call by the beautiful name of *Mutterkraut.*" Mr. Gallico, I thought, has certainly acquired a firm grip on local color.

Reading on, I discovered that Mr. Gallico's story has to do

with the *abfahrt*, one of the very few traditions of Liechtenstein that didn't originate with Baron von Falz-Fein. An *abfahrt* is a going-down—specifically that of Liechtenstein's three thousand cows from the high meadowlands where they spend the summer to the villages below, in autumn, and at the front of the *abfahrt* is the most lactiferous cow, cutting a figure in red, white, blue, silver, and gold ribbons, its milking stool on its head upside-down, and a laurel wreath on that. So attired, the *abfahrt* goes leisurely into a mountain tunnel, built, incidentally, by Franz Josef II, and out again into the sun, where every Liechtensteiner who can spare the time is waiting to greet it. Still reading, I'd come to this very point in Mr. Gallico's story—"Men waved their hats and shouted, women wept and sobbed . . . the brass band struck up the national anthem of Liechtenstein, the *Männerchor* burst into song, as did the *Sängerbund*"—and I'd made a mental note to ask about the national anthem, when I glanced up, and found myself staring into the icy eyes of Baroness von Falz-Fein. "You," she said, not yet screaming, "will want to meet Mr. Gallico, I believe, so there he is." Baroness von Falz-Fein pointed down the counter, hied herself to her customers again, and presently could be overheard to say, "*Here* is a lovely music box. It's 'O Mein Papa,' and which we are selling at eleven francs and . . ."

Well, Mr. Gallico *is* fantastic. His body is massive, his face is ponderous, his expression is that of a continuous harrumph—in all, a very formidable person. Here at the Quick Tourist Office, he was dressed in a fabulous blue pin-stripe double-breasted suit, a similar shirt, and a pre-eminent red tie; he was crouching low at a far counter, feinting with his left at the counter clerk. "Bong!" Mr. Gallico was saying as I approached him. "The fourteenth round, if you are following me," and the clerk, who was following Mr. Gallico, smiled wanly, jabbing him experimentally in the solar plexus. I bided my time and, when they had separated, introduced myself to the fantastic Mr. G., congratulated him on the appearance of *Ludmila*, his first book to be published in Liechtenstein, and asked how it

LIECHTENSTEIN

was doing. "Quite well," said Mr. Gallico, putting his dukes down and speaking in a *basso profondo* voice, "and thank you. Tomorrow, the Baroness and I shall be driving to England in regard to a movie. The younger baroness is there now, taking a screen test." Mr. Gallico explained that the younger baroness is four, is the daughter of Baron and Baroness von Falz-Fein, is able to speak German, English, and a little French, is most fortuitously named Ludmila, and is anxious to land the starring role, also Ludmila—not St. Ludmila, the statue, but Ludmila Vospelt, the principal biped in Mr. Gallico's story. When I had disentangled all these Ludmilas, I questioned Mr. Gallico about his chum and her father, the Baron, who still could be contemplated going hammer and tongs at the sand, cement, and gravel on Herren Street. "He," said Mr. Gallico decisively, "is running the whole country. See, Eddie is cleaning the street, but meantime he's talking to the Prime Minister." Then Mr. Gallico shook hands with me, touched mitts with the counter clerk, explained that he and Eddie were going for a stroll, and, stepping outside, took away Eddie's broom and his water hose, and together they strolled into the sunset on the now immaculate street. I gathered that Mr. Gallico was very proud to know somebody who knew the Prime Minister of Liechtenstein, and vice versa.

Soon afterwards, the Quick Tourist Office shut up, and I was hurried outside by the Baroness. I partook of some fine food at the Ratskellar Engel, listened to the zitherist there, took in the international floor show at the Schlössle, slept at the Pension Sonnenhof, a quiet, delightful place, and the next morning drove to the Quick Tourist Office's branch at the border, to keep my appointment with Baron von Falz-Fein. "What a morning!" he said as I arrived. "Two hundred people, and Freddie was in a flap, poor boy. Look at that, he couldn't even wind the cuckoo clocks." Freddie, the branch manager, a thin, relatively subdued man of twenty-five or so, smiled at me to indicate he was Freddie and precipitately began to wind the cuckoo clocks. As the decibels rose, Baron von Falz-Fein went over to his customers, bowed, and sought to interest them in a selection of Swiss cheeses, and I went over to Freddie.

We struck up a conversation. "I'm from Switzerland, and I ran into Baron von Falz-Fein at a movie in St. Moritz," said Freddie, still winding, "and he said, 'Come with me to Liechtenstein!' So I did, and look, he made me the branch manager. Every half an hour, cuckoo! cuckoo! cuckoo! and I used to go balmy, so now all of the cuckoo clocks are a different time. Here, this one's seven o'clock. Any moment now, the—"

"Cuckoo! Cuckoo!" said the clock.

"Eight dollars and fifty cents," said Freddie. "Also we've got a smaller model, if you're interested, and we've also got music boxes, Liechtenstein cow bells, ocarinas . . . I can give you a visa, too."

"The Baron mentioned about the visa," I said.

"Sure, can I have your passport? It's free," said Freddie, "only don't let anybody see it."

"Why not?" I asked.

"The Baron or you'll be fined—there's a government order against it."

"*What* government?" I asked.

"*All* governments," said Freddie, and as I hurriedly took my passport back, Baron von Falz-Fein reappeared. He was carrying a half-eaten banana, and he held it aloft, for all humanity to see.

"My lunch," said the Baron disgustedly. "What a morning! And next it'll be Mr. Gallico and my wife—so good-by, every cigarette in the store. They are driving to England, you know."

"I know. Yesterday," I said, "I was talking to Mr. Gallico. I'd meant to ask him, or someone, about the national anthem."

"Of Liechtenstein?" said the Baron. "It's the same as Switzerland's, '*Rufst du, mein Vaterland*'—the same music. Also it's the same as England's, 'God Save the Queen.'"

"In that case," I said, "it's the same as 'America,' also."

"Good lord! Popular, isn't it?" said the Baron, and he thereupon sang the national anthem of Liechtenstein, and, for those

LIECHTENSTEIN

readers of mine who'll want to do the same, I conscientiously noted the words:

> Oben am deutschen Rhein
> Lehnet sich Liechtenstein
> An Alpenhöh'n.
> Dies liebe Heimatland
> Im deutschen Vaterland
> Hat Gottes weise Hand
> Für uns ersehn.

When the Baron had finished, he hurried back to his customers, and I was left speculating on what in the world Liechtenstein was doing in a German fatherland. By and by, though, my thoughts were interrupted by the arrival of Mr. Gallico and the Baroness, in a big, hideous, black-and-ivory Bentley—custom made, with a silver PWG on its black-and-ivory door. Mr. Gallico eased the automobile to the curb, opened the door, disengaged himself from a safety belt, got out, and shook hands solemnly with Baron von Falz-Fein; the Baroness didn't budge. Mr. Gallico was dressed as fabulously as the day before, I noticed.

"Paul, I can't get out of this thing," said the Baroness. She was digging away at her safety belt, and looking very displeased.

"Tsk!" said Mr. Gallico, and untethered the Baroness; then they went into the Quick Tourist Office, and Mr. Gallico began to provision himself with chocolate bars. I took the opportunity to ask him why he lived in Liechtenstein.

"Why do I live here? Because it's quiet," said Mr. Gallico. "My home is higher than four thousand feet, and nobody else can find it." Mr. Gallico smiled sinisterly.

"*Please* don't talk to Mr. Gallico," cried the Baroness from across the room. "We're in a great hurry." Mr. Gallico shrugged and went back to the Bentley, and, presently, so did the Baroness, after gathering twenty packs of cigarettes from the shelf, giving a long, typewritten list of things to the Baron, and kiss-

"Why do I live here? Because it's quiet," said Mr. Gallico.

LIECHTENSTEIN

ing him perfunctorily. Then, safety belts were closed, contact was made.

"Drive carefully, Paul," said Baron von Falz-Fein.

"*Jawohl*," said Mr. Gallico, and away they went, and, as they did, along came Cook's in the other direction. Some prior arrangement must have been made, since the bus stopped dutifully, and right alongside the Quick Tourist Office.

"What a *morn*ing!" said Baron von Falz-Fein to Freddie, who was still winding the cuckoo clocks. "But yes, they're all like this, aren't they?" Freddie nodded.

The bus door had opened now, and a swarm of bluebottles alighted to begin their visit to Liechtenstein—a visit of twenty-odd minutes, to be sure, but long enough for Baron von Falz-Fein to deliver his message, and he started at once. Until now, the Baron had spoken a very creditable English, but now he seemed to have acquired a thick East European accent, and his talk was interpolated with phrases like "something who is more interesting," "forty or fifty hours a mile," and "I apologize, I cannot speak well English." ("Oh, *we* can understand you.") In this exotic idiom, which, for the sake of clarity, I shall omit, the Baron apprised his listeners that they were in Liechtenstein and, when the gasps of astonishment had subsided, went on to say, "Liechtenstein is a country with only eleven thousand people. 'Liechtenstein' is German for 'a bright stone'—which one, I do not know—and people have lived in Liechtenstein for five thousand years. In 1939, Germany tried to invade Liechtenstein, but Father Frommel and some of the *Pfadfinderkorps*, the Boy Scouts, were waiting here at the border, and Father Frommel said to the Germans, 'Go back. You aren't wanted in Liechtenstein,' and the Germans did. Twice Liechtenstein was invaded by Russia. The first time in 1815; the second time in 1945, but *they* only wanted, and got, political asylum in Liechtenstein." In such a vein, Baron von Falz-Fein spoke for another few minutes and concluded, "Now, if you'll want a souvenir of Liechtenstein, come inside. We have cuckoo clocks, a visa, and many things more, and *Ludmila*, a story by Mr. Gallico, who lives in Liechtenstein, which is autographed by Mr. Gallico."

Then, into the Quick Tourist Office went Baron Edward von Falz-Fein, into it went the swarm of bluebottles, and, presently, into it went I. Bluebottles, barons, and counter clerks were in a stupefying crush, and Freddie was saying, "Look, please, a lovely souvenir of Liechtenstein."

"How much is that in money?" said a lady.

"Four shillings tuppence," said the Baron.

"Aw, we get it in *every* country," said a boy.

"Cuckoo!" said a clock, and I stole away.

Everything that Baron von Falz-Fein told the tourists at the Quick Tourist Office is the oft-told, oft-heard anecdotage of Liechtenstein. When rearranged in topical, chronological, or (notably by Mr. Stockvis) alphabetical order, it's the lion's share of everything ever written about it—*Your Holiday in Switzerland,* for instance, where it's written how "Hitler, having carelessly forgotten to include the little state in his absorption of Austria, sent a detachment along to remedy the mistake. A gallant priest, along with a few unarmed boy scouts, met the invaders, however, on the border." I knew that all this anecdotage is old hat to the reading public, and so, determined to apprise them of something new, I went that afternoon to Father Frommel himself and asked of him the full, as yet untold particulars of the 1939 affair. The Father is sixty-five or seventy now, old, burly, and rather eccentric, and he lives alone in retirement outside of Vaduz: he doesn't shave but once a week, dresses in black trousers and a black turtleneck sweater, reads, paints, and waits quietly for death. The Father was experimenting on a gray cubist crucifixion when I arrived, and he commented that he's not often visited these days, although he's much spoken of. When I asked my question, he nodded, and said, "I tell you what happened. On March 25, 1939, I have anxiety, for, according to somebody, the Nazi soldier are coming here. So I travel with the auto to the *grenze* ... *grenze?*"

LIECHTENSTEIN

"Border," I said.

"—border, to see if the Nazi soldier are here. Seeing, at the border, there are no difficulty, I—"

"No difficulty?"

"No soldier. Seeing, at the border, there are no soldier, I return to here saying, '*Gut!* There are no soldier at the border.'"

And that, Father Frommel said, is sum and substance of his story, and how the Nazi detachment and the *Pfadfinderkorps* got into it he didn't know—but there they were, and nothing he said could exterminate them. At that, the Father gave me a hopeless look, returned to his gray cubist crucifixion, and awaited anew the call of immortality. A sadder and a wiser man, I departed, recollecting something that Thomas De Quincey had written a century ago but which, till that afternoon, I hadn't really believed: "All history," De Quincey had said, "being built partly, and some of it altogether, upon anecdotage, must be a tissue of lies."

Anyhow, the population of Liechtenstein is eleven thousand. And it's also true, according to archaeologists, that people were living there five thousand years ago, although they didn't think of themselves as Liechtensteiner, of course. Very little is known of this pre-Liechtensteiner crowd, even anecdotally, until the first century B.C. ones, the Celts, who are known for their "unkempt hair, smeared with soap," their "hanging mustaches," their "rough war cries, and their disdain of death"—all this from Poseidonios, a visiting journalist of long ago. "Always thirsty and quarrelsome," he wrote, "they sit in their round huts on the bare ground, drinking and boasting of their deeds and falling into sudden tempers that end in blood fights." Since then, the Liechtensteiner have certainly come a long way. They are quiet, peaceable, closer to the sober-sided people of Switzerland than to the hail-fellow-well-met Austrians (but noways close enough to satisfy the Swiss, who tell their children to eschew the sin, folly, and winebibbery of Liechtenstein, a hundred yards away). Today, hanging mustaches are out of vogue, but a gentleman's hair in Liechtenstein is still unkempt, and it's all the rage.

Another thing I have learned—to my surprise—about the Liechtensteiner is that only twenty percent of them are farmers, but fifty percent are working in factories. This figure, too, was given to me by Baron von Falz-Fein, and when I asked him what is being made in Liechtenstein, other than cuckoo clocks, he turned red and replied, "Er . . . no cuckoo clocks. The cuckoo clocks are from Germany, a wholesaler. Well, so what? We *used* to make cuckoo clocks, but now we are making false teeth, salami skins, adding machines, fruit squeezers, bed pillows, and sewing needles"—a far more diversified output, the Baron thought, and I certainly agree. Furthermore, he said, swelling in civic pride, the Ramco false-teeth factory has less than a dozen competitors, the only others being in England, France, Italy, Germany, Switzerland, and, for heaven's sake, Liechtenstein (a small one, under the art gallery), while the Elastin-Werk salami-skin factory has only three competitors, in Germany, Sweden, and Spain, the requirements of the Communist world being satisfied by a plant in Czechoslovakia. The Contina adding-machine factory, he continued, just about ready to burst, has no competitors in all the world, for it makes the Curta, and a finer, faster, more jim-dandy adding machine you couldn't find. Indeed, said Baron von Falz-Fein, the Curta —and he took one from behind his counter—can not only add, subtract, multiply, and divide but, if the owner is particularly savvy, can extract the square root, too, yet it weighs a trifling eight ounces, the smallest adding, subtracting, multiplying, dividing, and rooting machine on earth. "Only ninety-four dollars. Go, ask me a question," said Baron von Falz-Fein, so I asked him to divide 5,796,432 by 897. The Baron leered, and taking a firm, resolute grip on the Curta, which is smaller than a fist, black, and built like a pepper mill, he started to twirl its crank with a savage determination; a giddying flow of numbers appeared on every part of the pepper mill, and I saw that a Curta was clearly what Malcolm, Diana, and I had needed at Monte Carlo, especially if a little pepper had been made to sprinkle from the bottom. Then, "6,462.020!" cried Baron von Falz-

LIECHTENSTEIN

Fein, and though I haven't bothered to verify this, I think it's plausible, indeed. "And," said the Baron, when he got his composure back, "the Curta will divide anything up to ninety-nine billion, and now, because of its popularity, we are making a Model II to divide anything up to nine hundred and ninety-nine trillion"—and he hurried behind the counter, bent down, and reappeared instantaneously with the second smallest adding, subtracting, etc. machine on earth. "Go," he said, "ask—"

Regretfully, I told the Baron how there wasn't any number in the nine-hundred trillions that I particularly wished to see divided that morning, and, thanking him for the demonstration and everything else, I left him—and here, I'm sorry to say, Baron von Falz-Fein goes out of our story forever. (Another, equally spectacular baron is waiting for us in twenty-six pages.) Meanwhile, I drove to the Contina adding-machine factory itself to see how the heretofore rural Liechtensteiner are taking to factory life, and, appropriately, I found it smack in the middle of somebody's farm, as rural as all get-out—an eloquent juxtaposition of the old and the newer Liechtensteins. Here in its pastoral setting, the adding-machine factory is long, rectangular, and not especially pretty, and inside, as I discovered by going there, is an awful hullabaloo and a small, frantic assembly line, six girls. The nearest of them was tweezering a tiny, silver thing to a tiny black thing, and was functioning at a good clip; Numbers Two and Three were assembling the innards, also at double time; Numbers Four and Five were fitting the outers to the innards; and Number Six was giving the fully articulated Curtas the once-over, twiddling the cranks to see if they added right. Nearby, a score of lathes were making the welkin ring, and yellow oil was spattering every which way, like fat in a frying pan. Presently, a guided tour to all this commotion was given me by the foreman, Herr Arno Pfeifer, a smart, enthusiastic man of thirty-five who said he learned the adding-machine game in Zurich, Switzerland, and who continued, "In Liechtenstein, we make our adding machines one every twenty minutes, and directly it's off the assembly line, it's gobbled up. However, we cannot go any faster, for there are five hundred parts. Naturally you would like to know how an adding machine works, wouldn't you?" Naturally, I said; so Herr Pfeifer went over to Number Five, who had just put a Curta together, and, taking it away from her, started for my edification to take it apart again. "As you can see," Herr Pfeifer said, as Number Five looked daggers at us, "the crank, here, is connected to a *staffelwalze*, so now you know the secret, and Franz Josef II has bought the patent. When the crank is rotated, so does the *staffelwalze*, and the *staffelwalzezahnsegment* meshes with the *übertragungsachsezähne*, on the *übertragungsachse*, which makes the *fünfzack* turn, which, in turn, makes the *ziffernrollezähne* on the *ziffernrolle* turn, and that's where the numbers are. Observe!" Herr Pfeifer turned the crank, and I kept a steady eye on the *staffelwalze, staffelwalzezahnsegment, übertragungsachsezähne, übertragungsachse, fünfzack, ziffernrollezähne,* and *ziffernrolle* to see if they were turning; and by jiminy, they were. "Besides, we have a built-in *übertragungsachseschleudersperrscheibe*," Herr Pfeifer began, but before he could finish, the midday bell started to ring, and Numbers One, Two, Three, Four, Five, and Six dropped all five hundred parts at once and bolted from the factory like a football team. Herr Pfeifer looked at me beseechingly, so I bolted too.

Having found my visit to the adding-machine factory so enlightening, I decided to spend the afternoon in visits to the Ramco false-teeth factory, the Elastin-Werk salami-skin factory, the P.A.V. fruit-squeezer factory, the Hanauer & Schmidt bed-pillow factory, and the Press & Stanzwerk sewing-needle factory, the better to comprehend our new, industrial Liechtenstein. Of these, the most educational was the salami-skin factory, in Triesen, and I want to say something about it. Believe me, never till that afternoon had I seen so much salami skin— an uninterrupted mile of it, emerging at eleven inches a second from a big, red, otherwise indescribable device at the factory and slinking, like a python, into a chemical bath and then dragging its slow length across a vast, overheated room—one hun-

LIECHTENSTEIN

dred and twenty-five degrees, I learned, to dry the salami skin. The raw material for this, I also learned, is the subcutaneous hide of cows, which neither the butcher, the tanner, nor the milkman especially wants, and which is ninety-nine and six-tenths of a percent protein. (In America we use Cellophane.) All of these widely unappreciated facts were given me by Dr. Bruno Stahlberger, my guide, a quiet, scholarly man who is employed by Elastin-Werk as a research chemist and who, I discovered, is quite embarrassed that what he is dealing with are dead cows. Every day, Dr. Stahlberger said, eight hundred cows are slaughtered in the name of salami skin, and thereupon he dropped the subject, and, as we toured the factory, referred to the salami skin at all stages of its manufacture only as "the material."

"The material," Dr. Stahlberger was saying as we left it slithering in the vast, overheated room, "at this stage is ready to be marketed, but first, we at Elastin-Werk insist on testing it, something that cannot be said by our competitors. Here"—and Dr. Stahlberger opened the door—"is our testing laboratory. The young man over there, with the air pump, is inflating the material to fifteen-hundredths of a kilogram per square centimeter, and if there's a drop in air pressure, we know there's a hole somewhere, and the material is rejected. The thingumajig near him is an electric caliper: if the traffic light is red, the material is too big; and yellow, the material is too small; and green, the material is bung-ho. As you can see, the material is bung-ho." All of which, I'm afraid, has given my readers but a tiny inkling of what was happening in the testing laboratory, for the air pump was shrieking, the electric caliper was crackling, the traffic light was flashing a green, green, green, r . . . green, and the material—now like a *den* of pythons—was writhing deliriously in the last agonies of death. All was pandemonium, and I watched it fascinated, when suddenly—pop! And the air was full of shredded salami skin.

"Uh-oh. A blowout," said Dr. Stahlberger. "The gray flannel, was it a good suit?"

"It was already stained with rice, würst'l, and snowballs," I said.

"Ah. But nevertheless, we had better leave." Dr. Stahlberger led me outside, where freights of Elastin-Werk salami skin were being manifested for Europe, England, Australia, and the United States. "Now," he said, "do you have any further questions about the material?"

"Just one. Are we supposed to eat it?" I said.

"Why not?" said Dr. Stahlberger, and as I departed, he fell to.

Over and above the Liechtensteiner who work at salami-skin, false-teeth, etc. factories are the Liechtensteiner, all lawyers, who work at radio, locomotive, and two hundred other factories—ghost factories, whose total assets in Liechtenstein are seldom more than a manila envelope, but which have incorporated there because of the easy taxes. Over and above *them*, it is said, are the Liechtensteiner, dead and alive, who work at ghosting itself, for Liechtenstein, like Sark, is said to be mightily beset by supernatural beings. Naturally, I gave this matter my careful attention when I was in Liechtenstein, and I discovered that three distinct types of abominations may be encountered there, the *schrätlings*, the *tobelhockers*, and the miscellaneous ghosts. The schrätlings are living human beings, a kind of witch, and some night if you wake up choking, it shouldn't be discounted that a schrätling has gotten you; what to do then is to gasp the following poem, in German if possible, which is said to exorcise the most persistent schrätling:

> *I ban you from my house and home,*
> *I ban you from my sty and stall,*
> *I ban you from my bedstead....*
> *Climb over all the mountains,*
> *Climb over all the fences,*
> *Climb over all the rivers,*
> *Till daylight comes again.*

LIECHTENSTEIN

At present, a dozen-odd persons are known to be schrätlings, and recently a schrätling in the salami-skin village of Triesen emigrated, when her little game was discovered, to New York City, and what she is up to now, heaven knows. A quota of one hundred people was given to Liechtenstein in the McCarran-Walter Act, as many as to India, Pakistan, or China, but no safeguard was included against schrätlings.

Our second bugaboo, the tobelhockers, are found in two varieties, living and dead, but once a tobelhocker always a tobelhocker, and the living tobelhocker of today is the dead tobelhocker of tomorrow; as such, he isn't allowed in heaven or hell and is damned, instead, to a cold, gloomy, terrestrial chasm (a *tobel*), in which he will sit (he will *hocken*) to judgment day. I myself have visited this *tobel*—a forest primeval in the silent, icicle-wet mountains in back of Triesen—and though I didn't encounter a tobelhocker, I did encounter a person who knew a person who *did* once, and what he reported is that the tobelhockers were playing cards, silently, icicle-wet, and that, although they didn't try to choke him or anything, they were truly an unsettling sight. Afterwards, I did some research into the tobelhocker problem, and I discovered that tobelhockerism was unknown until the seventeenth century, when Liechtenstein—then the Manor of Schellenberg and the County of Vaduz—was afflicted with such things as fire, famine, and drought, to say nothing of the Plague and the Thirty Years' War. All this, of course, was blamed on the schrätlings, and the job of uncovering them was patriotically assumed by a committee, the "accusers," as they called themselves. From time to time, the "accusers" came forward with a list of five, ten, or a dozen card-carrying schrätlings, who were decapitated at once, as were their sons and daughters, guilty by association: they, however, are not the tobelhockers, for the whole idea boomeranged, the "accusers" were decapitated too, and *they* are the tobelhockers, and so are their descendants to the ninth generation. Today, one thousand tobelhockers are alive, principally in Triesen and Triesenberg, but none have emigrated to the

United States, thank God; we have quite enough of them already.

So much for the schrätlings and the tobelhockers. The miscellaneous ghosts, I learned, are totally dead, but how this is ascertained, I didn't. In Liechtenstein, I heard of a ghost who walked, talked, and shook hands with the living; of another ghost who delighted in würst'l and sauerkraut; of a third who was lifted bodily by a Capuchin monk and carried out of a haunted house; and when, in every instance, I inquired what it was that differentiated the ghost from a human being, I was given a shrug and was told, simply, *"er geisterte"*—"he ghosted." Nevertheless, I took a fancy to Liechtenstein's ghosts, who appear to be more affable and far less frightening than our American ones, and I'd like to tell the very unorthodox ghost story of one of them, closing my visit to Liechtenstein. The story was told originally by Frau Eberle, of Triesenberg, to her son, Josef, who put it in writing for his German class at Vaduz High School, who passed it along to you and me. Josef has titled the story "A Good Ghost," and I have translated it faithfully; and here it is.

A Good Ghost

Once upon a time there was a beautiful house. It stood in Triesenberg, and it belonged to a well-to-do family, a gentleman and his wife. However, there was a ghost in the house, and the family was so afraid it moved away.

The house was bought by a poor farmer for only a little money. "Look at our beautiful house," he said to his wife and children, "which I have bought for so little money." But his wife and children wouldn't go inside, for they were afraid of the ghost. Finally, the farmer said, "Tonight I will sleep in our house, and tomorrow I will tell you if any ghost is there."

Then the farmer went to his house, and when he opened the door, he saw that a ghost was really there. It was sitting on the stairs in the beautiful, empty house. The brave farmer went to the ghost and said, "I'm not afraid of you. But please, can't

LIECHTENSTEIN

you be invisible to my wife and children?" The ghost answered, "Yes, invisible I can be, and invisible I will be."

The farmer thanked him, and slept soundly all the night in his beautiful house. The next day he hurried to his wife and children. "I slept soundly," he said, "for there isn't any ghost at all inside our house. Now we can all move in."

Immediately they moved in. "Really," said the wife and children, "there wasn't any ghost at all"—for they couldn't see it, although the farmer could. So they lived in the house for many weeks—the farmer, his wife, their children, and the ghost.

One day, the farmer was at the ratskellar when he heard a knock at the window. When he went to the window, it was the ghost. "Run home," it said, "for a fire has broken out!" The farmer and the ghost ran home, and it was really so. However, the farmer put it out.

Another day, the farmer was in the woods. All of a sudden the ghost appeared and told him to hurry home again. "One of your cows is choking," said the ghost, and it was really so. The cow could still be saved.

Finally one day, the farmer was on a journey when the ghost came out of the floor. "Your wife is very ill," it said. On the way home, the ghost explained. "In all my lifetime," it explained, "I never stopped to help the needy, and now I've had to ghost it, until I met a man who wasn't afraid of me and who needed my help three times. I met you, and I helped you three times. Now you will live happily ever after, and I am saved."

The ghost disappeared and never came again. The farmer's wife got well. And truly, he and his family lived happily ever after.

*"I have sworn fidelity to . . .
the Republic of San Marino.
I renew the sacred oath!"*

—THE CAPTAIN REGENT OF SAN MARINO.

SAN MARINO

The Most Serene Republic of San Marino, an awesome, almost impregnable mountain of rock in northern Italy that is not only the oldest and smallest democracy in the world but, in the strictest sense of the word, is the only one, a year ago had a Communist government and, as everybody surely knows by now, it had a civil war and threw the rascals out. The reaction

SAN MARINO

to this in the American papers was one of almost eleutheromaniacal joy. The *Christian Science Monitor* called it "a victory"; the *New York Times* called it "an unprecedented triumph"; and what with all the hullabaloo, you'd think the Sammarinesi had fought their way out of slavery—out of the salt mines, perhaps. Well, I was in San Marino when the Communists were, and damned if I can see what the shouting is about. San Marino wasn't a police state by any means. The people I saw were happy and unafraid and seemed to be running their own affairs, peacefully and rather well. I was told, in San Marino, that the Communists there are not *really* Communists but something else, and the people I was told by were apparently right. The "Communists," who had been governing the place a dozen years, still hadn't nationalized the industries or collectivized the farms—"It would hurt production," they said. Their ties, if any, with the International Communist Conspiracy or even with the Russians were pretty tenuous: they had a consul general in New York City but nobody at all in Moscow, and I learned that the Russians abstained from voting when, in 1953, San Marino was approved for the International Court of Justice. (They voted "no" on Liechtenstein.) There was an opposition party in San Marino when I was there, the Christian Democrats, who flourished. Nobody in the Christian Democrats had been tortured, tried, shot, or sent to a labor camp, although a lawyer of theirs was stopped by the police in 1949 and asked to open his brief case: he told them to mind their own business, and they did. After much digging and prying, I was able to learn from the Christian Democrats a few cases of "Communist tyranny." At times, the Christian Democratic newspaper had been censored, once after saying the government was led by "traitors and infidels who have prostituted our country to evil and corruption and have caused the bones of our patron saint to tremble in his grave." An Italian priest who said it was led by murderers and assassins was told to go home. Signor Guidobaldi Gozi and two friends were put in jail after a Fascist demonstration; Signor Giuseppe Righi and a friend were put in jail after slandering the foreign minister; all of them were let out shortly after. Signor Cesare Bonelli, a tourist, was put in jail, and everybody was red as a beet. That is all. It's true, of course, that nobody is wholly free when any of this can happen, but even the most zealous of the Christian

SAN MARINO

Democrats that I saw agreed that things are considerably worse in Hungary.

All in all, the Most Serene Republic of San Marino seemed to be just that—most serene. The civil war that finally threw the Communists, or whatever they are, out, also seemed from the newspapers to be serene enough. A fist fight in the piazza was reliably reported, and somebody took a potshot at Giulio Massima. (He missed.) One of the papers reported that "a lot of trigger-happy guys [are] running around out there. Thank God most of them don't know where the triggers are." Apparently, the only sustained action of the war was seen by the mimeograph machines: the Communists were in the government palace with one of them, and the Christian Democrats were holed up in an iron foundry, four miles away, with another, and also with a few bottles of Chianti, some candles, a portable radio to get the war news on, and a total of eight rifles and submachine guns with a sign on them, DON'T TOUCH. The guns never were. The war was over in eight days, when the Communist mimeograph machine announced, "Overwhelmed . . . the people's government of San Marino ceases all vain resistance and offers this last service for the supreme good of the nation." The Communists are out of office now, and the Christian Democrats are in. "A victory," says the *Christian Science Monitor*. "An unprecedented triumph," says the *New York Times*. "San Marino . . . succeeds in setting itself free."

"*Così, così,*" is what I bet they're saying in San Marino.

Shortly before all this, I drove out of Liechtenstein and then to San Marino on the smooth, wide asphalt road running straight as an arrow from the Adriatic coast. The road is one of the best in Italy. After it crosses the Sammarinese frontier— where there was, incidentally, no customs or any other sign of an Iron Curtain—it starts to climb uphill in zigzags, crossing again and again the steep road it superseded. By car, it was a zesty fifteen-minute ride to the top of the mountain, where the capital city clings. San Marino, the city, was built as a fort,

117

with a city wall and narrow, cobbled streets that are terribly slippery in the rain, and still it's a thing of these gray and ponderous stones. It isn't at all colorless, though. The shop windows are bright with vases and postage stamps, for the tourists, and in each of the tiny piazzas is a rectangle of bills, pronunciamentos, and posters, an explosion of cubist color on a tawny, sun-parched wall. The posters overlap in a madcap way; their colors are red, pink, mauve, green, gray, black, all of them solid; the type is Gothic or Bodoni, clean-cut. The top layers, when I arrived, were ads for something called Cynar and for a music festival nearby in Rimini, Italy. Underneath were posters for the Miss Italy of 1956 elections, and underneath *them*, a bit raggedy at the edges and only partly visible, for San Marino's own elections a long time earlier—VOTA DEMOCRAZIA CRISTIANA; VOTA PARTITO COMMUNISTA; CONTRO LA GREPPIA, CONTRO IL MALCOSTUME, VOTA PER UN NUOVO GOVERNO.

Everywhere I went, I could see and hear reminders of San Marino's independence. One of these is the cubic, crenelated palace of the government, whose bells—what high-fidelity fans might call a woofer and a tweeter—woof and tweet in an utterly incomprehensible way on every quarter hour, and another is the fort on every high point of the city, defending it through the ages. Still another is the city itself; it feels to be hovering over the earth as Laputa, the flying island of *Gulliver's Travels*, had been, apparently free of any terrestrial stays. In San Marino—thirty-eight square miles, thirteen thousand people—I always knew I was in an independent country. The Sammarinesi were tickled pink to talk about it, to write about it, apparently even to think about it, and apparently they were tickled most of all to find some benighted soul who'd never even heard of the place and to buttonhole him at length. As soon as I got there, *I* was buttonholed by a concierge and was taken willy-nilly to one, another, and still another movie on San Marino. The movies were of a piece. They were full of those reminders of San Marino's independence, shown with pride—the palace, the forts, the inaugural parades, the country's flag.

SAN MARINO

One of them ended with a close-up of San Marino's coat-of-arms on one of San Marino's mailboxes, into which an endless line of tourists (to San Marino) put letters, all of them stickered with San Marino's stamps. At this point, martial music played, crescendo.

Here and there in the movies, I was shown the faces of Lincoln, Roosevelt, Napoleon, Garibaldi, and a very saintlike and bearded stonecutter, and I wondered, naturally, what such an unlikely crowd had to do with the Most Serene Republic of San Marino. The answer, I learned later, was not much. Lincoln wrote a letter to the country on May 7, 1861, thanking it for an honorary citizenship and saying that San Marino "has by its experience demonstrated the truth, so full of encouragement to the friends of Humanity, that Government founded on Republican principles is capable of being so administered as to be secure and enduring." FDR wrote a letter on January 17, 1945, saying that truer words than Lincoln's were never spoken. Napoleon discovered San Marino on a map in 1796, and is said to have said, "*Ma foi!* Let us preserve it as the model of a republic"; he did. (About Andorra he supposedly said, "*Ma foi!* Let us preserve it is a museum piece.") Garibaldi, at least, was *in* San Marino; the armies of Austria, Spain, France, and Naples chased him there in 1849, but he gave them the slip and went to America. This is hardly the stuff of which history is made in any more extensive country, but in San Marino, I gathered, they are the high points of an otherwise unspectacular millennium.

The saintly stonecutter, I learned, was none other than San Marino himself, who more or less founded the country in the fourth century and is its patron saint. A devout Christian, he fled from the lion arenas to what today is San Marino, and he lived in a cave still seen on the mountain there; soon he was joined by other Christians; and the owner of the mountain, Felicità, who at first regarded him as simply a trespasser, at length was converted, joined the colony and maybe even married him, and now is a saint herself. (So is Leo, Marino's best friend.) Marino, when he died, was buried on the mountain, but when he became a saint he was stolen by King Astolphus, who took him to Pavia, Italy, where he was stolen by Pepin the Short, who put him back; as of press time he was located, or so the Sammarinesi believe, in the altar of the big white basilica, high above the city. His skull is shown to everyone on September 4. Marino, it is said, has kept an active interest in the affairs of the republic, more than once getting it out of jams—notably by laying a fog in 1542 and, in 1740, by teaching Antonio Belzoppi how to swim, of which more in a few pages. A sentence of twenty days is prescribed for saying "San Marino" in vain.

The Marino legend says, furthermore, that he set up San Marino as a democracy, and for certain it was a democracy of the Athenian sort in the 1200's, almost everyone sitting in the legislature. (Women and children were out, as they were in Athens.) This body, the Arringo, still is meeting twice a year, and it's why San Marino can be called the only real democracy on earth. To be sure, nothing much happens in the Arringo these days; twenty or thirty men show up, petitioning it, and absentees are supposed to be fined one six-hundredth of an American cent, but never are. It's all over in thirty minutes. Actually, most of San Marino's laws are made by the Great and General Council, sixty men, which is what the election posters were all about. The Great and General Council, in turn, elects two people in it as captains regent, a kind of bicameral chief of state, like the Roman consuls. (Until 1945, the captains regent were chosen by lot—a child, usually blind, pulled their names from an urn—but the Communists decided this mode of selection was altogether too chancy.) The two men govern San Marino jointly for half a year, and can't be re-elected.

While I was in San Marino, two Captains Regent, Signori Augusto Maiani and Primo Bugli, a Communist and a left-wing Socialist, were inaugurated, and the inaugural was seen by something more than a hundred tourists, including me. The

SAN MARINO

tourists were Italians and Germans, mostly; they began appearing in San Marino in force on the night before, and the shopkeepers stayed up late, selling them postage stamps and vases. Black cars from Rome with diplomatic license plates were all about, and excitement was in the air. Besides me, there was one American there, a good-looking girl in a red cashmere sweater who said she was employed at our consulate in Florence, Italy, and that her name was Patricia. Later, as Patricia and I had a beer together at the Ristorante Garibaldi, she added she was there in a more-or-less official capacity, having been asked at the consulate to represent the United States at the inauguration, the consul being busy in Genoa. She was, in fact, the Acting American Minister to San Marino—a sort of *pro tempore* Clare Booth Luce. Patricia wasn't altogether sure of what was expected of her, but, she said, a concierge had promised to take her in tow, getting her to the right places at the right times. Some Sammarinesi there, at the Ristorante Garibaldi, bought us a round of beer, and a Belgian standing at the bar taught Patricia to curtsy, something, she said, she would doubtless be called upon to execute on the morrow.

The next day was crisp and a little overcast. After breakfast, I strolled to the cobbled piazza in front of the palace, where, I had understood, the day's activities would be centered, and where a small, determined knot of tourists was already standing about, toying with their exposure meters and waiting for something to happen. Nothing did until 9:45, when we heard the sound of drums, horns, and glockenspiels far away. The music grew nearer, and then a little band came into the piazza, trying not to look at their friends in the windows above and, rather desperately, to keep in step. Then came a column-by-two of riflemen; they were dressed in blue with chevrons of red, and they were of all shapes and ages, as if the Boy Scouts had run afoul somehow of the G.A.R. platoon. And lastly came a column-by-two of swordsmen, in flashy orange. A bouquet of white and powder-blue feathers was flouncing on each of their heads, growing, apparently, directly out of it, and the tourists hurried over to get a picture. At ten o'clock sharp, the bells, in their own mysterious fashion, gave a woof, woof, woof, woof and no tweets, the band struck up the national anthem, the swordsmen drew their swords, and a man in an utterly indescribable uniform raised the flag of San Marino, white and powder-blue. Then, he, the band, the riflemen, and the swordsmen went downhill, and everything was quiet for the next hour. The tourists were getting impatient, and were taking pictures of each other, and writing cards.

The band marched up again at eleven o'clock. (It spent the greater part of the day going up and down, I observed.) This time, a column-by-two of dignitaries was coming after it, some of them in striped pants and cutaways, and one of them in all this and a W-shaped beard, too. The Captains Regent were there, in black robes and floppy black hats, trimmed with ermine, and immense medals on ribbons of white and powder-blue, and the Captains Regent-to-be were right after them. And right after *them* was Patricia, looking lovely. She wore a blue suit, she carried a blue pocketbook by the strap, and, as she walked, she chatted with the Belgian of the night before, who had changed into a fine green uniform and a hat with a heap of feathers on top, like a Hoopoe bird. There were others like him, including, I was told, the Minister from S.M.O.M. (which started a new line of inquiry, of course, to be pursued in the next chapter), and there were other women, too, including the Acting Minister from Haiti. A few obvious ringers with Baby Brownie cameras were mixed in among this, and, at the end of the procession, some little boys were marching to the music. Now and then, the police would shoo them away, whereupon they'd go to a doorway and sulk, marking time.

The dignitaries went across the piazza and into the palace, where, I learned, they would be presented to the Captains Regent, and I imagined that Patricia would be called upon now to curtsy. (She was, but didn't, she told me later, having remembered at the last moment that Americans are only supposed to bow.) Outside, meanwhile, the crush of tourists was

SAN MARINO

so bad that the column of orange swordsmen couldn't turn around; it marched into the palace, reassembled, and marched out again, and the tourists took pictures of it coming and going. Presently, the dignitaries emerged, a terribly bald one holding Patricia by the arm and absolutely beaming; so was the sun, and the band was playing loudly, and everything was like a football game on a golden day at halftime.

Shortly afterwards, the Captains Regent took the oath of office. Someone—a Communist, I was told—gave a speech in Italian, and I picked up the words *"libertas,"* "Garibaldi," and "Abraham Lincoln"; a man behind him nodded vigorously, and there was a burst of applause when he finished. Then, a flourish, and the old Captains Regent took the medals on the white and powder-blue ribbons off, to lower them slowly on the new. The music hit a peak; the Captains Regent-to-be became the Captains Regent. *"Ecco! Ecco!"* cried a little girl beside me. I felt warm and patriotic, and didn't know why. And then, the crowd poured across the sun-drenched piazza; the band marched downhill, uphill, and down the hill again, and up again in the afternoon for a concert; the bells gave a woof and two tweets; and Patricia went off in a limousine, the man with the bald head waving and waving good-by.

The International Communist Conspiracy seemed far, far away—about five hundred years in the future.

A few days later, when they were comfortably settled in office, I paid a call on the Captains Regent and found them getting along fine together. They reminded me, in fact, of Tweedledum and Tweedledee—they not only looked alike, with swarthy round faces and oily hair, but they were dressed almost identically, in gray suits, gray socks, and those awful pearl-gray ties that diplomats wear. Whenever they spoke, it was always in bits and snatches, each of them interrupting the other, but the pieces, strung together by my interpreter, always seemed to make a coherent sentence. Signor Maiani, the Communist, said that prior to his election he worked on a farm, in a mine, and eventually at a tourist shop; Signor Bugli said he sold postage stamps. The two signori, although, they continued, they lived five miles apart and hadn't met before their inauguration, were already calling each other by their last names, having dropped the "Signor." Some of the things to be done for San Marino in the coming months, they said, still interrupting, were social security and public housing. (The Communists had already built many houses, as well as bringing about old-age pensions, full employment, and civil rights for women, who couldn't own any property till then, and still can't vote.) Neither of these seemed especially crucial, so Signor Bugli and I decided to talk about postage stamps, which he once sold. Signor Bugli, with some assistance from Signor Maiani, said that San Marino used at first the Kingdom of Sardinia's stamps and, after the unification, Italy's; the Sardinian ones are worth from twenty-four to four hundred dollars now when canceled by the Sammarinese post office, he said. The first Sammarinese stamps were in 1877, and philatelists, whose pricing policies I wouldn't even pretend to understand, are paying only thirty-six cents for some of them, and only sixteen cents if they aren't sticky. On the other hand, another of those stamps is worth as much as $9.68 sticky, $4.03 unsticky, and $6.45 canceled. An unscrupulous dealer who buys a gross of them and puts on stickum apparently makes a profit of $813.60, minus the cost of the stickum. Also, Signor Bugli told me, San Marino used to make its own money but doesn't any more.

A while later, positively fascinated by all this, I did some private research into the postage stamp matter, and I learned that San Marino made do with the 1877 stamps for half a dozen years, overprinting them CENTESIMI 5 and CENTESIMI 10 in 1892, and changing the colors a bit later. Now, though, like Lundy, Andorra, Monaco, and Liechtenstein, it is thinking them up at twenty or twenty-five a year and has issued no fewer than seven hundred and fifty-four kinds, including one hundred and seventeen airmail ones, although there isn't an airport in the whole country. The stamps commemorate such various things as

SAN MARINO

Columbus's birth and the opening of the Sammarinese railway, and depict such persons as San Marino, Garibaldi, Abraham Lincoln, Benjamin Franklin, and the Discus Thrower, and, needless to say, are bought up eagerly by philatelists in every land, adding $160,000 a year to the Sammarinese treasury. I also learned that the ink was hardly dry on the 1892 stamps—the ones with the overprint CENTESIMI 5—when the printers found that a considerable profit could be had by printing them all wrong. To the inexpressible delight of philatelists everywhere, they began to print CENTESIMI 5 rightside up, upside down, singly, doubly, doubly upside down, and doubly rightside up *and* upside down, and had even printed a set of GENTESIMI 5's, when somebody told them to lay off. (Today, the GENTESIMI 5's are worth $136 sticky and $72 dry, and if the "G" is especially fat they're worth $160 sticky, $80 dry. How people figure this out, I'll never know.) According to San Marino, someone is now assigned to the print shop to stop any similar malpractices, but I noted that since the war it has printed sixty-four kinds of stamps that are perforated wrong, ten that are centered wrong, and one that even is colored wrong, and in 1947 a stamp that was supposed to be overprinted GIORNATA FILATELICA wound up ꓤƆIꓶƎꓶA⟟ꓶIꓞ AꓔAИЯOIƉ. To make matters worse, a rascal in Italy has bought up Sammarinese stamps and messed them up on his own, overprinting 3 NOVEMBRE 1918 upside down on some of them, for instance, and making a killing.

San Marino's stamps are not its only source of revenue, I learned. There are taxes; and Italy gives it a rake-off on the Italian import duties, as it ought to. Nevertheless, I learned, the Communists were going further and further into the hole after the war, as their annual budgets neared a million dollars. Of course, the first thing they thought of doing about it was more postage stamps, including, in 1947, a series in honor of Franklin Delano Roosevelt, which they figured would be a wowser in the United States. (American philatelists who missed out in 1947 will be pleased to learn that Roosevelt can still be gotten for a penny and a half, sticky or dry, canceled or not. This is the re-tail price for the one-lira Roosevelt, on which is quoted his historic letter to San Marino. The President himself is shown in a very patriotic attitude on the five-lira stamp, a glorious thing in purple, brown, red, white, and blue. This Roosevelt is worth 2½¢ canceled, 2½¢ uncanceled, $2.40 if his bottom isn't perforated, $1.20 if his side isn't perforated, a nickel if he's overprinted, and heaven knows what if he's overprinted twice. He also comes in airmail.) Posthumously, FDR wasn't enough to balance San Marino's budget, though, and Italy, meanwhile, had aggravated things by not giving it the import duties, to start an economic crisis there, to get rid of the Communists. For a while, the country didn't know where to turn. At this critical juncture, there appeared in San Marino a terribly mysterious person, Mr. Maximo Maxim, who rented a bungalow, got himself a mistress, wore yellow velvet gloves, and talked all day on the long-distance phone, thereby giving rise to rumors not only in San Marino but in such remote quarters as *Time* and *Life* that he was a Communist spy, perhaps the Communist boss of Italy. Mr. Maxim, who said all along he was just a businessman, in vain, offered four hundred thousand dollars a year to San Marino to let him build a casino there. The Communists agreed—forgetting that the same offer had been made a hundred years before, and that the Captains Regent had refused it, exclaiming, "Citizens! It is not by the maintenance of material prosperity that the good name of free states is preserved. It is by means of the great virtues of proud and honest republicans, who know how to repulse riches, even in poverty."

Mr. Maxim's casino—a couple of baccarat tables and five roulette ones—opened in 1949, and soon it was making money hand over fist. At this point, re-enter Italy, still trying to get rid of the Communists. Italy said it wouldn't stand idly by while Italians were being "bled"; it put up a road block at San Marino's frontier, told the gamblers to get a passport, a visa, and a *carnet de passages*, and even after that it held them a few hours looking for marijuana in their hatbands. After seventeen months of

SAN MARINO

such harassment, San Marino gave up. The casino was closed; Mr. Maxim, arrested in Italy, was sent to Israel; and Italians had to travel considerably farther, to San Remo, to bleed. San Marino was eight hundred thousand dollars in the red, unable to pay its employees for three months. Since then, it has thought of making money as a kind of Mexico (divorcing people), a kind of Panama (registering ships), a kind of Liechtenstein (incorporating companies), and a kind of Andorra (building a radio station); it even tried being a kind of Kentucky, selling such titles as "the Count of Montelupe" for twenty-four thousand dollars and "the Duke of Peschiera" for thirty-seven thousand, but nothing has worked out right. The country still wasn't solvent when I was there. The casino was boarded up, and great hiatuses already were to be seen in the plasterwork.

Of all the places I visited, I liked San Marino best. (Then Punial.) Andorra, the only other democracy, has kept free by a rather sneaky way, I think, by truckling equally to France and Spain; San Marino has kept free by fighting for it. Time and again, it has been attacked by such people as the Borgias, the Wrongheads, the Bishops of Montefeltro, and even the Popes. The Pope invaded it in 1542 (but his army got lost in a fog, produced, it is said, by San Marino himself), and the gypsies invaded it in 1559; the Masons wanted it in 1790, apparently. Most of these wars were against the Roman Catholic Church, the most noted of them being in 1739, when Cardinal Alberoni conquered San Marino and held it one hundred and five days.

Alberoni is the villain of San Marino's history. There, it's hard to get a dispassionate account of why he invaded it and what he did there, but, having read a few books about it, I think I have the story straight. Giulio Cardinal Alberoni, I learned, was the illegitimate son of a gardener and a spinning girl, and according to no less an authority than the Pope he was like "a glutton, who after a good meal would fain have some brown bread." In early life, he was an apprentice cook, but he rose fast, becoming the prime minister and also the primate of Spain. The next several years, he made a pest of himself stirring up rebellions in Austria, in Southern France, in Scotland—heaven knows what he had in mind, but he was fired. The Pope sent him into the sticks as legate to the Romagna. There, Cardinal Alberoni looked around for other worlds to conquer, and discovered San Marino.

The books in which I was reading this admit that San Marino was, then, in a pretty bad way, but surely it wasn't so awful as Alberoni said. "San Marino," he wrote to the Pope, "is a very Geneva in the heart of the Papal States, harboring the enemies of God and the Saints alike, a hotbed of tyrants, and if any hostile prince should seize it, he would make of it a strong standpoint from which to attack the Pontifical dominions. Moreover, San Marino is a beam in the Holy eye, a nest of dissensions, robbery, and rapine, which it is necessary to suppress; and, moreover, it is the sincere wish of the people to be incorporated in Your Holiness' territory." The Pope (Clement XII) told Alberoni to take it easy, but Alberoni laid siege to the little country and, after it ran out of food, marched into it with his soldiers, archers, and executioners behind. The next day, he ordered the Sammarinesi to the big white basilica where the saint is, and from the altar he called for an oath of allegiance to the Papal States. One or two people gave it, while the choir sang hallelujahs, and then it was the turn of the Captain Regent, old Giangi. Giangi turned the tide, shouting, "I have sworn fidelity to my lawful prince, the Republic of San Marino. I renew the sacred oath!" Giuseppe Onofri said the same, and Girolamo Gozi cried enthusiastically, "Long live San Marino! Long live liberty!" The others took up the cry, including the priests, and Alberoni looked simply awful. A chronicler who was there says, "It was an anger more befitting a gardener of Piacenza than an ex-prime minister of Spain, a prince of the Roman Church, and a papal legate." The service ended "amidst a confusion and hubbub which didn't belong to religion."

Later in the day, Giangi, Onofri, Gozi, and several others

SAN MARINO

were put in jail and their houses ransacked. (An inkwell, a silver snuffbox, and a candlestick were taken out of Gozi's.) Other Sammarinesi, though, secretly went to the Pope and protested, and the French ambassador also did so, being quoted in one of the books I read as saying, "The king, my master, will never permit the subjection of a free and independent nation—at least, not without his authority." Baffled by all this conflicting intelligence, the Pope sent a friend of his to San Marino to take a poll, as it were, and the result, in words of one syllable, was that "there were few lovers of Roman sovereignty but many lovers of liberty." Hearing this, the Pope set San Marino free. That day—February 5, 1740—is still a national holiday, with a parade of girls and boys carrying a banner with the word LIBERTY. Nowadays it is celebrated on September 3, when more tourists are about.

Giulio Cardinal Alberoni, to finish my story, was sent to Bologna, where he spent the rest of his life saying nasty things about San Marino. Giangi, Onofri, and Gozi are national heroes, second in the Sammarinesi's hearts only to Garibaldi, Roosevelt, and San Marino himself. Another hero of the Alberoni days was Antonio Belzoppi, and a few words about him are in order. Antonio Belzoppi, when all this was going on, had hurried to Venice to get some aid, and three murderers, in Alberoni's pay, hurried to Venice to get Belzoppi. Belzoppi and the murderers encountered at night; thereupon, our man jumped into a gondola and paddled for all he was worth, and, after hailing another gondola, the murderers gave him chase. (I rather like to think they shouted, "Follow that gondola!" but history doesn't bear this out.) Belzoppi made for the next canal, the murderers in hot pursuit . . . and then for the Grand Canal . . . the Lagoon . . . and then he was caught! Antonio Belzoppi, though, took a stiletto out, and he killed the three murderers as well as their gondolier, a fleeting figure on the pages of history, who, as far as a disinterested researcher can learn, was only trying to make a fare. At this point, Antonio Belzoppi fell in the Lagoon. But San Marino, the saint, he said, appeared in the sky

129

miraculously and taught him to swim, and the story ends as he's back in San Marino the republic, the Captain Regent. The Belzoppi family is still going strong there, and it was a Belzoppi who let Garibaldi in, in 1849.

San Marino has been invaded only once since then—1944, when it was used as a battlefield by the Germans and the British. A bit earlier, the British had bombed it too, believing, in error, that ammunition was being stored there; sixty-two people were killed and a million dollars of damage was done, greater than all the other invasions together. San Marino has been asking for compensation ever since. So far, the British are willing to pay only seventy-two thousand dollars—reckoned, I was told, at forty dollars for each fatality, four cents for bomb disposal, and other damages—and San Marino refuses to take so little. Its notes to the Foreign Office are getting firmer and firmer, now being written in plain English instead of Latin, as before. There's no telling how it will end, really, but I was assured in San Marino that a resort to force is out of the question.

When I was there, the Christian Democrats were talking it up that to get a million dollars from England, the Christian Democrats would have to do it. This was one of their biggest selling points in the last election—indeed, it was almost the only one. The next election, and the next chance for a Communist comeback, is in September, and now the Christian Democrats are talking up the women's right to vote, their idea being that women are better Christians than men and likelier to vote for Christian Democrats. And even the Communists are being given pause by signs like "The women have the right to elect and be elected—*Article 137, Russian Constitution*" in the piazzas. The Committee for the Emancipation of the Sammarinese Lady is hard at work, and it may be the determining factor in September.

I wonder how it'll turn out, the election. I think it'll be close. In San Marino, an election is just about as up-for-grabs as a corporation proxy fight, what with the Communists hurrying about

SAN MARINO

the docks of Genoa and the coal mines of Belgium to round up Sammarinesi of voting age, and the Christian Democrats going as far afield as Hoboken, New Jersey, for theirs. There aren't any residency requirements in San Marino, and these bring-'em-back-alive tactics are legal, although decried by each of the parties when practiced by the other. (At the last election, more than a thousand dockers, coal miners, and factory hands poured into San Marino by bus, voted Communist, got free beer and baloney sandwiches at party headquarters, and tumbled out again the same day. The Christian Democrats' Sammarinesi came by Pan American World Airways from New York.) Something like this is sure to happen in September. And when it's over and done with, the newspapers, in sorrow or in joy, will be giving San Marino a "Communist" or a "Christian Democratic" stamp —but the stamp is one of the unsticky ones, and it's worth a dime a dozen. "Communist" or "Democratic," I daresay it won't make a big difference in the Most Serene Republic of San Marino.

It's the rest of the world I'm worried about.

"Allora, smetto di cantare."
—THE CHANCELLOR OF THE S.M.O.M.

THE S.M.O.M.

The smallest country in the world is half as big, approximately, as a football field and is located in downtown Rome two or three blocks from American Express, and next door to Cucci's, the haberdasher. Its flag is red-and-white, a lot like Denmark's, and its name is rather immoderate, I think: the Sovereign and Military Order of Saint John of Jerusalem, Rhodes,

THE S.M.O.M.

and Malta, which is abbreviated at all but the most ceremonious of state occasions to the Sovereign and Military Order of Malta, or the S.M.O.M. That the Sovereign and Military Order of Malta, or S.M.O.M., is truly sovereign is shown by its being recognized by Italy, the Vatican, San Marino, Austria, Spain, Portugal, the Dominican Republic, Haiti, Panama, Costa Rica, Nicaragua, El Salvador, Ecuador, Colombia, Paraguay, Argentina, Chile, Peru, Brazil and Lebanon, and that it's truly military is shown by an air force bigger than most of these places'—one hundred and twenty planes, of which three, at the very least, are said to be in sufficient repair to permit them to leave the ground. The S.M.O.M. has a minister in each of the twenty countries that recognize it, and vice versa, and while it would be nonsense for me to suggest that he has anything to do, I can suggest how he sometime *might*. Put the case that Signor Cucci, the haberdasher, is murdered today by a disgruntled client, who flees across the border into the S.M.O.M.: the only recourse now for the Italian police is to extradite the man, something that would be done, of necessity, through the Italian Minister to the S.M.O.M., and the S.M.O.M.ian Minister to Italy.

What the Sovereign and Military Order of Saint John of Jerusalem, Rhodes, and Malta lacks in territory, it also lacks in population, being inhabited at the last census by two people, Brother Paternó and Baron Apor. (There used to be a third—Prince Chigi, who was the grand master, or sovereign, of the S.M.O.M., but who died in 1951 and hasn't been replaced yet.) Brother Paternó is the lieutenant grand master, and, as such, is kept so awfully busy with matters of state that I couldn't see him, while Baron Apor, whom I did see and chatted with for quite a while, in fact, is the chancellor—a small, animated, merry old gaffer who wears a black homburg and carries a black umbrella, and is ever losing himself in old jokes and reminiscences, a characteristic one being of the fellow who learned, from his doctor, that wine, women, and song were killing him, and who replied, *"Allora, smetto di cantare"*—"Okay, I'll give up singing." Between such jokes as these, the Baron told me he doesn't pay taxes

The smallest country in the world is located in downtown Rome two or three blocks from American Express.

THE S.M.O.M.

to Italy, being a citizen of the S.M.O.M., and that he brings in cigarettes, liquor, and suchlike free of duty; and he offered me a free-of-duty Chesterfield. He travels, said the Baron, on a passport of the S.M.O.M., and he graciously let me see the thing: it was red-and-white and very natty, and the page that is signed by Mr. Dulles on *my* passport was signed by Baron Apor, himself, on his, and carried the words, "His Eminent Highness, Fra Ludovico Chigi Albani Della Rovere, Prince and Grand Master of the Sovereign Military Order of Malta, request all to whom it may concern to allow the bearer, Baron Gabriel Apor, to pass freely and to afford him such assistance and protection of which he may stand in need." The next several pages were full of visas. Hereupon, the Baron observed that nothing except the discovery of bootleg gold will cause such a to-do at the international borders of Europe as the arrival there of himself or Brother Paternó with an S.M.O.M.ian passport, it being treated by the customs people as if it were practically radioactive. That the passport is allowed, eventually, at all of these borders, the Baron said, is a proof positive of the sovereignty of the S.M.O.M. He added that the S.M.O.M. doesn't give any visas of its own, but can; that it doesn't mint any money of its own, but did; and that it doesn't print any stamps of its own, but will—at some as yet undetermined time in the future, after the proper arrangements are made with the International Postal Union and an adequate place, if any, is found for a mailbox on the S.M.O.M.'s soil.

Well, I think this is very unusual. How it managed to come about is a long story, and, with the reader's indulgence, I'd like to make it as long as possible, as there's so very little I can say about the S.M.O.M. of today. The fact is that the S.M.O.M. has been a country ever since 1048, but, unlike such countries of those days as Slavonia, Catalonia, Lower Lorraine, and the Caliphate of Cordova, it manages to be with us in the twentieth century by having put its lock, stock, and population on a dozen or so ships whenever it was conquered, and popping up somewhere else in Europe or Asia. Six hundred and twenty-six years of this peripateticism are noted, in chronological order, in the very name of the S.M.O.M.—the Sovereign and Military Order of Saint John of Jerusalem (one hundred and forty-three years), Rhodes (two hundred and fourteen years), and Malta (two hundred and sixty-nine years)—the omissions being a hundred years at Acre, eighteen years on Cyprus, forty-two years getting from one of these places to another, and, of course, all of this century and most of the last in Rome. I suppose there's no reason why a nation shouldn't behave this way—my dictionary says a nation should have "a more or less compact territory," and in the case of the S.M.O.M. it's less—but, I think, it's altogether too trying on the rest of us, and sometimes the S.M.O.M. was gadding about so much that even its citizens didn't know where it was: at the turn of the nineteenth century they thought it was in Leningrad, of all places, and elected the czar as grand master. In spite of its aberrations, the S.M.O.M. was one of the great countries of Europe for much of the millennium, owning a half-dozen forts along the Mediterranean, one hundred and forty estates in Palestine, and nineteen thousand in Europe, and in protocol always coming the first.

In those days, the S.M.O.M.ians were known as the Hospitalers, for as a hospital the S.M.O.M. had begun—in 1048 or thereabouts, in Jerusalem, to care for the pilgrims. The Hospital of St. John the Baptist was given a kind of extraterritoriality by the Moslems, making it a kind of Vatican City, and it stayed so after the Moslems left and the Crusaders came, in 1087. On that day, ten thousand people were killed in the Mosque of Omar alone, and their bodies floated out in the blood; the hospital had much to do; and later it was given money by many of the Crusaders it cared for, growing in power and population. Its first grand master was the Blessed Raymond du Puy, who made the S.M.O.M. a military, as well as a sovereign, state, and sent it into the Crusades, and who prescribed for it the religious rule it still uses: "Firstly, I ordain that all the brethren, engaging in the service of the poor and the defense of the Catholic faith, should keep the three things with the aid of God that they have

THE S.M.O.M.

promised to God: that is to say, chastity and obedience, which means whatever thing is commanded to them by their masters, and to live without property of their own: because God will require these three things of them at the Last Judgment. And let them not claim more as their due than bread and water, and raiment, which things are promised to them. And their clothing should be humble, because Our Lord's poor, whose servants we confess ourselves to be, go naked and miserably clad. And it is a wrong thing for a servant that he should be proud, and his Lord should be humble." The grand masters after the Blessed Raymond du Puy realized, though, that a nation founded on chastity would be rather a flash-in-the-pan, so just a few of the citizens took the vows. Those who did were Knights of Justice, and those who didn't were Knights of Honor and Devotion or Knights of Magistral Grace, and this differentiation obtains in the S.M.O.M. today. Baron Apor is a Knight of Honor and Devotion, and Brother Paternó is a Knight of Justice.

Jerusalem fell again to the Moslems in 1271, and, it's written, the nuns of the S.M.O.M. chose death to dishonor: they couldn't commit suicide, but they could cut their noses off, and they made themselves so hideous doing so that they were killed, and weren't raped, by the Moslems. The rest of the S.M.O.M. had already taken its kit and caboodle, as it would often in the future, and had relocated to the north of Jerusalem, at Acre; it was run out of there in 1291, and it wasn't seen in the Holy Land again until 1954, when it opened the legation in Lebanon. From Jerusalem to Acre; from Acre to Cyprus; from Cyprus to Rhodes, by which time even the grand master was so bewildered as to where, if anywhere, the S.M.O.M. would materialize next that he was thirteen years in catching up. Presently, the grand master was Deodato de Gozon. It's said in many histories of the S.M.O.M.—almost all of which, incidentally, are called *A Short History of the Order* (or *Knights*) *of Saint John of Jerusalem*—that Deodato de Gozon nominated himself and voted for himself and was, even so, spoken of as a modest man—and little wonder, for Deodato de Gozon had been the first S.M.O.M.ian to slay a dragon. According to the many *Short Histories*, the dragon, after eating up women and children for several years, was slain by Deodato de Gozon and a pair of English bulldogs, which, during the encounter, had held the dragon at bay, having been specially trained for the purpose on a wooden, facsimile dragon. Generally, I'm not one to put any stock in dragons, but this particular one is pretty well documented, de Gozon's own tombstone saying, in Latin, "Skill is the conqueror of force: Deodato de Gozon, knight, slew an enormous dragon." The stone was put there by people who should have known, and we can only conclude that a terrible sort of animal was prowling about in the Middle Ages and, mercifully, has gone extinct. (Even the Bible has talk of dragons—the Seventy-fourth Psalm.)

In 1444, the Sultan of Egypt laid siege to the S.M.O.M.; it was lifted, but many of the knights were dead, the fortifications were out, earthquakes and a tidal wave were making them worse, and the S.M.O.M.ians were in a funk. Then, Sultan Suleiman the Magnificent, of the Ottoman Empire, laid siege again, and the people reacted in a way quite unimaginable today—by worrying about the enemy within, and all but forgetting the enemy without. A lady of Spain, a pilgrim, got to be something of a celebrity by going around barefoot and putting the finger on people in high places, not naming any names, however; the first to be killed was a Turkish slave, and then a Jewish doctor, and things were far enough along for the Chancellor himself to be tortured, tried, and decapitated, when Suleiman the Magnificent opened fire and conquered the S.M.O.M. "There has been nothing in the world so well lost as Rhodes," said Charles V of the Holy Roman Empire, incorrectly, and gave it Malta.

Charles V was to get a falcon every year in return, and he seems, at first, to have had the better of the deal. Malta was like a no-man's land when the S.M.O.M. got there; its castle had gone to seed, but the S.M.O.M., under the grand mastery of Jean Parisot de la Valette, worked for thirty-six years to fix it—even the women, and even la Valette, were carrying stone to the para-

THE S.M.O.M.

pets—and the S.M.O.M. had its powder dry when Suleiman the Magnificent, who conquered it in Rhodes at the start of his reign, said he'd conquer it in Malta at the end. In 1565, he laid siege—one of the great sieges of history, fought a third of a year by thirty thousand Turks and only eight or nine thousand S.M.O.M.ians. And fought savagely, too: the Turks cut a Maltese cross into their prisoners and sent the bodies downstream to the S.M.O.M., and the S.M.O.M., in turn, decapitated its prisoners and fired a fusillade of human heads onto the Turks, "and from that day onwards, no quarter was given on either side," in the words of a *Short History*. They used to throw hoops and crockery pots of wildfire, like hand grenades, at one another, and there were frogman fights at sea. La Valette was told to surrender; he pointed to the trenches, saying, "There is the only ground that I will surrender, and that as a grave for the Turkish army."

The catastrophe was at hand. The S.M.O.M. was reinforced, to a degree, by a Mesquita, the Governor of Notabile, who stormed the Turkish hospitals when nobody was about, and the Turks were reinforced by Hassan, the Begler Beg of Algeria, and on Thursday, August 23, they assaulted every part of the S.M.O.M. at once. The S.M.O.M. had been forewarned—someone had shot an arrow in with THURSDAY on it—and almost every knight was out of the hospital, at the battlements. They held for a week, and then eighty-five hundred reinforcements came from Spain, and the Turks skedaddled in panic, many of them being killed, as they did so, by their very general. Suleiman the Magnificent hit the ceiling when he heard of this, and resolved, at the age of seventy, to lead the army himself, and he sent a letter to la Valette swearing "by the god wch hath mayd heaven and yearth and by our xxvj Proffites and the foure Musaphi which fell downe out of heaven and by our chief proffit Mahomet" that nobody would be hurt if the S.M.O.M. surrendered. "But yf," Suleiman added in his second sentence—his first sentence had been two hundred and seventy-nine words long—"but yf you will not yeald yor selves as wee have said

139

wee will roote out the foundacion of your castell upsid downe, and make you slaves and to die an evell death according to our pleasure as wee have dann to manny others and of this be you right well assured." La Valette, after reading this, sent a few men to Constantinople and blew up the Turkish navy, and that was the end of that.

Suleiman the Magnificent died in mortification the same year, and Jean Parisot de la Valette died, of sunstroke, two years later, and after that the Ottoman Empire and the S.M.O.M. took a brodie. The S.M.O.M.ians gave in to luxury and vice, and Malta, won by bravery on August 23, 1565, was lost by cowardice on Meadow 23, 6—to use the language of Napoleon's communiqué. Chiefly, the cowardice was that of the Grand Master, Ferdinand Joseph Anthony Herman Lewis von Hompesch, who, as Napoleon hove up with fourteen sail-of-the-line, thirty frigates, and three hundred cargo ships, did nothing at all, and the S.M.O.M. was conquered apace. ("How fortunate," said one of Napoleon's staff, "since a couple of dozen men could have held the city against us.") Von Hompesch's only worry was to keep his chinaware and jewelry safe; he didn't, and he died unable to pay for a funeral. The other S.M.O.M.ians took kit and caboodle once again and went, in a quandary, to Austria, England, and Russia, and the ones in Russia, as I have already said, elected the czar as their seventieth grand master. (That a czar should take the vows of chastity, obedience, and poverty, and still remain a czar, hadn't seemed at all irregular to the S.M.O.M. since the thirteenth century, when it took in the King of Hungary and got, in gratitude, seven hundred silver marks a year.) After a while, the S.M.O.M. was given the half acre of downtown Rome that is, still, its only territory, but as part of the bargain only three men—the grand master, the lieutenant grand master, and the chancellor—could be citizens there. The other S.M.O.M.ians were to be citizens of the country they lived in. Today, there are five thousand of these in the Order of Malta, and, for them, it's very like the Order of Odd Fellows or the Benevolent and Protective Order of Elks, except if they get to

THE S.M.O.M.

be ministers; a few in the United States are Francis Cardinal Spellman, Mr. Frank Leahy, Mr. Frank Folsom, and Mr. Henry Ford II.

The two contemporary citizens of the S.M.O.M., Brother Paternó and Baron Apor, are well-behaved, exemplary men, and there isn't any need in the S.M.O.M. to have any laws or law courts, and, if we wish to learn of that aspect of the S.M.O.M., we must study it when it was more heavily populated, on Malta. Those days, it was against the law to throw rocks into a window or dirt onto a door, or go to the ballet; slavery wasn't against the law (there was a big market in the capital city), but cowardice was, and a General St. Clement, who ordered a withdrawal, was found guilty of it in the sixteenth century. It was against the law to duel, but there was a narrow street, the Strada Stretta—the Narrow Street—where the S.M.O.M.ians used to get jostled, at times, and fly extemporaneously off the handle, and it was the legal fiction that a duel fought on the Strada Stretta really wasn't, just as slander spoken in the United States Senate really isn't. Eventually, anybody who cared to duel did so on the Strada Stretta, it being closed to pedestrian traffic by the seconds. A common punishment for much of this was starvation; torture was legal, and General St. Clement, the coward, was strangled to death and thrown in a burlap bag into the Mediterranean. The S. M. O. M. gave sanctuary to the civil criminals of other countries—Caravaggio, the artist, a murderer, was one of them—and the S.M.O.M.'s hospital gave sanctuary to the civil criminals of the S.M.O.M., although, in the course of time, conspirators, traitors, murderers, perjurers, poisoners, pillagers, sodomites, arsonites, assassins, debtors, highwaymen, and thieves were barred from the hospital by one regulation or another.

Historically, the S.M.O.M.'s hospital was that of 1048—part of the caboodle taken from Jerusalem to Acre, Cyprus, Rhodes, and Malta. The hospital seems to have taken a brodie as the S.M.O.M. did; it was visited in the eighteenth century by John Howard, the philanthropist, who said it was "so dirty and offensive as to create the necessity of perfuming [the beds—of which there were seven hundred and forty-five, by the way] and yet I observed that the physician in going his rounds was obliged to keep a handkerchief to his face," while the hospital staff were "the most dirty, ragged, unfeeling and inhuman persons I ever saw. I once saw eight or nine of them highly entertained by a delirious, dying patient." He also complained that the vermicelli was dirty and the bread moldy, but, Baron Apor has assured me, this latter was on the menu for its penicillin content, the drug having been known, but not isolated, by the S.M.O.M.'s hospital in the fifteenth century. The hospital was run in every century by a high officer of the S. M. O. M., the Hospitaler, also known as the Pillar of the French Tongue. The Pillar of the Italian Tongue was the Admiral, and the Pillar of our own, English Tongue was the Turcopolier—the "son of a Turk" in the Latin tongue, who commanded the light cavalry at first, getting the coast guard afterwards. That the Grand Commander was the Pillar of the Provençal Tongue, and that the Spanish Tongue was pillared by the Drapier till 1462, after which it was pillared partly by the Drapier, in his capacity as Pillar of the Aragonese Tongue, and partly by the Grand Chancellor, as Pillar of the Castilian and Portuguese Tongue, is, I think, as obscure a bit of incidental intelligence as anyone could know, and might well be committed to memory by people (like me) who generally make a hobby of such things.

All of which brings us to the Sovereign and Military Order of Saint John of Jerusalem, Rhodes, and Malta today—Brother Paternó and Baron Apor. The latter of these has an apartment in the Italian quarter of Rome, but the former is living on S.M.O.M.ian soil, in the Order of Malta Palace, 68 Via Condotti, a solemn, gray, four-floored building that takes up *all* the S.M.O.M.ian soil. The palace, a minute's walk from the bottom of the Spanish Steps, may be readily identified by the letters CVCCI in front, in gold, which I took at first for some sort of Roman numeral but soon realized was a sign for Signor

THE S.M.O.M.

Cucci, the haberdasher. Here at the front of the palace, Signor Cucci has rented a store, filling the windows of it with silken bathrobes and ties, and the several other stores in the palace have pearls, coral, gold tea services, and Buddhas of jade in their windows; none of the stores have extraterritoriality. Between the door to Cucci's and the door to Rapi's is the ponderous door to the S.M.O.M., indicated by a small silver plaque, SOVRANO INTERNAZIONALE MILITARE ORDINE DI MALTA, and by another, INTERNATIONAL MILITARY SOVEREIGN ORDER OF MALTA—two further variations on the name of the country that, according to Baron Apor, are erroneous, as is the variation on his own passport—and beyond the door is a court, smaller than a tennis court but surely large enough for the mailbox that Baron Apor envisages. The court is full of automobiles by day, some of them with S.M.O.M. plates, and is rather pretty by night: a Maltese cross, in red-and-white, is floodlit at the far end, and a gargoyle is spewing water into a pool of goldfish; and the whole thing can be appreciated until 1 A.M. from the Via Condotti, in Italy.

There is a concierge at the border of all this, but he graciously let me by, without any trouble, on the day I visited Baron Apor. The Baron's office is on the palace's third floor; it is well-appointed, but, unfortunately, it doesn't look into the courtyard but onto a typical scene of back-yard Italy, a *pasticcio* of dirty wood and rickety balconies, one above the other and populated, for the most part, by white, restless pieces of laundry, like mountain sheep. For five or ten minutes, I sat in the anteroom and looked at this—a cat lurked, a woman in black drew the laundry in—until, presently, I was shown to the chambers of Baron Apor, who greeted me enthusiastically in English and Italian, told me the story about wine, women, and song of which I've already apprised the reader, told me several facts about the S.M.O.M. of which I've also apprised the reader, gave some hurried orders to a secretary standing by with a pyramid of state papers in his hands, and took me, directly, on a furious tour of the S.M.O.M. itself—a red-and-gold hall of state in which the

Peruvian ambassador had presented his papers a week earlier; a red-and-gold dining room in medieval tapestries; a green-and-gold room where the delegates of the S.M.O.M.ians who don't have citizenship will meet, sometime soon, to elect a grand master; and last but not least the S.M.O.M.'s hospital, in the back rooms of the palace. All of these rooms were tidy, shipshape, and decorated by paintings and maps of Malta, and of the seventy-six grand masters—Deodato de Gozon, who slew the dragon, looking like Man Mountain Dean, and Prince Chigi, who died in 1951, looking like a perfect old man, bald-headed and white-goateed.

The hospital was excellent, I thought. Its waiting room was lit by ultraviolet, germicidal light, and I learned that the one hundred or so patients passing through it every day are given the newest of the miracle drugs—isolated, at long last—and the best of dietary food (a far cry from the eighteenth century, when the S.M.O.M.'s hospital specified a diet of "the best soup, made of fowls, herbs, vermicelli, rice, etc., and every sort of meat . . . such as chickens, pigeons, poultry, beef, veal, game, hashes, fricassees, stews, sausages etc. in such quantities as are necessary; also fresh eggs, pomegranates, plums, and grapes, and every kind of freshment allowed to sick people; such as biscuits, apples, fruit, sugar, and all sorts of confectionery, each according to his wants"). This is the same hospital with us, interruptedly, for nine centuries, but, as I learned from Baron Apor, the S.M.O.M. also has a number of hospitals on foreign soil, some of them larger than the S.M.O.M. and as far afield as London and Schleswig-Holstein, Germany, where, at first, the flags of the S.M.O.M. were thought to be Denmark's by the Schleswig-Holsteiner, who figured the Danes weren't up to any good.

Before I left, I learned from Baron Apor of two other things the S.M.O.M. does in this twentieth century: to fly pilgrims from Italy, Ireland, and Sardinia to Lourdes, and to fly missionaries out of Africa for what in the United States Army is called R&R, a Rest & Recreation leave. For these purposes, the S.M.O.M uses its air force, such as it is, which is kept on Italian

THE S.M.O.M.

soil, is flown by Italians, and, as a matter of fact, was gotten gratis from Italy at the end of World War II. The S.M.O.M. was strictly neutral in that war, as in every war since the Napoleonic ones, and its ambulances went north and south of the battleline, and even today the S.M.O.M. considers itself on friendly terms with every country on earth—except one, a country two hundred times as large and scarcely a mile away, Vatican City. The cause of the falling-out of these two Roman Catholic neighbors is that root of all evil, money: the Vatican has wanted the S.M.O.M.'s, or, at least, the right to audit it, ever since the S.M.O.M. went into the red a decade ago, when all of its navy —a rented navy—disappeared on the Atlantic Ocean with ten thousand bushels of wheat. It turned out that a Count Thun, a federal employee at the S.M.O.M., was using the S.M.O.M.'s money to play the wheat market, and it also turned out that someone else at the S.M.O.M. was playing the stock market, and that someone *else* was smuggling radios from the United States to Italy, via the S.M.O.M., in boxes that were labeled PENICILLIN. Prince Chigi, the grand master, died of a broken heart when he heard of this, and the Vatican investigated; today, though, the S.M.O.M. is in the black, and has written a secret one-hundred page paper telling the Vatican to make itself scarce. What will come of this is hard to say, for relations between the S.M.O.M. and the Vatican have been off-again, on-again since the thirteenth century, when Pope Gregory IX threatened to excommunicate it. (Pope Gregory thought it was in cahoots with the Order of Assassins, a Moslem one, and the S.M.O.M. didn't help any by going to war, soon afterwards, with the Order of the Temple, a Catholic one.) Relations between the S.M.O.M. and the non-sovereign, non-military Order of the Holy Sepulcher also aren't so good; *they* have been off-again, on-again since the eleventh century, when, according to the Church of the Holy Sepulcher, the Church of the S.M.O.M. was ringing its bells too loud. Nowadays, the schism is over real estate, some profitable land at Sorrento that the S.M.O.M. and the Order of the Holy Sepulcher lay claim to. The Grand Commander of the

Order of the Holy Sepulcher and enemy of the Order of Malta is Nicola Cardinal Canali, who was, nevertheless, named by the Vatican to investigate the Order of Malta, and who, moreover, is *in* the Order of Malta—a pretty kettle of fish, I think, and one that I wouldn't dare to elucidate any further.

By now, I suspect that several readers who have been to Italy and the Vatican City are cursing themselves for having been only a block away and missing the chance of doing a third country, the S.M.O.M. They will be comforted to know, accordingly, that, if they saw everything in Rome expected of them as tourists, they *have* done the S.M.O.M.—unwittingly. They will recollect being taken to a shady hill by the Tiber, and being directed, by the American Express man, to peek through a keyhole in a big wooden door; and what they saw was a lovely thing, a long, green avenue of trees and the dome of St. Peter's a mile beyond. The dome of St. Peter's is part of Vatican City, of course, and the keyhole is part of Italy—indeed, a national monument—but the door in which the keyhole is and the avenue of trees are part of the S.M.O.M.: it's the summer villa of the grand master, and, like the summer villa of the pope, at Castelgandolfo, it's extraterritorial.

I haven't any idea how the Pope would feel about it, but, I'm pleased to report, the grand masters of the S.M.O.M. have never taken exception to the thousands of tourists who visit their summer villa and peek into the keyhole. The door itself is not opened for the tourists, though: it is opened only for the grand master, when there is a grand master, and for those people, like me, who are given what amounts to a visa by Baron Apor, and it is opened on these occasions by Signor Cesare Giacchetti, a kindly old Italian who has opened the door, closed the door, cleaned the fluff out of the national monument, pruned the avenue of trees and some persimmon trees, out of sight, and dusted the villa of the grand master since the end of World War I. Signor Giacchetti performed the first two of these functions for me, and said he uses a penknife to perform the third, the

THE S.M.O.M.

fluff being put into the national monument by a couple of young imps in the neighborhood; he also observed that, until recently, the scene to be contemplated at the end of the avenue of trees wasn't St. Peter's Cathedral but an Italian smokestack: there was an outcry in the Italian press, and the indignity was taken down. Signor Giacchetti and I had been chatting of these matters in the garden of the grand master's villa for barely a minute, when one of those tinted, air-conditioned buses arrived, and lo! another swarm of bluebottles alighted, to peek into the keyhole; and Signor Giacchetti and I peeked back.

The bluebottles had the better peek. It encompassed not only Signor Giacchetti, me, and a national monument or two, but no fewer than three countries: Italy, the S.M.O.M., and Vatican City. It is, I think, the most extraordinary panorama of its sort to be seen anywhere on the Continent but the summit of Mt. Blanc, and I heartily commend it to the vacationist in Rome.

"Quiet! Quiet! Quiet!"

—THE PROTOEPISTATIS OF ATHOS.

ATHOS

"To begin with, I cut off my breasts."

Thus Mlle. Maryse Choisy begins the story of her visit to Athos, a country on the north shore of the Aegean Sea where no woman of any race, creed, color, or religion has been allowed for almost a thousand years. In Athos, the only people are twenty-two hundred monks of the Orthodox Church and two

ATHOS

hundred "civilians," all of them males, and all of them certain to blow their tops if anyone of the opposite sex is discovered there. The ban applies not only to female hominidae but to female dogs, cats, horses, and cows, and, with notably less success, to birds, fishes, and insects too, the idea being that sex, even when practiced by the lower species, is "an outlandish spectacle to souls which detest all forms of indecency." Mlle. Choisy, something of an outlandish spectacle herself, was one of the few devil-may-care adventuresses able to violate it. In most of these cases, the consequences were rather drastic. For example, the story is told of how an ill-fated female dog strayed into a monastery there in 1821, immediately died, and turned into a doorknocker, while in 1930 a female human by the name of Alice Diplarakou—Miss Europe of 1930—strayed into another, and though she didn't turn into a doorknocker or anything, a monk, discovering the brave new world of Miss Diplarakou's, fell head over heels in love: he broke his vows, followed Miss D. to Athens, asked her to marry him, and learned, for the first time, that she already was. Shortly afterwards, he went insane.

The latest border incident was in 1952, when a Miss Cora Miller, an American teacher of home economics in nearby Salonika, Greece, put ashore in Athos for a few fleeting seconds: she pottered about the dock, returned to her boat, and sailed away, but the country's government was so incensed by the outrage that it passed a law, still in effect, sentencing any such undesirable aliens to three months in jail—a Greek jail, there being none in Athos itself. Apparently this is okay with Greece, which keeps a paternal eye on Athonite affairs, although, with a legislature of twenty monks and a sort of president, the protoepistatis, and without any taxes, the country itself is pretty independent. Of the twenty monasteries in Athos, seventeen are full of Greeks, and the others of Serbians, Bulgarians, and Russians; the international set is completed by a passell of Rumanians who, having come too late to have a monastery, have a skite, a cross between a monastery and a hermitage. There are six hundred skites and hermitages in Athos, as well as the small seaport of Daphni and the capital town of Karyes—in English, "Nuts."

The Russians in Athos aren't at all Communists but Czarists, and recently, when a man from the Kremlin visited them at their monastery, Russiko, to see what was up, they were found saying prayers for Nicholas II. Nevertheless, the Russian presence there is in the Stalinist tradition. In 1839, Russia made up its mind to take over, offered a dozen-and-a-half monks to Russiko Monastery—then a Greek one—promising to end it there, but no sooner were they in than the Russians tore up the promise, a practice not unheard of in their homeland today, set up a puppet abbot, and began to make monks of their flunkies, helpers, and hired hands until there were four hundred Russians at Russiko. The Greeks appealed to the Ecumenical Patriarch, at Constantinople, but, it's said, the Russians slipped him eighty-eight thousand dollars and a twenty-two-thousand-dollar cross, and paid off the Holy Synod to vote straight. By this century, there were forty-five hundred Russians at Russiko, as many monks as in all the rest of Athos, which was fast being infiltrated. Now the wheel has come full circle, or almost. Russia, under the Communists, has let out nary a monk since 1928, and Russiko, its lifeline cut off, has shriveled to eighty graybeards, most of them older than seventy and half of them in the hospital. They while away the hours by dusting the skulls of the dear departed, and dreaming of the days when Athos was nearly theirs.

The sad state of Russiko is echoed in the other nineteen monasteries. Athos is in a bad way; it loses an eighth of its population a year, and the Athonites who haven't died do little but eat and pray, and precious little of that. The creative ones are few and far between: a dozen who paint; a botanist somewhere; a man who copies books awfully well; and the only person in the world who writes in Early Byzantine, the language of Early Byzantium. Athos has lost the dynamism that made it, even recently, a center of Orthodox culture, and now it's only memories and museums—but magnificent ones indeed. Its paintings, frescoes, robes, and especially its Byzantine manuscripts, many

ATHOS

of them bound in gold and studded with diamonds, rubies, emeralds, and amethysts, are worth a staggering sum, while in the way of relics it's still the principal repository of the True Cross, there being 878.36 cubic centimeters in Athos, at the last tally, as against 537.587 cubic centimeters in Rome and 516.09 in Brussels. (Next are Venice, Ghent, and Paris. Some people say there's enough True Cross in the world to build a cathedral, but really there isn't more than a six-inch cube, a tiny fraction of the Cross itself, found in Jerusalem by Constantine's mother in 326.) Some of the other relics in Athos are the brains of St. John the Baptist; the blood of St. Demetrius; the skull of Isaiah; the tusks of St. Christopher, who, according to the Orthodox Church, had them; the left foot of Mary Magdalen; the crown of thorns; the gold, myrrh, and frankincense; and the robe, or part of it. At Vatopedi, the largest monastery, there is a belt of camel's hair reputedly worn by the Virgin Mary and known for its healing powers in all the Orthodox world: in 1872 it was sent to Constantinople to stop a cholera epidemic, and did, while in 1884 it proved its efficacy in the vegetable as well as the animal kingdom by arresting a lemon blight on Chios, in the Aegean Sea.

A million dollars, I am told, was offered for something in Athos—the crown and robes of a Byzantine emperor—and certainly some of the old, jewelly Bibles there are also worth a million. Athos won't sell. It holds stubbornly to priceless books that are seldom seen, never opened, the sale of which would feather its nest; indeed, the only way to get at these treasures is to steal them, something being done with such consistency, and such a rare critical sense, by the visitors that books and pages pilfered from Athos can now be found at the leading libraries of Europe, there being an especially fine Bible at the British Museum. In Athos, the security measures are haphazard at best: priceless works of art are stuck in cupboards, whatnots, and bureau drawers, and, the way they're left about, it's terribly clear that anybody with a crowbar could put ashore in Athos this very evening, a suitable place being Iveron Monastery, and shove off, presently, with a million dollars of swag. Whenever Greece is reminded of this, it gets the heebie-jeebies, and once it wanted to seize the entire art and lock it up in Athens. As the whole operation smacked of something illicit, though, it reconsidered, and in 1954 it sent a committee of art experts there instead to save and safeguard the stuff, leaving it where it is. Arriving in Athos, the experts all were dismayed to find worms in the manuscripts, soot on the icons, dust on the Bibles, and an exquisite portrait of St. Mark in a trash can; in the Byzantine manuscripts a thousand pages were gone, stolen not only by the visitors and Turkish soldiers, who used them as gunwad in the 1820's, but, it is whispered, by some the monks themselves, who used them as fishbait. The experts have fallen to with a will, dusting, scraping, locking, chaining, fumigating, and rejuvenating, and today, from many a vault in the medieval monasteries of Athos, there comes, anachronistically, the antiseptic smell of DDT.

Athos is one hundred and twenty-four square miles in area, a long, spindly peninsula of Macedonia, lush, rugged, and seagirt. It's pretty easy to go there from Salonika, gentlemen, so I did, and I did so the only sensible way, by boat, as there isn't any road on the whole peninsula except for mules and human feet. By now, I'd been traveling a year: it was October, 1956, and Athos was everywhere sunset-colored, and the monks appeared as little black sunspots on it. From the boat, as from everywhere else, Athos was dominated by a stony gray mountain at its southern end. (Indeed, the country is properly called the Holy Mountain of Athos.) Higher than Mt. Washington, Mt. Athos is, I thought as I neared it, a mountain for mountaineers rather than monks, who nevertheless have built a chapel at the top. On it, long ago, a beacon fire told of the fall of Troy; against it an invasion fleet of Persia's was shipwrecked; and later, to avoid another tragedy like that, the Persians cut a canal across the peninsula and sailed in back of, instead of

ATHOS

around, Mt. Athos. Later still, according to a legend, the Virgin Mary herself was shipwrecked there.

Dochiariou was the first monastery I went to. It is an average one, not very large, not very small, and according to the monks who met me at the pier it was built in 950, though I suspect they were piling it on a bit. Dochiariou is built around a patio, the center of which is a church, a rather pretty thing in pastel pink, and the rest of Dochiariou is full of pastels, flowerpots, and red tile roofs, almost, from some angles, like a Mediterranean villa. First I was taken to its reception room, which might be the salon of any small, spiritless pension, and was given water, candy, coffee, and *ouzo*, a powerful Greek wine that I almost had to chug-a-lug, it being the custom in Greece, apparently, to pick up the empties in two shakes of a lamb's tail. Presently, the Abbot of Dochiariou, Father Daniel, hurried in to greet me, saying, "It's rather chilly today, do you want the window closed?" Father Daniel had a Santa Claus beard, a pigtail down his neck, and a gold tooth that twinkled whenever he smiled, which was often; he wore a dusty black robe and a black hat—not a skullcap, but the kind of hat that bellhops wear. He looked, indeed, like everyone else at Dochiariou. He said a total of twenty-five monks were there, although he had room for seventy; he himself had come in 1897 to visit an uncle, and he liked it so much he stayed (the uncle, I learned later, having promised him a private cell and several acres of farmland). In time, Father Daniel became a deacon, a priest, a chief of priests, and an abbot, as well as the representative from Dochiariou in the country's legislature, the Holy Community.

One thing that puzzled me at Dochiariou was its clock, which was ticking merrily but which otherwise seemed to be at sixes and sevens. (Specifically it was at 6:15, though my own watch and intuition said noon.) I asked Father Daniel about this, and learned that the clock itself was on the up-and-up, but that the monks at Dochiariou start counting time at sunrise, not midnight; thus, 6 A.M. Standard Time is 12 P.M. Monk Time, unless the sun rises earlier, or later, than 6 A.M., which it usually does. Eighteen of the monasteries are on Monk Time, I was told; Vatopedi, which is terribly up-to-date and is even called the Paris of Athos, is on Standard Time; and the Russians, a troublemaker in any crowd, are on Russian Monk Time, which begins at sunset instead of sunrise. To make matters worse, if they can be, the Russians have a skite several miles away on Standard, or Vatopedi, Time, so that a Russian who leaves the monastery at noon reaches the skite at 10 A.M., or even sooner if he takes a mule. Ten A.M. at the skite is 3 P.M. at Russiko if the sun sets at 7 P.M., and it's 4 A.M. at Dochiariou if the sun rises at 6 A.M.; if the sun sets at 8 P.M., which is 3 P.M. at Dochiariou if the sun rises at 5 A.M., then 10 A.M. at the skite is 10 A.M. at Vatopedi, 2 P.M. at Russiko, 5 A.M. at Dochiariou, and 3 A.M. in New York. This sort of thing, so reminiscent of the cuckoo clocks in Liechtenstein, doesn't confuse the monks as much as it confuses me, for they, as I realized after a few days in Athos, are scarcely aware of time at all, and are living, it would seem, in the Middle Ages and all other ages as much as in 1959. It's quite bewildering to listen to them; if they're talking, say, of the Crusaders who tortured them in the thirteenth century, they wince in pain, and if they're talking of the Great Fire of Simopetra Monastery, which, one learns, was extinguished in the sixteenth century, they shudder as if they had only yesterday been plucked from the flames. At Russiko, I saw a desk calendar open to May 8, 1911, and at Dochiariou I saw a truncheon to fight the pirates with; at Chiliandari, I learned, the gate is locked on Sundays, for somewhere in the dark backward and abysm of time, on a Sunday, somebody had dreamt of danger then. A spectacular case of this timelessness in Athos is told by another visitor, who records the following conversation:

"We want to bathe, Father Stephen. Are there any sharks here?"

"Sharks? They abound."

"Have you seen them?"

"I? No. But they ate a deacon two hundred and fifty years ago."

ATHOS

If time seems to be standing still in Athos, it seems so only to the monks. Actually, the place has had a turbulent history, having been invaded by the Crusaders, Catalans, Turks, and Nazis, and twice by the Communists. (This was in 1944 and 1947, when two hundred guerrillas shot up the capital town of Karyes. "You haven't come to worship," one of the monks said, as bullets flew hither and yon. "You will come to a sorry end." And so they did; the Greek Army trapped them and wiped them out.) The history of Athos, I was told, began in the ninth century, when Euthymius of Salonika and Peter the Athonite went there to get away from it all. Peter the Athonite lived as San Marino did, in "a cave extremely dark and surrounded by thick vegetation, in which the crowd of beasts was such that it surpassed the multitude of the heavenly stars," to quote his biographer, while Euthymius, not to be outdone, was crawling around on hands and knees, eating grass. More and more hermits came to Athos; a monastery was built in 963; and a constitution was drawn up in 972, on goatskin, proclaiming it a free and independent nation and banning women forever and ever. (Several hundred of them came anyhow, but were shooed away.) Athos grew rich, it being the custom to give it immense lands and monies, a kind of bribe to heaven. The Emperor of Byzantium built a monastery there; the Emperor of Trapezus built another; the Despot of Serbia gave it a heap of Serbian countryside after visiting it with his *wife*, for Pete's sake; the Czar of Russia gave it a heap of Moscow; and so it went, century after century, until it owned four thousand plantations in Rumania alone. Now the crowned heads of Europe are more enlightened about public land policy, and, since 1863, they've been busy taking it all back. Today, the foreign holdings of Athos are pitiful indeed: the Hotel Vienna in Salonika, the flats at 30 Pavlou Mela Street, a few other buildings here and there, and two-fifths of the fish in Lake Bourou. Athos manages to squeak by financially by selling its wood to Greece, whose telephone poles usually come from there.

Throughout its history, Athos had a unique place in the Orthodox Church, which calls it a "monastic republic"—just as important, in its own way, as Vatican City or the S.M.O.M. to the Roman Church. Some of the gravest theological disputes in Orthodoxy have started there—for example, the memorable Quarrel of the Kollyva, a kind of porridge that some of the monks boiled on Saturday and others on Sunday, all of them being agonized for one-and-a-half centuries by the question of which day, Saturday or Sunday, was more suitable from a spiritual point of view. (Eventually, the Ecumenical Patriarch said any old day was fine by him.) In the Middle Ages, something happened in Athos to tear apart the Orthodox world for a century. Gregory Palamas, one of the monks, announced after looking at his navel several days that he saw a divine light there, the specific instructions, for those who dabble in this sort of thing, being "Sit down in a corner, shut your door, and raise your spirit above everything vain and temporary; then bend your beard forward on your breast, and with all your soul open the perceiving eye which is in the middle of your body." This done, "Force yourself to find the exact site of the heart, where all the forces of your soul are destined to live. First you will encounter darkness, and the resistance of impenetrable masses; but if you persevere and continue this work day and night, you will finish by feeling an inexpressible joy; because as soon as you have found the site of the heart, the spirit sees that which it could never realize previously. It sees the air between it and the heart glowing, clearly and perceptibly and with a miraculous light." According to Palamas, the light was uncreated, like God, and the other monks in Athos said he was certainly right. Diametrically opposed to this school of thought was that of John Barlaam, the tutor of Petrarch and Boccaccio, who, calling the whole thing a heap of pious nonsense, said the light in Palamas's tummy *was* created. (A third possibility—that there wasn't any light—seemed to suggest itself to no one.) Barlaam wrote a flier against "the navel-souled ones," the Emperor of Byzantium and the Ecumenical Patriarch were dragged in, and four councils were called to settle the thing. At last, the Great Council of

ATHOS

1351, at Constantinople, decided for the uncreated light, and peace returned to the Holy Mountain of Athos. John Barlaam was convicted of heresy, and even today, when the awful list of the cursed is read in the Orthodox Church on Orthodoxy Sunday, his name leads all the rest: "To them that . . . confess not, according to the inspired teaching of the saints and the pious belief of the church, that that most divine light was not a creature, nor the essence of God, but an uncreated and physical grace, and forth-shining, and energy, which ever inseparably proceedeth from the divine essence itself—*anathema, anathema, anathema.*"

The Holy Orthodox Catholic Apostolic Eastern Church is rather like the Roman one, emphasizing, though, Easter and the Holy Ghost. In fact, it was an argument over the Holy Ghost—the Romans saying that He proceedeth from Jesus, and the Orthodoxes saying that He doesn't—that brought about the schism beween them, in 1054, when the Pope excommunicated every man, woman, and child in the Orthodox Church. (The Orthodox Church has had its revenge, in a way. It holds that no one is baptized until he is under three times, apparently damning everyone in the Roman Church to limbo.) The Orthodox cathedrals, too, are rather like the Roman ones, an obvious difference being the use of icons instead of statues. In Athos, I must have seen a thousand of these—portraits of Jesus and Mary, of martyrs and saints, a halo of gold, gilt, or gilded brass around their heads and often studded with jewels—hanging in the cathedrals on every inch of wall space. Some of them are called miraculous, like one, at Vatopedi, that started bleeding a few hundred years ago when an ill-natured monk stabbed it in the cheek. The monk fell to the floor hysterical and, for the next three years, sat in a cupboard until the icon forgave him. His wicked hand was never forgiven, though: it was cut off, and even today it is shown to tourists, who have stolen some of the fingers.

Aesthetically, I didn't care for the icons. The hodge-podge of gilt, paint, and jewels, to say nothing of dust and candle soot, was rather trashy, I thought; the faces were lifeless, the postures banal. Maybe I'm just a Philistine: the monks, showing me this, never failed to "ooh" and "aah" at every icon, to view them from the choicest angles, and to lecture me about such icon artists as Panseelinos, who, having something or other that Raphael didn't, was the greatest in history, and Theophanis, the second greatest. Be that as it may, the art of iconoplasty has clearly fallen off, icon after humdrum icon now being manufactured in Athos *à la* Willow Run. Once, I visited some of the icon artists at their skite, and they, as they painted, said they were hanging in New York, Chicago, and San Antonio, Texas; that London had just applied for an icon of St. Mamas a hundred centimeters by seventy; and that Mamas looked like anyone else, sitting on a lion, though. "We love to paint icons," the monks said, painting icons, "and that is why we came to Athos"—and that, in turn, brought up why the other two thousand came to Athos. The artists thought about this and said, presently, that piety wasn't the only reason, as far as they could tell: a number of monks are there because their friends are there, and others, apparently, had a hard time at home; others are afraid of hell. Afterwards, I learned that two or three monks are criminals, lying low, while a few misguided souls took the vows because of Greek girls going for monks in a big way.

To me, the surprising thing isn't that two thousand people should decide to give up wine, women, and song and live in a monastery, but that *only* two thousand should. If Christianity teaches that to kiss a girl, to have a beer, to wash a car or play a little one-o'-cat on Sundays, to do anything fun, is wrong, and that the wrongdoers are to spend eternity in a blast furnace, it seems to me that every man, woman, and child in Christianity would drop everything and buzz over to Athos on the next plane. Since most of them don't, it's some shrift to hear reports that the Athonites aren't altogether holier

ATHOS

than the rest of us. Here's a rather restrained example of what you hear tell—in a book by Ralph H. Brewster:

> "What do you mean? Do you mean to say such things really happen here?"
> "I should think they do! There's hardly a monk on Athos who isn't like that!"
> "Well, well. That is interesting. Tell me more."
> "There is not much to tell; they're all like that, and not easily satisfied either! They want all sorts of refinements. There is one monk in a monastery here, who gives me 200 drachmas each time I visit him."
> "Really, in what monastery is that?"
> "Ah, I can't tell you. I am sorry, but I promised not to tell."

Well, if there are two thousand men living together on a mountain, there's sure to be talk. In Greece, the monks are everywhere said to be homosexuals, and many people wouldn't put a thing past the holy fathers, accusing them, for instance, of kidnaping little boys and whisking them off to the monasteries. In 1933, a Mr. Themistocles Kornaros went to Athos in disguise and wrote a book about it, *The Saints Unmasked,* in which he accused them of drug addiction, alcoholism, misanthropy, perversion, and pederasty, among other things. As a matter of fact, a little of this occurs there, as everywhere, but Mr. Kornaros was stretching the point. "On the beautiful shores of the Athonite peninsula," he wrote, "one sees the floating prostitution boats, [and] one meets the father who drags his twelve- or thirteen-year-old child from cell to cell, renting it to the monks. . . . For such beings, of whom even the name beast would have been mild if it weren't an insult to the working beasts, we have sacrificed and are sacrificing lives, entire populations, civilization, morality, human existence." When I was in Athos, I asked, of course, about this curious book, and the monks replied that Mr. Kornaros is a Communist, this sort of answer being just as adequate in Athos as in our own country. However, the monks wouldn't deny that some of them are worldlier than they

If there are two thousand men living together on a mountain, there's sure to be talk.

might be—than, say, Euthymius of Salonika or Peter the Athonite. Today, the newspaper comes to Athos every day, and some of the fathers have radios, too, often tuning in the Voice of America, while some of them in Karyes sell incense, icons, pipes, perfume, picture postcards, nail clippers, napkin rings, knives, spoons, salad forks, canes, combs, crosses, and Chinese back scratchers stamped ATHOS or SOUVENIR OF ATHOS, and, whenever the tourists come to their shops, can higgle and haggle with the best of them. Little wonder that Richard

ATHOS

Halliburton, after going to Athos in the 1930's, said, "In all probability [it] will develop into one of the most ideal summer resorts in Europe."

The Friar Tucks are a common sight in Athos. Such a one is Father Theomides, of Lavra Monastery, a jolly, fat little man who made like a picture postcard as I took his photograph, holding a lettuce up like the Statue of Liberty. Father Theomides had been to America; he spoke a little English, but he had the curious notion that people in monasteries, such as himself, were "monkeys," and he laughed when I set him straight. That night, Theomides took me to his cell and, rather slyly, reached among the raggedy books and the cobwebs and pulled a bottle of wine out, and as we drank he said he'd been in America less than a year, in 1906, as a short-order cook in Joliet, Illinois; Galveston, Texas; and New York City; and that he'd left us at eighteen, going straightway to Athos. Father Theomides volunteered to tell me a little of his life there. Every day, he gets up at 2 A.M., Standard Time, said Father Theomides, when the sound of a wooden mallet calls the monks to prayer; at 8 A.M. church lets out, and after a cup of coffee he goes to work in the grape arbor, staying until 2 P.M. Then, back to his cell for lunch, a quick siesta, and another hour in church; at 5 P.M. the grape arbor; at 8 P.M. supper; and at 10 P.M. bed. (At 2 A.M. church.) No meat is served at mealtimes, and only one slice of bread. In such a way, Father Theomides has lived for half a century.

Besides Dochiariou, Russiko, and Lavra, I visited Chiliandari, Iveron, Koutloumoussiou, Pantokrator, and Vatopedi, sleeping at some and chug-a-lugging water, candy, coffee, and ouzo at all. Everything was on the cuff, of course, as in monasteries anywhere; a fellow could live in Athos for nothing at all, and, I learned, a hundred or so rascally, impecunious Greeks are doing just that. There, as nowhere else on earth, the hundred or so have perfected the fine art of free-loading in a monastery: having gotten hold of the Calendar of the Saints and using it like a *Fielding's Guide to Europe,* they go from monastery to monastery for the feast days of each, when the refectory tables are groaning with steak, fish, eggs, cheese, lobster, and the best of wines. A kind of fierce pride obtains in these fellows; they call themselves the Order of Mount Athos and are rather snooty about whom they let in, and don't, membership being closed to all but the very rabble—i.e., those who haven't any job, any shoes, any socks, any luggage; anything, indeed, but a heartfelt desire to mooch in the monasteries. The Order of Mount Athos isn't above petty thievery—a drachma here, an icon there—and it's quite a headache to the country's cops, thirty-five men on loan from Greece, who, but for them, wouldn't have anything to do. The monks themselves never get into trouble, or so I was told.

Having visited all these monasteries, I decided to pay a call on their president, the Protoepistatis, a quiet, scholarly man with a delicate face, a black goatee, and black horn-rimmed glasses, whom I found at his desk in Karyes under a clock on Monk Time. The Protoepistatis of Athos said hello, and, while jangling some keys absently in his hand, observed that he was born in a suburb of Istanbul, that his father was a shipping agent, that he came to Athos out of piety in 1910, and that he'd be the protoepistatis a year, having been elected such by the Holy Community, over whom he presided. The Holy Community, he went on, isn't unlike a legislature in the secular world, and the debates are often so spirited, the monks shouting and banging the tables and yanking one another's beards, that he, the Protoepistatis, has to ring a bell to get some peace and quiet. A characteristic squabble, he recalled, was that of Dochiariou and Xerophontos, both of them laying claim to two hundred and fifty acres of Athos, some chestnut and walnut trees. To support its case in the Holy Community of the Holy Mountain of Athos, Dochiariou produced a few papers from the thirteenth, fourteenth, and seventeenth centuries and quoted decisions of the Byzantine and Ottomanic courts; Xerophontos also had papers, but, to the immense good fortune

ATHOS

of Dochiariou, they were copies, for Xerophontos had burned down in 1819. All of these allegations were going hot and heavy when Dochiariou played its trump, a 1939 decision by a Turkish court in its favor, the contemporaneity of which—it was, after all, in the very same century—all but stunned the Holy Community and carried the day for Dochiariou. In the Holy Community, the contentious Dochiariou has also fallen out with Vatopedi, while forty years ago Simopetra and Xeropotamou had so ferocious a tiff, over port rights, that the Holy Community threw up its hands and told them to go to court in Turkey, which they did, at a cost of $170,000.

The intramural feuds in the Holy Community are like zephyrs compared to its bicker with Greece, which has been going fast and furious for nine hundred and fourteen years. The two countries lay claim to twenty-five acres of pasture land at their common border; the issue was joined in 1045 A.D., but, because of congested calendars and the law's delay, it didn't come into court until 1936. A decision, I was told, is imminent. The Holy Community of the Holy Mountain of, and the Protoepistatis of, Athos, believe the case is crucial for two reasons: one, because a few women have been seen on the disputed acres and it isn't clear whether to throw them in jail, and two, because a few monks are brewing a little mountain ouzo there, which is quite illicit if the land belongs to Greece, but quite okay if it belongs to Athos. Having already been accused of kidnaping, fornication, and sodomy, the holy fathers believe that to be found guilty of moonshining would come as a culminating indignity, so they have retained a city lawyer, Mr. Athanasius Gerochristos of Gerochristos, Gerochristos & Gerochristos, and are waiting for the verdict with baited breath. When it's handed down, they will know, finally, where Athos is, but, I reflected as I flew on to Arabia, the more important questions of why it is, what it is, and what it will be, now that money and monks are petering out, are sure to beset the Holy Mountain of Athos for dozens of years to come.

"Asaf ala ayam madhat."
—THE SHEIK OF SHARJA.

SHARJA

The Sheik of Sharja and I sat together at his palace and had some coffee in the afternoon. His palace is white; it smoldered in the sand-hot sun, and the flag of Sharja hung like a damp handkerchief on the flagpole over it—Sharja being a country on the Persian Gulf. Outside, in the palace's shadow, a thousand men and women celebrated the end of Ramadan, the month in

SHARJA

which nothing can be eaten from dawn to sunset; it now was Shawwal, and things aplenty were being eaten by the people in the palace's shadow, and their voices carried like sea-shell sounds to where the Sheik and I were sitting. Dark men from Persia and Pakistan sang in a high, unearthly wail and swayed giddily from side to side, as a cobra charmer might, and others of them beat a tom-tom with loose, boneless hands; they wore the diaphanous robes of the desert, white headgear, and a black *agal*—a coil of braid that formerly was a camel fetter—to hold the headgear down. The Arabs looking on were dressed the same, and the children were frolicking in the tree (there is only one tree of any size) or on half a dozen swings, beneath it, and their mothers sat like hawks on the sands nearby. The mothers of Sharja wear iridescent, hawklike masks to cover the eyes and nose, instead of veils; their lips are dyed with henna, and their eyes are made moonlight-bright by belladonna drops; and their robes are altogether black. The Sheik was dressed in white, but his robe was trimmed in gold, and his *agal*, too, was golden; he carried a sword, a dagger in his sword belt, and the scabbard of each was filigreed in gold.

The Sheik of Sharja is the Honorable Saqr bin Sultan, or, more fully, Saqr bin Sultan bin Saqr bin Khaled bin Sultan bin Saqr bin Rashid . . . al Qawasim. ("Bin," in Arabic, is equal to "ben" in Hebrew and "son of" in English, and "Qawasim" is the family name.) He is a small, dark, prideful man, with bushy brows and a goatee as tough as a rasp, and he sat beside me, on an overstuffed sofa, as our coffee was served the Arabian way. A coffee maker—a human being, not a utensil—carried it ceremoniously into the room, in a golden urn, and poured it into our golden coffee cups with many ceremonious clicks of gold upon gold, and the Sheik of Sharja and I partook of three coffee cupfuls apiece, it being woefully bad manners in Arabia to have any less. The coffee was tart and powerful, and, after our three mandatory drams, we waggled our cups at the coffee maker as a signal we had had our fill—this, too, being the proper manners in Arabia. Both of these fine points of etiquette, and others, had been taught to me by several of the Englishmen in town, who also had briefed me on the proper way of speaking to the Sheik of Sharja, which, in words of one syllable, is not to. The Arabian custom, they had said, is to exchange at the Sheik's afternoon coffee hour what, in America, would be nothing more than the bare civilities, the first in chronological order being "Peace be with you" ("And with you," the Sheik replies prescriptively), the second being "How are you?" ("Good," or "Bad"), and the third and last being "Allah be thanked" if the Sheik is good, or "Allah has willed it" if the Sheik is bad. This is followed, invariably, by a great deal of silence, which is broken after ten or fifteen minutes when the Sheik of Sharja says, "And how are *you?*" ("Good," or "Bad") and "Allah be thanked" or "Allah has willed it." Then, coffee is served in triplicate, and such fruits as pineapple are eaten from the right hand, since, in Arabia, the left is thought to be unclean, and employing it at the table is again bad manners; "How are you?" and "Allah, etc." are said again, rose water is sprinkled on the hands and sandalwood incense is wafted to the face, and, without any further ado, the visitor takes his leave. The Englishmen instructing me in all this remembered the case of Mr. Basil Lermitte, a businessman who had lived in Sharja, who had achieved success for his firm by his uncanny ability to sit with the Sheik of Sharja two or three hours, never saying a word. Mr. Lermitte, I was informed, had "an understanding silence."

Well, my friends will testify that an understanding silence is a quality I don't possess at all, and, after trying to sustain one a dozen or so minutes, I decided to throw precedent to the winds, and I made so bold as to ask the Sheik of Sharja how *Sharja* was. It was so-so, said the Sheik: the Japanese were cutting into the pearl business of late, and Sharja's economy was on the skids. "Allah has willed it," I replied, and steeled myself for another quarter hour of silence, but the Sheik, apparently, was delighted at the new turn his afternoon coffee hour had taken, for he pressed me with questions of his own—What did

SHARJA

I think of Sharja? What did Americans think of Sharja? And what did Americans think of sheiks? Surmising it's bad manners to say that ninety-nine out of a hundred Americans seldom think of Sharja at all, I did say what we think of sheiks: as dark, seductive men, sleeping on the desert in tents and hurrying across it on Arabian horses. "*La, la,*" said the Sheik, laughing and shaking his head, and he waved his arm at his palace and his 1955 Buick outside; and I concluded that sheiks have fallen upon better days since those of Rudolph Valentino.

After this unprecedented conversation, the Sheik of Sharja and I went away the best of friends. He showed me a few Kodachromes of his trip to Egypt, and I invited him, in my unofficial capacity, to make one to the United States; "I shall try to," said the Sheik, and "Allah be thanked," said I; rose water was sprinkled on our hands, and sandalwood incense was wafted to our faces, and we walked outside into the lengthening shadow of the palace and joined in the joys of Ramadan's end. The dark men from Persia and Pakistan beat the tom-toms ever faster and danced with willow wands, throwing them from shoulder to shoulder limply, in time with the tom-toms; the children swung beneath the tree, from sunshine to shadow, shadow to sun, and their mothers were like hawks upon the sand. One after another, the Sharjawis approached the Sheik, said "Peace be with you"—"*Salaam aleikum*"—and kissed him on the nose and forehead, and the Sheik endured it silently. (It was too hot, really, for these embraces.) I myself was approached by Ghulam, a servant at the fort I was staying in. "Merry Christmas, sir!" he said.

"Merry Christmas, Ghulam," I replied, for it certainly was.

Ghulam and the thousand other bons vivants at Sharja were Sharjawis, mostly, but many had come the half-a-dozen miles from Dubai, yet another tiny independent country on the Persian Gulf. The Ramadan is ended, in these countries, whenever the new moon is seen by the reigning sheik: it was seen by the Sheik of Sharja but, pitiably, not by the Sheik of Dubai, who is eighty years old and getting pretty myopic, so the Sheik of Dubai's people had hurried to Sharja, to the month of Shawwal, and to food in anything going across the desert—jeeps, camels, trucks, and taxis. (A dozen or so taxis go between the two countries, the oldest of them a New York City Sky-View somehow far astray.) A few of the bons vivants came from the other nearby sheikdoms, seven in all: Sharja and Dubai are the only ones with any population to speak of, but all seven are tiny, independent countries ruled by seven independent sheiks, who, like Prince Rainier of Monaco, have the unqualified power of life and death. Unlike Rainier, though, the Sheik of Sharja cut a man's hand off as lately as 1952, the Sheik of Dubai put a man's eyes out with a red-hot needle, and the Sheik of Ras al Khaima did so with his own thumbs; the Sheik of Sharja hasn't, to my knowledge, killed a man, but the Sheik of Ajman has killed two. Such idiosyncrasies of the seven sheiks are a favorite conversational item for the Englishmen in town, and, after listening for several evenings and doing a bit of verification, I learned, in addition, that the Sheik of Ajman is very poor, traveling in a Chevrolet pick-up truck; that the Sheik of Abu Dhabi is very rich, burying money in the floor and sitting determinedly on top of it; that the Sheik of Umm al Qaiwain is diabetic; and that the Sheik of Fujaira is hunky-dory, but hypochondrial: he's always in the hospital, and he's never willing to sign a state paper unless he is given glasses. (He is given sunglasses.) The Sheik of Abu Dhabi, too, has been troubled by mental ills, notably by a delusion that his coffee maker would murder him. In 1953, his paranoia became so acute that he went to be treated in London by Her Majesty's physician, but, deciding after two or three appointments that the fellow was in his enemies' pay, he fled to Paris, and what happened there to the Sheik of Abu Dhabi, and to his coffee maker, is still recollected fondly on winter evenings by the Englishmen in Abu Dhabi itself, and, for that matter, by the Sheik. (The coffee maker was with the Sheik of Abu Dhabi all

SHARJA

along, the Sheik feeling, apparently, that his good qualities as a coffee maker outweighed his bad.) In substance, the story is that the two travelers, after chopping up the floor of their hotel room to make kindling—to make coffee—were expelled from it, and, after building a fire under the bathtub of another hotel room to make hot water, from *it;* that they went in high dudgeon to Cairo, liking it much more; and that, in time, the Sheik returned to Abu Dhabi without any trace of his mental diseases, but with a social one. Something else about this innocence abroad that I didn't learn in Sharja but in *Holiday,* which has sources of its own, is that the Sheik of Abu Dhabi was particularly impressed, in Paris, by the oil derrick on the Left Bank, the highest he'd ever seen. It was obvious, the Sheik had said, why France was economically so better off than Abu Dhabi.

In all fairness to the Honorable Shakbut bin Sultan, the Sheik of Abu Dhabi, his worries as to his coffee maker weren't altogether irrational, for the same fellows had murdered every Sheik of Abu Dhabi since 1912, three in all. The history of Abu Dhabi since the late eighteenth century shows a similar pattern: eight of the sheiks were murdered, two of them made their getaway in time, two were cashiered but not at all murdered, and two died in office of natural causes, while the destiny of the Honorable Shakbut bin Sultan, the incumbent, remains to be seen. The histories of Sharja and the other countries are more or less the same: the conventional way to become a sheik was to murder the last one, something not only done by members of the family but also by casual acquaintances, and even by tourists—a case in point being Mr. Thomas Horton, of Newcastle-on-Tyne, England, who got to be Sheik of Kishma late in the eighteenth century by choking his predecessor to death and marrying his wife, having come to Kishma by way of Sweden, where he murdered his captain in the Swedish army; Russia, where he murdered his wife; Iraq, where he murdered the governor; and the Persian Gulf, where he murdered the whole crew of a British East India Company ship. (As Sheik of Kishma, the Honorable Thomas Horton was known for his lofty motives, though several said they didn't approve of his methods. Once, he entertained the one hundred and twenty men of a British sloop, the Hope, and, far from murdering them, he gave them an equal number of Negro girls to marry; "the girls were naturally delighted," according to the papers where I learned all this, "but not so the captain, who knowing the mischief one woman often caused in a ship, wondered whatever he should do with one hundred and twenty on board." He let them off at Bombay.) In Arabia, there isn't any longer

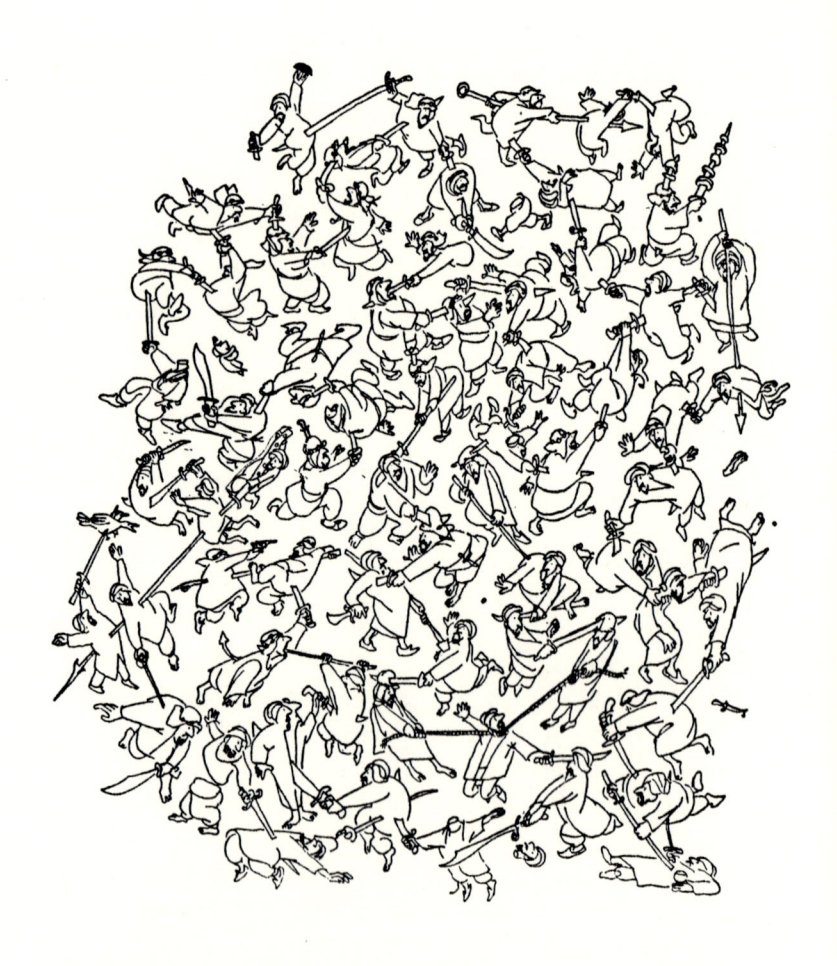

SHARJA

a Sheik of Kishma, and one supposes all the candidates were murdered in the course of time. The most recent murder hereabouts was in 1951—that of the Sheik of Kalba, by his son—while in Sharja itself the most recent murder, as of going to press, was in 1921, the Sheik's eyes being put out with a red-hot poker and his throat being slit, all of this going on at the very palace where Sheik Saqr bin Sultan and I had coffee together.

None of this, to my way of seeing it, reflects any credit on the Sheik of Sharja. To be sure, he didn't murder anyone to get his incumbency, but (lest it be thought he's above this sort of thing) he was trying hard to murder the Sheik of Dubai in 1939; he even declared war. The war wasn't taken seriously, though, by anyone but the sheiks, and was so apathetically prosecuted that after a year of it exactly two people had been hurt, and both by accident. In fact, the war used to be called off several times a day whenever a pearl, fish, or rug merchant went by taxi from one country to the other, or whenever a Pan American plane full of non-belligerents was due at the airport. (Sharja was a fueling stop for Pan American, which is still flying over it every morning.) I'm afraid that Arabian wars, as well as Arabian sheiks, have lost a lot of glamour since the days of Rudolph Valentino. The war of Sharja vs. Dubai wasn't one of Bedouin horsemen, as we'd have hoped—on the average there are 1.14 horses a sheikdom—but of artillerymen, who let fly rusty, age-old cannonballs from the Sheik of Sharja's palace to the Sheik of Dubai's, and vice versa. For gunpowder, the artillerymen used a blend of saltpeter and cactus that imparted to the cannonballs a very low muzzle velocity, if any, the balls never really getting to their targets but settling into the sand, a mile short. At night, they were picked up and fired in the other direction, until, by normal attrition, no more cannonballs were to be found, and the War of Sharja vs. Dubai was declared over. Its last shot was fired by Mr. Juma bin Thani, who, after a futile search on the desert for second-hand balls, remembered a high explosive shell that hit the palace in 1908 but didn't go off; digging it up, he thrust it into his cannon with the usual wad of saltpeter and cactus, and it was in the ensuing explosion, I learned, that the war's only casualties occurred.

Since then, a number of other inter-sheik wars have been held—Dubai vs. Abu Dhabi in 1947, Abu Dhabi vs. Ajman in 1948—but they, too, are nothing to get alarmed about, and their principal effect is to keep the Rand McNally people at wit's end. Happily, a more or less permanent map of the seven countries is now being essayed, at their suggestion, by Mr. Julian Walker, a young, eager, disinterested Englishman who, to my very good fortune, was a passenger on the tiny, crackajack plane taking me to Sharja from Bahrain Island, in the Persian Gulf. While we were aloft, he told me some of the difficulties of his work. There are, Mr. Walker said, many stretches of desert that three, four, or even five countries lay claim to, such that Fujaira would be all gone if the claims of Sharja were allowed, Dubai would be all gone if the claims of Sharja and Abu Dhabi were allowed, and peradventure *he* would be all gone if any claim *weren't* allowed. Mr. Walker said he was sitting on claim and counterclaim as a one-man court of international justice, and, digging into his brief case, he showed me his latest try to make head or tail of them, a vast, tentative, pen-and-ink map of the seven countries. For the next hour, as our plane neared the Sharja coast, I studied Mr. Walker's map and tried to make head or tail of *it*, while Mr. Walker compounded my confusion by observing that Sharja, not unlike the countries of the Holy Roman Empire, was broken into four pieces, with trackless miles of Fujaira (in three pieces) and Ras al Khaima (in a piece) in between, and that Dubai was broken into two pieces, with trackless miles of one of the four Sharjas, one of the three Ajmans (the others being in one of the four Sharjas and *the* Ras al Khaima), and the Sultanate of Oman in between, and that Umm al Qaiwain was—oh, the hell with it. Anyhow, Mr. Walker said, the whole damn thing was tentative, for the seven sheiks hadn't seen the map and, when they did, would surely recollect a heap of new claims and counterclaims.

SHARJA

Next, Mr. Walker observed that the contiguity of the Sultanate of Oman to six of the seven countries (and the contiguity of Qatar, another country, to one) is nothing to worry about, as these boundaries are cut-and-dried, but that the contiguity of Saudi Arabia, in the hinterlands, is worrying everyone from the United Nations on down. The Saudis, he said, are claiming so much of Abu Dhabi that scarcely any is left, and even have sent a number of soldiers, under an emir, to seize an Abu Dhabi oasis, this being the Buraimi Crisis of which I'd surely been reading in the newspapers. Mr. Walker said emphatically that Abu Dhabi was right and Saudi Arabia wrong, and asked me to apprise my readers of this. "You see," he explained, "the Sheik of Abu Dhabi has a palm-tree tax, and King Saud of Arabia has a camel tax, so the nomads who live *here*"— he pointed to the disputed area on his map—"don't pay any taxes to Abu Dhabi, as they don't have any palm trees, being nomads, but they do pay taxes to Saudi Arabia, one goat per every ten camels, and I must say they're jolly glad to, because a goat is worth thirty or forty rupees, and whenever the Saudi Arabian tax collector takes a goat away, he gives them a hundred and fifty rupees back, as a 'gift.' I might add it's *Ameri*can rupees, from the Arabian-American Oil Company, and it's all being used to bribe the nomads." Mr. Walker waited while I got this down, and then observed that the entire crisis—camels, goats, palm trees, emirs, nomads, and who's paying taxes to whom—was being arbitrated by five well-paid lawyers from England, Saudi Arabia, Belgium, Pakistan, and Cuba, and that the lawyers, when last heard of, had convened on the French Riviera, and that the English lawyer had walked out because the Arabian lawyer was biased. Meanwhile, the Rand McNally people are calling it all a bad job, and are pretending, on their latest maps of the Middle East, that the seven countries aren't even there—an attitude Mr. Walker thought was cavalier at best, and maybe even scandalous. The best that other cartographers do, he concluded, is to draw two or three sporadic borders disappearing into the desert as into quicksand, and to label the whole forty thousand square miles as the Trucial Oman, the Trucial States, or the Trucial Coast.

"Trucial" is a word that doesn't exist except on maps, and means, I gather, "of or pertaining to a truce"—a truce in the last century that ended a forty years' war with England. Until then, the area was known in England as the Pirate Coast, but, once the truce had been signed, it was clear that piracy couldn't occur any longer, and the word "Trucial," to replace "Pirate," was happily coined by Captain Prideaux of the Royal Navy, and since then the area is the "Trucial Coast," and acts of piracy "maritime irregularities." The Trucial, Pirate Coast—Sharja in particular—was a pirates' den even before the Exodus, a version of the Koran says, and certainly since the first century, when Pliny, the Roman, wrote that "voyages are made from Egypt to Arabia every year, and companies of archers are carried on board, as those seas are greatly infested with pirates." In the fourteenth century, Sharja blockaded the Persian Gulf, says Marco Polo, and in the eighteenth century it seized a British East India Company ship and sold its crew into slavery, which is how the war began. That the Sheikdom of Sharja could hold off the British Empire for the next forty years is due, I learned, to the British policy then, appeasement. After twenty years of being pirated by the country, the British were still selling it ammunition. In 1797, some of this ammunition was sold by Captain Carruthers, of the *Viper,* and straightway was used to kill Captain Carruthers, to kill or wound one-half of his crew, and nearly to sink the *Viper* itself; the Foreign Office was more than embarrassed, but it took the Sharjawis' word—that Captain Carruthers had fired first—and ordered the Royal Navy never to fire unless fired upon. This was followed to the letter by Lieutenant Graham, of the *Sylph,* who didn't fire a shot as the Sharjawis climbed on board, and everyone's throat was cut on the gangway in Allah's name: *"Allah o akbar"* ("Allah is great"). The order *wasn't* followed by Lieutenant Gowan, of the *Fury,* who fired first, scared the Sharjawis off, and was cen-

SHARJA

sured personally by the Governor of Bombay for doing so—"for daring to molest the innocent and unoffending Arabs of these seas."

By now, Sharja had a thousand ships and twenty thousand pirates on them, and there were murmurs, in England, that its policy of appeasement was not an unqualified success. The next policy tried was a police action: the Navy, in 1805, was sent against the Sharjawis with orders "to act with the greatest moderation," not to offend them. This, too, wasn't an unqualified success; nor was the Expedition of 1809, which landed and killed "seventy to eighty of these vagabonds," according to its communiqué, and went home; nor the Expedition of 1816, which threw its weight around by shooting three hundred and fifty cannonballs into the Persian Gulf. Unabashed, Sharja was soon putting the whacks to India itself, and, after thinking about this another two years, England decided, at last, that there isn't any substitute for victory, and sent Sir W. Grant Keir, a dozen warships, and seven thousand men to invade it. The shame! Sharja had been a paper tiger all along, and its sheik surrendered right off, followed by the Sheik of Dubai, who turned out to be nine years old. Five Englishmen had been killed, as against untold hundreds in the appeasement years.

Well, some people never learn. In England, it was now decided to keep so hard-gotten a peace by that most rigorous of means, a treaty, and so the Treaty of 1820 was signed with the sheiks, who, presently, tied up a dozen Englishmen to a grapnel and threw it into the Persian Gulf. The Foreign Office saw that another treaty was called for, and soon it was signing them at two a year, all of this ending in 1853 with the Treaty of Peace in Perpetuity—peace in our time and everyone else's. A century later, in 1953, the Sharjawis got word of a schooner passing by, took it, and marooned its crew on the desert; but usually they aren't any longer pirates. (It wasn't the Treaty of Peace in Perpetuity that put them out of business, it was the steamboat.) Instead, the Sharjawis go to movies like *Treasure Island* and get nostalgic, and the old ones still gather at twilight along the cool, wet shores of Sharja and reminisce; *"Asaf ala ayam mad-hat,"* they say to each other, or, as a Scotsman like Captain Kidd might have worded it, "For days of auld lang syne."

What has replaced piracy as the main industry of Sharja, Dubai, etc., is smuggling—mostly of Indian tea, Hong Kong silk, and suchlike from the seaport of Dubai, where the tariff is four-and-a-half percent, to those of Pakistan and Persia, where it's twenty-five percent or more. (Nobody knows how the Sheik of Dubai hit on four-and-a-half percent. It's assumed he saw it in a bank or somewhere and adopted it as a pat, businesslike number.) A lot of pearling is done, but it's being hurt by the Japanese, as the Sheik of Sharja said; some of the people fish, and some of them grow dates, even wheat and tobacco. As can be well imagined, the white hope of the sheiks in this industrial age is to make an honest living at last by striking oil, and, accordingly, they have signed a contract going well into the twenty-first century with Petroleum Development (Trucial Coast) Ltd. For a number of years, the Petroleum Development (Trucial Coast) Ltd. people have been digging holes in the desert to see what's under it, if anything, and some raw, suntanned seismologists from America, which owns a quarter of P.D.(T.C.) Ltd., have been setting off T.N.T. offshore, to the irritation of some unenlightened natives who think their white hope is to catch more fish. Almost all of these holes are being dug into Abu Dhabi's soil, for Abu Dhabi is next to Qatar, a country that was mentioned parenthetically once before, is pronounced like "gutter," and is so full of oil underground that its ruler has 1955 Buicks to give away—to the Sheik of Sharja, for one. The Sheik of Qatar enjoys, too, what is thought to be the only television set on the Arabian peninsula—mercifully he can't see anything on it, the nearest TV station being in Turkey—and he's sorely envied by the seven sheiks I'm writing of, who wait impatiently for a big black gusher of their own to soar from the desert sands.

One evening in Sharja, I was talking oil with some of the Englishmen there, and I asked, naturally, if the sheiks had any

176

SHARJA

chance of striking it. The evening was hot, as always, and my English friends were drinking Scotch on the rocks, mostly rocks, and were dressed, as always in the evenings, in white ducks, white open-collar shirts, and black cummerbunds—this, a slight nod to the proprieties of civilized life. One of the Englishmen so attired was just back from the Abu Dhabi oil fields, so I directed my question to him. He hemmed and hawed a few moments, and shifted his Scotch to the other hand, and presently he said, "Well, what I'm permitted to report is that we have drilled to six thousand feet, and we have encountered some unexpected difficulties."

"Quite," said one other Englishman. "No oil."

Almost all of my English friends on the Trucial Coast are like Mr. Walker, the cartographer—young, eager, and red-faced, without a hint of a suntan after several years in Arabia—and, in their black-and-white evening habits, rather difficult to tell apart. I bet there are a hundred of them, working for the Red Cross, the airport, the Foreign Office, and the bank, as well as for Petroleum Development (Trucial Coast) Ltd., and while they'd all allow that much of the world is gayer, and certainly cooler, than the Trucial Coast, they seem to be rather fond of it. This, however, is tempered by an uneasy feeling the world doesn't care about the Trucial Coast, and nothing pleases them as being reminded it does, as happened, for example, a half-dozen years ago, when none other than Winston Churchill sent a telegram there. Whatever the Prime Minister of Great Britain had to communicate to the Trucial Coast is secret, and nobody would apprise me of it, but they did recall, and with considerable pride, that, at the height of the Buraimi Crisis, a London newspaper had asked in its weekly news quiz as to what Buraimi was —an oasis, a race horse, or a kind of spaghetti—and that an M.P. had asked in the House of Commons as to *where* Buraimi was, and upon being told it's somewhere on the Trucial Coast, as to where the Trucial Coast was. This exchange, showing, as it did, that the Trucial Coast was not forgotten by the busiest deliberative body in England, was fast communicated to the foreign colony there by somebody witnessing it, and all week it brightened the evening hours at Sharja, Dubai, and Abu Dhabi that would otherwise be spent in talking oil, talking the idiosyncrasies of the seven sheiks, drinking Scotch on the rocks, and wearing cummerbunds.

The most important of the young, eager, and untanned Englishmen in these parts is Mr. Peter Tripp, of the Foreign Office. England has been in more or less hegemony since it beat the pirates (Persia, in 1888, and France, in 1891, tried to muscle in by giving away flags, but they didn't get very far), and, by treaty with the seven countries, it handles their foreign affairs, so Mr. Tripp isn't the Minister or the Ambassador but the Political Agent, the "P.A." The foreign affairs of Sharja, by and large, are with Abu Dhabi, Dubai, Ajman, Umm al Qaiwain, Ras al Khaima, and Fujaira, and what with thirty-six other combinations the P.A. is really kept busy: he worries about the inter-sheik wars, the inter-sheikdom borders, the claims and the counterclaims of the seven sheiks, several of whom he must visit a day, drink three cups of coffee with, and assume an understanding silence, and also get the red carpets out whenever they go traveling, and *also* keep the pearl merchants, fish mongers, and other pillars of the community happy, bestowing a title like "khan sahib" on them. He got glasses for the Sheik of Dubai, he got sunglasses for the Sheik of Fujaira, he got a coronation ticket for the Sheik of Abu Dhabi, and when the Sheik of Abu Dhabi fled to Paris, he got it canceled. All of this, and suchlike, he does one-and-a-half years without a vacation, and, the P.A. says, he nearly resigned when pulled from a happy life in the Anglo-Egyptian Sudan and told to do it.

One of the P.A.'s compensations is that he's the only Englishman in the world today to emancipate slaves. By the sheiks' permission, he is sort of an allie-allie in-free for the several thousand Arab, Negro, and Pakistani slaves in the sheikdoms, and any managing to reach him morning, afternoon, or night will get a personal emancipation proclamation from him, a piece of red-white-and-blue paper that says, in Arabic and English,

SHARJA

"Be it known to all who may see this that the bearer ... has been manumitted and no one has a right to interfere with his/her liberty." Although, each week, one or two slaves go to the P.A., get this, and hurry off to the Qatar or Abu Dhabi oil fields, the great majority are happy with their lot: they get bed and board, and sometimes pay, and, not having to worry about being fired, they don't work especially hard: they are born as slaves and marry slaves, begetting boys and girls who are slaves *de jure*, and once in a blue moon the prettier ones are sold to a Saudi Arabian prince, marry him, and bring their families to Saudi Arabia in a DC-3—it really happened, I'm told. At present, the selling price for a slave girl is two hundred and seventy dollars, and those of my readers who wish to obtain one should go to Hamasa, Sultanate of Oman, any day but Friday, most of the business there being done in Pakistani rupees, and privately. In the past, the slaves at Hamasa were kidnaped from Pakistan, Persia, or the seven sheikdoms, but this is frowned upon now by the sheiks, and anyone indulging is apt to be jailed, or maybe deprived, slowly, of his right hand, the Mohammedan punishment for thievery. Such a thing happened shortly before I got to Sharja, when the P.A., scorching across the desert in a jeep, overtook a slaver and the four girls he had kidnaped; the slaver was jailed, and the slave girls (who said he had raped them) were manumitted, and they hugged and kissed the P.A. for joy. According to the P.A., the girls were quite beautiful—but he has been in Arabia a long time.

One of Sharja's pillars of the community who was proclaimed a khan sahib by the P.A. is Mr. Hussain bin Hasan Amad, a fine, gentle, fatherly man who is generally known, in Sharja, as the Khan Sahib. He is a pearl merchant, and one afternoon I visited his cool, wind-swept home on the waterfront to learn what I could of this business. The Khan Sahib met me warmly in his sitting room, on the second floor, and clapped his hands for coffee, and as we drank it, in triplicate, he observed that pearling is done in the twentieth century pretty much as in the tenth: an Arab, in almost nothing, gets a deep breath and goes underwater, at times for twenty-five yards, and when he surfaces one-and-a-half minutes later for coffee or a quick cigarette, he has a big black bag of oysters, any pearl in it being given to the ship's captain, and sooner or later to the Khan Sahib. A diving suit is illegal—it would put too many citizens out of work. Something that does put citizens out of work is sawfish, the Khan Sahib went on, the largest of these having a six-foot saw, enough to slice a man in two, and something else again is *zar,* a very odd disease. The Khan Sahib recalled a Mr. Brahim, who came down with the *zar* on one of his pearling ships one day, whereupon he fell to the deck, saw the future—rightly, as it turned out—ate a red-hot charcoal, drank six quarts of sea water, and passed out; the next day he was working again, fit as a fiddle. The Khan Sahib said it was just like the *Arabian Nights,* and he could offer no reasonable explanation for it.

While all of these matters were being told me by the Khan Sahib, we had been joined, in the sitting room, by many of his ship's captains and by other men-about-town, and presently the dozen of us sat down on the floor, cross-legged, to an Arab lunch. It came on a whopping big platter—a pyramid of rice, raisins, corn, potatoes, and mutton meat, brains, and eyeballs, all to be eaten with the bare right hand, the Arab custom. All of us fell to while the Khan Sahib observed, for my benefit, that the whopping big platter was also an Arab custom: the leftovers would be given to any poor people needing it, and if more was needed, more would be gotten. Such is Arab hospitality, which even extends to the enemy within the gates, illustrating which the Khan Sahib told me how a sheik, some years ago, wined and dined a visiting fireman who had murdered a half dozen of his people, it being inhospitable not to. Soon, the Khan Sahib was speaking of other sheiks, of how *they* had murdered, of assassinations, usurpations, and treachery, of cut-away hands, of eyes made blind by red-hot pokers, and of war, of how a brother met brother in the 1947 war, killed him, and kissed his forehead, until, by the meal's end, I was thoroughly bewildered. The Arab's personality is its own antithesis, I thought, as strange as the Japanese's—or, perhaps, as God's of the Old Testament, loving and compassionate at most times, relentless when pushed too far.

It is a personality I don't pretend to understand, but I respect it. Missionaries of other persuasions who try to change it—to make it like God's of the New Testament, perhaps—have not been very successful in Sharja. There is, there, a Presbyterian mission called the American Mission Hospital and run by three American ladies, and, having heard many unkind things about it from the Sharjawis, I decided on my last afternoon there to visit it myself. I was met by Dr. Sarah L. Hosmon, the director, a slight woman of seventy or eighty whose face is taut, severe, and American Gothic, and who, after inviting me for tea in her living room, said that she's been on the Arabian peninsula since 1911, in Sharja since 1952, that two dozen or so patients come to the hospital each morning, and that, after a Bible lesson, they are treated by herself and the other two ladies at a nominal fee. "Either they listen to the Bible or they won't be treated," Dr. Hosmon said. "That's what'll save them—not the medicine—and either they listen or away they go. These people brag how they pray to God five times a day. Well, what I tell them is God doesn't listen to their praying, because it isn't done through Jesus Christ. *That* gives 'em something to chew on. Sometimes I read the Sermon on the Mount, or I prove that Jesus is the Son of God. Or—"

"Prove?" I said, almost unconsciously.

"Yes." Dr. Hosmon got up and fetched, for my benefit, a pen-and-ink chart from a nearby cupboard. It showed the genealogical tree of Jesus from the Virgin Mary and St. Anne upwards, and, using it, Dr. Hosmon set about her proof, and when, after five or ten minutes, she had finished it, I asked her whether she manages to get across to the Arabs at her hospital.

"That isn't important," she said. "My instructions are 'Go ye and preach the gospel'—that's all, and whether they believe it isn't my business. Only we don't want these people, when they're sent to Hell, to be crying, 'But nobody *told* us.'"

I thanked Dr. Hosmon for the interview and the tea, and left. I have neglected to say that she hasn't won any converts.

"And I'm the supreme court of appeals, too."

—THE WALI OF SWAT.

SWAT

Swat, a little country not far from Afghanistan, is trying to drum up the tourist trade these days, and just look! It had two hundred tourists in 1950, and nine hundred tourists the next year, and fifteen hundred the next year, and three thousand the *next* year, and the Swatis are tickled to death. Already they have built the Swat Hotel, and now they're building a sports arena and still another hotel, and they're talking of a

SWAT

ski lift in the Himalayas, which, in Swat, get higher than nineteen thousand feet. They have printed two tourist pamphlets—their "propaganda," as they call it. One of these, a colorful flier called *Visit This Enchanting Mountain State*, is available as far afield as Peshawar, Pakistan; the other, *Glimpses of Swat*, is harder to come by, but it's an outstanding publication from the very first sentence: "Swat constitutes one of the rare regions of the vast and extensive land which Almighty gives to a country only to inspire man with enthusiastic and melting heart, good spirits, purity of vision, ambitious ideas and chaste and sublime meditations by a scintillation of its eternal beauty and graceful nature."

Swat has been eulogized by the tourists, too. "A dreamland!" said Mrs. Mary Cawthorn, of Karachi, writing in the guest register of the Swat Hotel. "Beautiful!" said Mr. William Astell, of Kabul, Afghanistan. "A hidden dream that lurks on the fringe of imagination," said Mr. Harrison P. Johnson, Jr., of Cleveland, Ohio. "It was a long drive from 'Pindi, and," said an Air Force officer, "an entirely official visit, but, after reaching here, I suddenly felt so unofficial and inert that I could hardly pursue my official business. I want to see more of it—ever more." And finally Mr. William D. Weeks, of New York City, was moved to poetry, writing,

> *Greetings to this Grand Hotel*
> *Greetings too from Lord Nobel*
> *Greetings from all the whole darn lot*
> *To your verily handsome land of Swat.*
> *Thanks for the Service and the Maccaroons Sweet,*
> *That weren't had again for the love of Pete*
> *Thanks for hot water, flowers, and chai*
> *Thanks for everything, goodbye, Banzai*
> *You're always in heaven and never in hell*
> *When you come to the Wali Sahib's Swat Hotel.*

In Swat, a carbon of Mr. Weeks's poem is found everywhere, and an abridged version is printed in *Glimpses*:

*Greetings to this Grand Hotel
Greetings too from Lord Nobel.*

Debrett's *Peerage, Baronetage, Knightage, and Companionage* doesn't list a Lord Nobel, unfortunately, and I couldn't discover who he is, or why he cared to greet Swat. However, I did identify the Wali Sahib: he's Ala-Hazrat Ghazi-e-Millat Brigadier Miangul Abdul Haq Jahan Zeb, the Wali of Swat—"the pillar of cloud by day, and," according to *Glimpses* again, "the pillar of fire by night." An absolute monarch, the Wali of Swat is authorized to kill any or everybody in Swat, including tourists, but, I also learned, he's a very benevolent dictator who builds schools, highways, and hospitals for his people and only kills ten or a dozen of them a year, all of them criminals, and none of them tourists. "No, the day is not far," continues *Glimpses*, "when this land will flow with milk and honey"—and indeed, in 1957 Swat was flowing with honey, so much honey that several thousand jars of it were exported, each of them, according to its seal, APPROVED BY ALA-HAZRAT WALI SAHIB SWAT. The approbation of honey jars, I learned, is only part of the Wali's duties, for he also audits the treasury, sets the speed limits, reads the galley proofs of *Visit This Enchanting Mountain State*, tries murderers, plays tennis with the tourists, and, as the legislative, executive, and judicial branch of the Swati government, has two or three hundred appointments daily. He himself designed the Jahanzeb College there, a fanciful building with a spiral staircase, like a minaret, on every corner, as well as two wings on the Swat Hotel; it now holds thirty-three tourists at once. The Wali of Swat is deeply interested in tourism, and he's liable to swoop into the Swat Hotel morning, afternoon, or night to inspect it. On such occasions, he has criticized the toilet drains, the BX cable, the quarter rounds, the curtain rods, the electric plugs, the bathtub plugs, the bathtubs, the washtubs, the wash, the candlesticks, the flowers, the grass, the trees, the hinge on a closet door, and, almost always, the alignment of photo-

SWAT

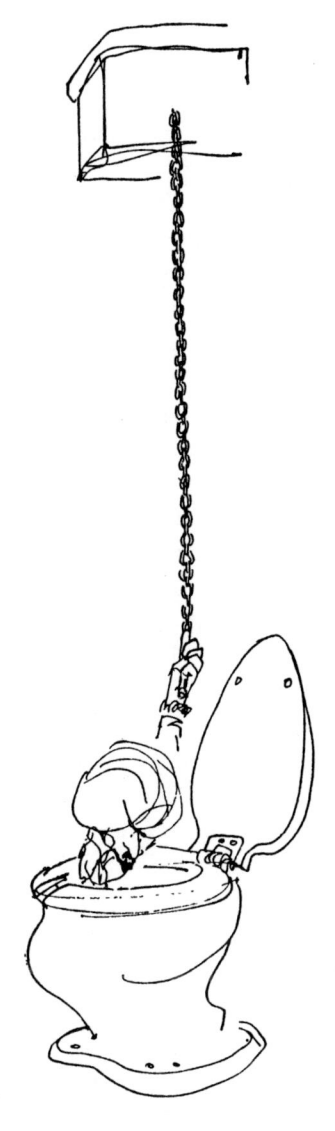

On such occasions, the Wali has inspected the toilet drains.

graphs in the lobby, depicting Rio de Janeiro, Monument Valley, and the Wali of Swat.

After I visited Sharja, I visited Swat, and I visited it at the solicitation of the United States Consulate General in Lahore, Pakistan. All week there, the temperature had been a hundred and eight, the cold water at my hotel had been scalding, and I had been sitting near, or in, the only place in Lahore for human life to exist—the swimming pool of our consulate general—when the wife of the consul, who, after all, owned the swimming pool and didn't care to have every overheated American in Pakistan in it, stopped by for a chat. "Listen," she said very politely, but very pointedly, "if it's too hot in Pakistan, why don't you go to Swat?"

I lowered my gin-and-tonic and answered, "Swat?"

"Swat," she continued, "is cooool"—a country, she said, a hundred miles long and fifty miles wide situated to the north of Pakistan, or *in* the north of Pakistan, depending on how you felt about it, like Lundy. Swat, she added, is east of Dir, another country of the same size and shape; south of Russia, a thin sliver of Afghanistan, and Chitral, still another country; and west of Amb, a country so small and so utterly insignificant that the next chapter is all about it. Swat's population is a half-million people, who cultivate corn, wheat, and rice, export a few thousand jars of honey, and manufacture serapes for the tourists. *Eve*rybody, said the consul general's wife, at the consulate general, the embassy in Karachi, and the embassy in Kabul, Afghanistan, had been to Swat, usually to cool off, and she concluded by saying "Go! It's the thing to do, you know."

Okay, I can take a hint, and I started for Swat the next day—luckily not in a bus, or what passes for a bus hereabouts, but in the spiffy green Chevrolet of the Wali himself. The Wali, a quiet, neighborly man with a strong, determined upper lip and a swarthy face, and wearing, on this occasion, a pin-stripe suit, a vest, and a cap of Persian lamb, was in Lahore on business, and I stumbled upon him at my hotel, in the lobby, where he was sit-

SWAT

ting contentedly on an overstuffed sofa and reading the Lahore *Civil and Military Gazette*. When I'd introduced myself and asked about a hitch, he said he'd be delighted, and we left at six o'clock in the morning. Our car was SWT1, and a gun-toting bodyguard drove it at seventy-five miles an hour: he dusted everyone in northern Pakistan and sped out of Malakand Pass, where Gunga Din had fought, to Swat's low, khaki border country and its international customs there. This—like its army, its taxes, and its flag, a white blockhouse on a field of green—suggests that Swat is independent of Pakistan, and the Wali himself told me, with a shy, embarrassed smile, "I'm the supreme authority. I can sentence anyone to death. And then I'm the supreme court of appeals, too." However, the Wali says he's a citizen of Pakistan. Proponents of the Swat-in-Pakistan theory say, too, that the international customs isn't *really* an international customs, and point, as proof, to page three of *Visit This Enchanting, etc.*, where it says, "If he should pause at the customs barrier at the State boundary, the traveler will find himself at a vantage point for surveying . . . the swiftly flowing water." In most countries, of course, the customs barrier isn't a matter of "if" or "should": the traveler jolly well pauses, swiftly flowing water or no. There's much to be said on both sides, I guess. I myself didn't pause there, or even slow down, but then I was traveling with a wali.

The road was dusty and hotter than I'd expected, but far off, at least, was a range of cool, snow-gabled mountains that I hadn't seen in Pakistan, and closer, in the valley, were some wet, seductive fields of green. A sign on the roadside carried the words, in English, IN SAIDU STAY AT THE SWAT HOTEL. Saidu, or Saidu Sharif, is the capital of Swat, and the Swat Hotel, where the Wali dropped me with a cheery good-by and without bothering to swoop inside, is one story high, white, and clean, like an unassuming American motel. A man in a turban took my suitcase, and I chatted awhile with the manager, Mr. Mohammed Sharif Butt, who, as he sleepily brushed a fly away, reminisced that he worked in the hotel business thirty years in Rawalpindi, Peshawar, Delhi, and Simla, and that he was in Simla when, in 1950, the Wali spotted him and whisked him away to Swat. It's an easy life here, Mr. Butt said, brushing another fly. The Swatis are Mohammedans, he said, and go to mosque on Friday; and Thursday is also a holiday, so that everybody will rest and go to mosque on Friday; and the Wali takes Sunday off, too.

Later in the afternoon, I took a stroll in Saidu Sharif, finding it rather a quiet town, quite drab, but without any signs of poverty. Some of the people had cars or motorcycles, but most of them walked, often with a terra-cotta jug sitting delicately on their turbans, or they poked along in *tongas*, a kind of one-horse shay, horizontal only when nobody was in it. Some plumes of red, yellow, and green on the tongas, and here and there on the horses, added a little color to Saidu Sharif, but really it was like the preponderancy of this earth of ours: narrow, rutted streets, houses of mud and twigs, and the lingering smell of sewage—to me, by now, a rather agreeable one. Almost everybody was wearing *pyjamas*, a billowy white kind of leggings from which our own pyjamas—the word, and the pyjamas themselves—are derived, and also a nightshirt, as we'd call it, reaching to below their knees; the children were wearing nightshirts and no pyjamas at all. Half of these children amused themselves by slinging stones at the birds, a peril to the other half of these children, who amused themselves by sitting in the trees; the two halves were thoroughly friendly, crying out "Welcome!" as I walked along. (Indeed, one of the children cried out, "Welcome, my darling!") The women, if they were up and about, were covered top-to-toe in a heavy white sheet, as if a tent had collapsed on them. It must be very uncomfortable in the summer, I decided, when the temperature goes above a hundred, but the women haven't made a complaint—anyhow, not an organized one—and the United Nations Commission on the Status of Women, in the area several years ago, reported to our consul general that it's much worse in Central Africa. Telling me this, our consul had added a word of warning: "Ignore the women. If ever you see a woman without a veil on, look away."

"Otherwise?" I had asked.

SWAT

"Otherwise"—and here our consul general had shaken his head, despondently and slowly—"otherwise, I'm afraid, you will see a very ugly woman." The consul general has been in the Middle East a long time, but not as long as the P.A.

The Swatis talk in Pushtu, a language of Afghanistan, but "Swat" itself is Arabic, meaning "black," the color of the clothes the Swatis once wore. "Wali" is Arabic too, meaning "ruler," and therein lies a tale, for the word is a chary compromise between the Swatis and the British, who recognized them in 1926. The Swatis liked a "Shah of Swat," but the British didn't: a shah, they said, is more important than a king; anyway it *sounded* so. The British held out for a "Nawab of Swat," but a nawab, the Swatis said, is less important than a shah. A "Khan of Swat" and a "Jam of Swat" sounded a little like those honey jars; a "Sultan of Swat" sounded like Babe Ruth; and then somebody thought up "Wali of Swat," and everybody was happy. In days gone by, there also were an Akhoond of Swat and a Badshah of Swat. The Akhoond was immortalized in the last century by Edward Lear, who wrote,

> *Who, or why, or which, or what*
> *Is the Akond of Swat?*
> *Is he tall or short, or dark or fair?*
> *Does he sit on a stool or a sofa or chair,*
>   *or* SQUAT?

The Akhoond of Swat, Mr. Lear, was tall and dark, and he led the Swatis against the British in 1863; the participants were mostly killed, and the British commander, Brigadier Neville Chamberlain, was hurt. Neville Chamberlain was the grandfather of *the* Neville Chamberlain, and the Akhoond of Swat was the grandfather of the Badshah of Swat. The Badshah built the Swat of today. A terrifying figure charging on a black horse and shaking a Martini-Henry rifle in the air, he led the Swatis to victory against—to quote from *Glimpses*—"the mountainous area . . . the riparian area . . . other areas . . . uncivilized residents . . .

mischief mongers . . . conspiring elements . . . a few tyrannical Khawanin . . . those Khawanin who refused to submit . . . danger from the Dir side . . . the North . . . the West . . . Khudu Khel, Savoy, and Gadun." The Badshah of Swat is still alive, a bald, toothless, spry old man with a frazzled beard, who likes to play checkers and crack his knuckles. He lives in a castle, reads the Koran day and night, and has given the government to his son, the Wali of Swat.

Of these three—the Akhoond, the Badshah, and the Wali— the Akhoond was the most religious; like San Marino, Euthymius of Salonika, and Peter the Athonite, he lived by himself a dozen years, meditating and eating nothing but herbs. The Badshah, too, is a devout man, fasting from dawn to sunset not only in Ramadan, like other Mohammedans, but every month of the year, and staying away from the movies as "graven images." The Wali pays lip service to Mohammedanism, as every wali must, but, it is felt, his heart isn't in it, and when he flew to Europe in 1954—his first trip abroad—it was whispered in the most daring quarters of Swat that he did so just to escape the Ramadan. Indeed, he left the day it began. (Incidentally, the Wali traveled on a Pakistani passport; the Sheik of Abu Dhabi had had no end of trouble on his Government of Abu Dhabi one.) The Wali has European, not Swati, ideas. Unlike the Sheik of Sharja, he hasn't put anyone's eyes out, or cut anyone's hands off, saying that the Sharia law "an eye for an eye and a tooth for a tooth" means for the punishment to fit the crime, not to re-enact it. Some time ago, for example, a Mr. Abdul Aziz killed a man horribly, and the bereaved family demanded an ear for an ear, a nose for a nose, a tooth for a tooth, and a leg for a leg; the Wali of Swat, though, decreed that this was cruel and unusual (Sherif Khan v. Abdul Aziz) and, handing Mr. Aziz over to the family, told them to shoot him, that's all. Sometimes murder, in the Wali's eyes, can be forgiven: when Mr. Shazad Gul saw his wife in a stranger's arms, he killed the two of them, but the Wali acquitted him (The People v. Shazad Gul) and, in his unanimous opinion, said Mr. Gul couldn't be blamed a bit.

The Wali believes in democracy, but the Swatis believe in

SWAT

walis, and, as a professor there told me, shrugging, "They've got to have a strong one, or they'll get another." The professor, too, believed in democracy, but he thought the Wali was doing okay —at least at present, when litigation is a question of who shot whom and who stole what, although the professor looked with alarm to the day Swat learns of interlocking corporations, fiduciaries, and double indemnity clauses. At present, a trial under the Wali is fair, free, and fast. One morning, I watched him get through seven in an hour, meanwhile answering a dozen phone calls, conferring with the chief secretary on matters of the budget, and appointing two teachers to a school in the hills. The courtroom was the Wali's office, a pleasant room whose décor included elk, deer, and antelope horns, a map of Swat, a bran-and-blue rug in shreds under the Wali's swivel chair, a fireplace, a silver spittoon, a Koran, a life of Mohammed, two copies of *Glimpses*, twenty of *Visit This Enchanting Mountain State*, a carbon of Mr. Weeks's poem, and a penholder inscribed A.C.C. —for Associated Cement Company, I was told. No lawyers were allowed there: only the accused, the accuser, and the Wali, and everybody looked too scared to lie, what with the Wali himself staring down his throat. "After all," he told me later, "I've been around for fifty years. I know who to believe, and who's for hire."

In Swat, everybody loves the Wali and told me so, yet he has a bodyguard of two thousand men, and night and day, from a hundred blockhouses like the ones of Revolutionary America, they are keeping watch. Wherever the Wali goes, they go too; and wherever he goes, he goes in secret. Eyes alert, hands on their Bren guns, the bodyguards prowl in and around his office, and as the Wali prays in his garden, they peer suspiciously over the hedges at the tongas going by. Why do they worry? What are they afraid of? They're afraid of the Nawab of Dir.

The Wali's eyes got cold, and his upper lip got tighter, as he told me of the Nawab. "He is cruel. He is uneducated. His ideas," said the Wali, "are primitive ideas. *I* am prepared to be friendly, but *he* is not prepared." The Nawab, uneducated, unprepared, rules the country of Dir, and what a difference! for, although there are fifty-six schools, a college, and seven hospitals in Swat, Dir, on its very border, hasn't even a kindergarten, and its only hospital is for dogs—the Nawab's forty dogs, which, next to his forty wives, are his favorite amusement. A satyr and a dissipater, the Nawab has taken drugs the greater part of his life, until his face, I'm told, is running to "rather a bluish green." To argue with the Nawab, to ask him why he doesn't build a school, or, indeed, to look without permission at his blue-green face, is death, and whenever the Diris go walking by his castle in Dir, Dir, they go quickly, all hunched over, eyes upon the ground. While the rest of us were fighting World War I, Dir and Swat, too, were at each other's throats, and now, forty years later, neither has forgotten it. Even today, a Diri's cow will chomp on a Swati's grass; "Son of a devil!" cries the Swati; "Weaver!" cries the Diri; and the fight is on. Maliciously, too, the Diris will sneak across the border to carry off a Swati cow, even a Swati wife, and, when the Wali of Swat protests, the Nawab of Dir will investigate and reply, like so many people these days, "The aggression was from *your* side." The Nawab of Dir and the Wali of Swat, themselves, have never met.

In happy Swat, everyone is sorry for the Diris—"Swat," I was told there, "is coming up, and famous far and wide, while they, the Diris, are still uncivilized." For the Diris, the only hope is when the Nawab is gone, and he is going fast. His eldest son and heir apparent is a quiet, benevolent fellow, who, it is thought, will usher an era of peace into Dir, Swat, and the Afghan border if he survives. (The Nawab has been trying to murder him a dozen years now—so far, however, with little success.) The Wali's son, too, is young, handsome, and devoted to Swati affairs, but alas! the heyday of waliism is almost over, and now the Wali has fifteen elected assemblymen to "advise" him. "And when I'm the wali," says the Wali of Swat's son, a little sadly, in words recalling the Prince of Liechtenstein, "I'll have nothing to do but sign, sign, sign."

*"Tell me where you are—
Pakistan or Amb?"*

—THE NAWAB OF AMB.

AMB

The trouble with Amb is that it's very, very small, and people who run across it on maps are apt to think it's a cartographers' abbreviation for "ambush," "ambiguous," or even "ambary," a plant that grows in patches thereabouts, instead of what it really is—Amb, an independent but utterly insignificant country on the Indus River, and smack in the middle of Western Pakistan.

Not only is Amb so small it's hardly worth mentioning but, to make matters worse, it's getting smaller at an average rate of two-and-a-quarter acres an hour, and if it keeps losing ground like this, it will be all gone by September. It started diminishing a dozen years ago, when Pakistan passed a law against the *jagirs*, or fiefs, in Pakistani territory; thirty square miles of Amb were *jagirs*, and Pakistan took it back. A second, even more stunning blow was in 1950, when, after coming across some eighty-year-old papers, Pakistan laid claim to the whole left bank of the Indus, two hundred and ninety square miles of Amb, and away it went. At the same time, Pakistan took away a vassalage of Amb's, the Khanate of Phulra, pronounced like "pool room" without the "m"—twenty square miles. The upshot of all this aggrandizement is that Amb, as of today, consists of only fourteen square miles and four thousand people, all four thousand and fourteen of them on the good-for-nothing right bank of the Indus, and even there the rule of Mohammed Farid Khan, the Nawab of Amb, is shaky indeed. The people are restive; some of them want to go Pakistan; and the Nawab, I understand, is so unsure of their loyalties that he hasn't been to Amb for several years, staying instead in a palace in Pakistan and, with a pair of high-powered field glasses, looking at Amb warily.

In the light of all this, I decided, after I'd visited Swat, it was now or never to visit Amb, and I hurried east on a couple of "buses" and was delighted to find it still there. The country itself was no delight, though: it was a hundred and twenty in the shade, as hot as a salami-skin factory in Liechtenstein, so outrageously hot, indeed, that most of the Ambis were sitting up to their necks in the Indus River. The Ambis are Mohammedans, I learned, who lived in Afghanistan six hundred years ago; they talk in Tanawali, dye their beards red, and, whenever they aren't sitting in the Indus or swimming to Pakistan—aided, incidentally, by water wings of buffalo skin—they dress in turbans, nightshirts, and pyjamas if they are men, nightshirts if they are children, and heavy, lubberly white sheets if they are women. On this

AMB

outrageous morning, the Ambis greeted me by laughing hysterically. It's a rather odd custom, I thought, apt, after a while, to get on a person's nerves, and I never was given a satisfactory explanation of it. According to someone, the Ambis are awfully shy and were giggling hard, but according to someone else the Ambis are awfully friendly and were smiling hard. Whichever it was, I confess to being rather annoyed with the Ambis, and Amb itself, by the time I got to the Nawab's guest house. There, I was shown to my room, a rather fashionable one with a stained-glass window, a Persian rug, a canopied bed, and a fireplace, of all things; it was just as hot as anywhere else. A servant gave me the most appalling glass of water I've ever seen —it came from the Indus River, and it was opaque—and, after dropping a Halazone pill into this, waiting a half hour, and throwing it away, I fell into the canopied bed and fell asleep.

By four o'clock, it was somewhat cooler, and I paid a call on the Nawab himself, at his palace in what is yesterday's Amb, is today's Pakistan. The Nawab of Amb reminded me of Ed Wynn: a rather silly face, a sillier grin, and a chin indistinguishable from a neck; a gray bell-bottomed jacket over a potbelly; a turban of powder blue; and a loose end of it up like an aerial— the vogue in this part of the world, but quite silly to look at. The Nawab was pleasant enough, but, I was told, he's liable to temper tantrums, and then he'll jump on his subjects (literally), rape them, or push them a foot further into the Indus River. His first words, after the usual pleasantries and *salaam aleikums*, were, "Tell me where you are—Pakistan or Amb?"

"I'm in Amb," I said amiably.

"Right!" said the Nawab, grinning. "And why the Pakistanis have taken it away, I'll never know. It's worse than the Russians." Wistfully, he looked across the river at what's left of Amb, idly fingering his field glasses, and said, "The people there, they *love* me. Day in, day out, do you know what I do? Philanthropy. Philanthropy. I give away money." So saying, he shot a glance at his secretary, a thin, red-bearded man—a khan sahib, incidentally, who was doing the translating—who picked up a little brown bag and let me squeeze it; I gathered it was full of rupees. "This afternoon," the Nawab said, "I gave away money to twenty people," his largess, he continued, amounting to 90¢ to a beggar; 90¢ to another beggar; $3.60 to an orphange; $17.20 to Mr. Haji Baz Gul, who was starving; $3.60 to Mr. Omar Khan, whose daughter had drowned as she sat in the Indus River; and comparable sums to other needy cases. "Also," said the Nawab, "I have granaries, and if ever the people are hungry, I give them grain."

"Where do you get it all?" I asked.

"For the most part, taxes. The agricultural tax is a bushel out of every two."

"One out of *two*?"

"Well, in certain cases, one out of three." The Nawab of Amb returned to the matter of philanthropy. "A few years ago, for example, I threw open a granary, and I gave away the best part of a ton. The people were starving."

"I wouldn't doubt it," I said.

*"Day in, day out,
do you know what I do?
Philanthropy.
Philanthropy,"
said the Nawab of Amb.*

Now it was evening, a Moslem time for prayer, and, after somebody sprayed the floor with DDT and somebody else unrolled a Persian rug, the Nawab kneeled, and started to salaam to Mecca, and as he did, another man pulled up and down on a rope attached to a huge, burlap fan on the ceiling above, and other men swatted flies. After five minutes of this, the Nawab of Amb stood up, huffing and puffing. He put a cigarette in his mouth, but he never got around to lighting it.

"The palace," I remarked, "is terribly hot."

"Here and there, I have a half-dozen others," said the Nawab of Amb, "—and much, much cooler."

After talking to the Nawab, I felt the Pakistanis were only right in dispossessing him, and too bad it wasn't sooner, but after talking to the Pakistanis, I felt like calling a plague on both their houses. The Pakistani side of the story was given me several days later by Mr. Abdul Qayum Khan, a politician, at his hot, musty office in the *Civil and Military Gazette* building, back in Lahore. For years, Mr. Khan had been a sort of Pakistani Cato, shouting, "Amb must be destroyed!" until, in 1950, he had his way, and those two hundred and ninety square miles were invaded by the Pakistani police. ("AMB IS LIBERATED," said the *Civil and Military Gazette*.) At the time, Mr. Khan said he was acting out of pity for the Ambis, promising them a lower tax, suffrage, and everything nice. Anyhow, the Ambis held an election soon after their deliverance, and a single solitary name was on the ballot —Abdul Qayum Khan.

"What I did," Mr. Khan was telling me, in Lahore, "was to liberate sixty thousand people. Under the Nawab, they were subjected to all sorts of tortures, to feudal excesses, and other unspeakable excesses which I couldn't even mention." Mr. Khan's face was fat, heavily jowled, and his eyes were pig eyes, lost under a beetling brow.

"Tortures?" I said.

"Unspeakable tortures."

"Which?"

"They're unspeakable."

"Oh."

"After I had apprised Pakistan of these unspeakable tortures, and of other feudal excesses, we were duty bound, of course, to liberate Amb."

"Please, would you tell me *one* torture?" I said.

"Well . . ." Mr. Khan leaned over conspiratorially, and whispered.

"Not really!" I said.

"Don't quote me," said Mr. Abdul Qayum Khan.

After he'd won the election, Mr. Khan had risen quickly. In three years, I learned, he was Pakistan's minister of industries and bucking for prime minister; then there was a cabinet crisis, he was kicked upstairs, the party wouldn't support him, and he's back where he started. So, in fact, are the sixty thousand people he liberated, who—seeing how the Nawab is still the owner, if not the ruler, of their land—are paying taxes to Pakistan *and* rent to the Nawab, and, apparently, are worse off than ever, except they can vote for Abdul Qayum Khan. Meanwhile, the Nawab has gone to court to get his country back, but even as he's filing suit for some of it, Pakistan is taking more of it away. The result of all this litigation is that the Nawab's lawyer, Mr. Sajjad Ahmad Jan, is twenty-one thousand dollars richer and is living in Abbottabad, the Pakistani equivalent of Beverly Hills. According to Mr. Jan, the Nawab hasn't a chance; according to the Nawab, Mr. Jan has a father-in-law who's a federal judge, *and*. . . ; and according to Pakistan, it's a quibble over words. "My goodness," a Pakistani official told me once, "the Nawab says it's his state, we say it's his *estate*. So what's all the fuss about?"

The withering-away of Amb has been paralleled by a withering-away of its ruling family. The last nawab was a warrior known all over as Zaman the Lion Hearted, with, in a photograph I saw, a terrifying mustache and a *sumo* wrestler's face—a fine illustration, I'd thought, for Abdul the Bulbul Amir. His son, the present nawab, reminded me of Ed Wynn, and *his* son, the heir apparent to what he persists in calling "the throne of Amb," reminded me of the people in upstairs bowling alleys: thin, oily, eczematous, and possessed of a frail, gigolo mustache. The Nawab Zada is a college freshman; he's been one, in fact, several years, having been kicked out of Burnhall Missionary College, in Abbottabad, where he spent his time drinking, gambling, and wenching—particularly wenching—and out of Gordon Missionary College, in Rawalpindi, where, although he lived the same way, he took the precaution of giving thirty-six dollars to the mimeograph man for a peek at the final exams. Gordon Missionary College found out, and now the Nawab Zada is applying to Harvard—and this, if it comes as a shock to Mr. Wilbur J. Bender, the Dean of Admissions there, I'll take the blame for. Having put the notion of Harvard into the Nawab Zada's head, I couldn't get it out.

Rawalpindi, Pakistan, is where I met the Nawab Zada, still a student at Gordon Missionary College. I had the devil's own time doing so, because the Nawab Zada wasn't in his dormitory, he wasn't in the dining hall, he wasn't in class, and his classmates seemed rather amused that I should seek him there, volunteering, instead, a list of Rawalpindi's fancier bawdy houses, at which, they advised me, the Nawab Zada might reasonably be sought. By leaving calling cards at such places, I arranged, at last, to see him at my hotel at teatime, and, when he got there, I shook his hand and asked if he cared for a beer—it's against the law for Mohammedans, but foreigners can get it—and the Nawab Zada said, "Of course."

His hair was slick, and yet he hadn't shaved in several days. He began by saying he wasn't helping to govern Amb, as yet, but that, as soon as he finished college, his father would teach him how. Gordon College wasn't for *him*, the Nawab Zada said; it was run by missionaries who were awfully touchy about some things; he wanted to go to school in America; did I have any suggestions?

"Well . . . Harvard or Columbia for foreigners," I said.

"That way, you can see the girls," said the Nawab Zada.

"Which is the best? As the son of a nawab, I want the best."

"It depends on what you're interested in."

"Well, besides to study," said the Nawab Zada, "a thing I'm interested in are girls."

"There're a lot of interesting girls at Harvard."

"Good." The Nawab Zada sighed, and he gazed out the window at the hot, dusty streets of Rawalpindi. "In Pakistan," he resumed, "there are two kinds of girls. There are the kind, if they see you coming they pull that black thing over their face. Also there are the kind, if you pay them you can enjoy them, if you know what I mean."

"I know what you mean," I said, a bit uneasily.

"But if you enjoy *them*, they don't enjoy *it*, so you really don't enjoy it, do you?"

"Of course not," I said.

"Of course." The Nawab Zada gazed out the window once again, and I hurriedly drank my beer; then, turning to me with an obscene smile, he said, "Is it easy to have a girl in the United States?"

"Of course it is. Everyone does."

"I mean," said the Nawab Zada, "is it easy to *have* a girl in the United States?"

"Oh! Well, it isn't against the law, but—"
"But?"
"But the girls—"
"I was only worried about the law," said the Nawab Zada. He had a look of unruffled confidence. I thought it was high time to change the subject.

"Do you think there'll be anything left of Amb by the time you're the nawab of it?" I asked.

"Pakistan will give it back," he said emphatically. "It must!"

"It won't. But even if you can't be a great nawab, you can be a good one, and that's more important."

The Nawab Zada reflected on this a while. "When I'm the nawab," he said presently, "what I want to do is abolish the veils. That way, you can see the girls." He grinned lasciviously, winked, and took another slug of beer.

"Apricots, of course."
—THE RAH OF PUNIAL.

PUNIAL

I'm the only tourist in history who's gone to Punial, one of three independent countries appearing on maps as a kind of listless blur in Kashmir, and the reason for the others staying away with such unanimity is, I think, the bridge at Punial's capital and only worthwhile place to go, Sher Qila. The bridge is made of vines; it hangs like a jump rope over a pretty terrifying river,

PUNIAL

and you've got to inch across it with an almost prehensile gait to get to Sher Qila from, say, the United States. Although the tourist trade is staying away from Punial accordingly, it is visiting the other two countries—Hunza and Nagar—in droves, and is giving them so much publicity that the Punialis are apt to feel rather slighted. Some people from *Life* were in Hunza to write it up; some people from the *National Geographic* were there; the Cinerama people were there to do *Search for Paradise;* Mrs. Roosevelt wasn't far away; and Justice Douglas, after being a few hours in Swat and writing a chapter in *Beyond the High Himalayas* about it, was a few minutes in Hunza, writing *two* chapters about it. Generally, the reason for all these people being in Hunza is that they'd seen its genial, peripatetic ruler, the Mir, at a bar somewhere, and he had asked them up. The Mir is an Ismaili Mohammedan, is allowed to drink, and does, and the Hunzakuts are, are allowed, and do the same, but the Nagarkuts are Sunni Mohammedans and never touch the stuff, and the Punialis are half-and-half. The three peoples are most unalike, although the three countries are close together. The Hunzakuts are happy, hardy, and hard-working, the Nagarkuts are lazy galoots, and the Punialis are lazy too, but happy too. The Mir of Hunza is able to make it rain, and the Hunzakuts are rather teed off whenever he does; the Mir of Nagar, too, has a few tricks up his sleeve; but the Rah of Punial, Khan Bahadur Rah Muhammad Anwar Khan, O.B.E., can't do anything out of the ordinary. He reigns but does not rain, it might be said, but he is nevertheless well-liked, the Punialis calling him "Chhalo"—"well-liked." The Punialis talk in Shina, a language of the Pisaca group, Indic branch, Aryan subfamily, Satem division of the Indo-European languages—some languages like it are Chitrali (see page 186) and Kafiri—and the Hunzakuts and the Nagarkuts talk in Burushaski, a language like nothing else on earth, and so difficult to learn it's almost a scandal. Burushaski has four genders, and forms its plurals by adding such various things as *ho, daro, tsero, i, hingas,* and *ougushans*, or by changing *hin* to *iwanchz*. Shina, which forms its plurals by adding *e* or *ei*, is easy as pie.

Historically, Shina is the language of the Shins, a people living on the near side of the bridge, but it's also spoken by the Yashkuns, on the other side. The Shins and the Yashkuns are the two kinds of Punialis, the Yashkuns being in the majority. The Yashkuns are the drinking ones—a gay, frolicsome people who like to wear daisies in their caps—while the Shins, on the wagon, apparently are the meanest people in the world. The Shins are out for the long green, I was told, and after getting it they bury it on the mountainside and never say where, even to their families, and it's still on the mountainside when they die. In the past, the Shins had a singular, to say the least, old-age program that ran quite against the Asian ideas of filial piety: whenever a Shin grew old, he was put into a basket by his eldest son and thrown over a cliff. Then *"Male kare puchete,"* as the Shins say—"The father's basket is also the son's"—and a generation later *he* was thrown over the cliff, until, as more and more sons realized this, the practice died out. Myself, if I were a Shin I'd try to keep it quiet, but no: they are given to beating their chests and ranting, "I am a Shin!," making everyone hate them all the more. The Yashkuns call them *bewaquf*—fools.

Pakistan, which runs the foreign affairs, such as they are, of Hunza, Nagar, and Punial, readily admits that Hunza and Nagar are independent countries, but it won't come clean about Punial. It calls Punial a "political district," not a country, although, to my mind, it's just as independent as the others: it's ruled by a hereditary rah, who is absolute, and it doesn't pay any taxes to Pakistan. There are other "political districts" in this neck of the woods—Yasin, Gupis, and Ishkuman, and each of them has a rah; these rahs, however, are appointed by Pakistan, can be recalled at will, and they do pay taxes. (Also in the neighborhood are the "sub agencies" of Astor, Chilas, and Gilgit, the "tribal areas" of Darel and Tangir, and the "attached agency" of Skardu, but you'll have to ask about these sometime else.) Ishkuman, as you might expect, is ruled by a rah who looks like Salvador Dali, and

PUNIAL

Gupis is known for its dragons, which used to eat women and children but which, like the S.M.O.M.'s one, were exterminated by a *buzurg*, a dragon-exterminator, and Yasin is where Mr. George Hayward, the British explorer, was bumped off in 1879—the whole bloody affair being memorialized by Sir Henry Newbolt in the poem "He Fell Among Thieves." Sir Henry would have us think that Mr. Hayward killed five of these thieves, whereupon:

> *He laugh'd*: "*If one may settle the score for five,*
> *I am ready; but let the reckoning stand till day:*
> *I have loved the sunlight as dearly as any alive.*"
> "*You shall die at dawn,*" *said they.*

Really, Sir Henry! Mr. Hayward didn't raise a finger, and he certainly didn't laugh; he said "Spare me, and I'll give you everything," and the thieves replied "We already have it," and off went Mr. Hayward's head. The language in these "political districts" is Shina, but Burushaski is spoken in parts of Yasin, and Chitrali (see page 203) is spoken in parts of Yasin, Ishkuman, and Gupis. In Gupis and Punial they put cream in their tea, but in Yasin and Ishkuman they don't. In Yasin and Gupis they aren't practical jokers, but in Ishkuman and Punial they are. In Hunza, if you're following me, they are also practical jokers; and the Mir of Hunza is such an inveterate wag, that, even if he's talking about Hunza, you couldn't tell truth from fiction, which is why I went to Punial instead. Once, talking about Hunza to the *Life* people, the Mir observed that a honeymoon couple there is always a man, a bride, and a third party, his mother-in-law, who teaches them the art of making love. This preposterous story was printed by *Life* with a straight face, and the Mir hasn't stopped laughing since. The Mir also told *Life* that in 1947, when the British got out of Pakistan, he hurried to the American Embassy in Karachi and asked to become the forty-ninth state, or at least a territory; the embassy said no, the Mir told *Life*. Whether this is true or not, I couldn't say, but according to the Mir it was just another gag.

There is a practical joker in Punial as well-known, in Punial, as Mr. Hugh Troy in our own country. His name is Mr. Qabul Khan, he is a farmer, and, though I never had a chance to meet him, I learned a few of his escapades, which made me feel that Yashkuns and Yankees aren't very different, after all. Mr. Qabul Khan is a Yashkun, and the people he picks on are Shins, especially the few who drink. One of these is Mr. Dar Besh, a rather stingy fellow who, in 1954, received a visit from Mr. Qabul Khan in the dead of winter. "I come from the Rah," said Mr. Qabul Khan imperiously. "He requires three bottles of your finest wine, and that at once!" Mr. Besh handed them over meekly, whereupon Mr. Qabul Khan left, bolted the door from outside, and, while sitting on the stoop and laughing, drank the bottles dry.

In Punial, a miser even worse than Mr. Besh is Mr. Khojai Khan, who would always serve wine to himself and water to his guests, and how Mr. Qabul Khan got even with *him* is almost a classic of practical jokery. At a bazaar, Mr. Qabul Khan bought himself a sheet, a turban, a pair of sunglasses, and a false beard, and, dressing himself in these and tucking some Korans under his arm, he hurried to the miser's home and announced himself as an Arabian seer. "Can you tell my fortune?" said the old curmudgeon.

"Of course—your palm, please." Then, peering at the life lines and love lines as best he could through the sunglasses, and speaking in Shina with an Arabic accent, Mr. Qabul Khan perceived, "You have six sons, two daughters, and seven cows."

"Correct!" said the miser.

"Your father's name was Sharif Khan, and he came from Gulapur, the village."

"Incredible!"

"In two years' time, I discern, you will be named a grand vizier, and you will be given many costly gifts."

"Not really!" The miser's eyes were like golf balls.

PUNIAL

"But only," added Mr. Qabul Khan, as he explored the tiniest crannies of thumb and forefinger, "—but only if you give, to the first man who visits you tomorrow, a pure black goat, ten pounds of ghee, and eighty pounds of wine."

"I will, I will!" shouted the miser, and he did, too, and—need I say?—the man who got it all, at the next day's crack of dawn, was Mr. Qabul Khan.

With fellows like Mr. Khan and the Mir around, it isn't easy to learn the customs—the real ones—of Hunza, Nagar, and Punial, but there are a few things I could document. In these places, I learned, they never eat butter fresh, but bury it under an irrigation ditch for ten or even twenty years; although it turns red and burns the throat going down, it's held in esteem. Usually it's dug up for weddings and funerals, or for sick people. A dead man, hereabouts, is commemorated by a roadside lean-to, called a *baldi*, or by a water hole, a *ghurk*. At weddings there is a dowry, but it's given by the groom to the bride—sometimes a gun, one-and-a-half ounces of gold, and twenty yards of calico, as well as some gewgaws to her relatives, such as six yards of cloth to her mother's brothers to make a turban with. After the wedding, the happy couple is pelted with rice and also with stones, rubbish, and dirt; there isn't any honeymoon, notwithstanding *Life*, for where would they go? A man who discovers his wife in another's arms, and shoots him, is guilty of murder, but if he shoots *her* nobody will say a thing. A dead woman is commemorated by a rockpile, called a *man*. Whenever a woman has a baby, an ibex horn is roasted in the fire, pulverized, and smeared on her face, thereby lessening the chance of her catching cold, it is said, and telling the world of a blessed event. A baby who cries is told the blue fairy will cut his ears off, and then he cries even harder. A baby of the Mir of Hunza, the Mir of Nagar, or the Rah of Punial is farmed out to another family for fear that he'd kill his father, or be himself killed. (Until a few years ago, this used to happen regularly, and in 1886 the Prince of Hunza murdered his father, poisoned his mother, threw two brothers off a cliff, and sent a note to the Maharajah of Kashmir saying, "By the will of Allah and the decree of fate, my late father and I recently fell out.") To the fun-loving Punialis, there are only two constellations in the summer sky, the Bed and the Pillow. The Bed, which was pointed out to me by the Rah on a balmy spring evening, is the Big Dipper to us; the Pillow hadn't risen, but I think it's the Great Square of Pegasus. In winter there are the Seven Brothers—to us, the Seven Sisters. Three, eight, thirteen, eighteen, twenty-three, and twenty-eight are unlucky numbers; so are owls; it's bad luck to break a mirror; and when someone sneezes, the others say "Allah bless you."

Polo is the national game of these countries, and the national food is the apricot. Hunza, Nagar, and Punial are simply teeming with apricots; Nagar says it's "the land of gold and apricots," and Hunza, said to have the healthiest people in the world, says it's because of apricots. For breakfast, the people have a bowl of stewed apricots, cooked over apricot wood, and a glass of milk coming, no doubt, from a cow born and raised on apricot leaves. The rest of the day, the people chew apricots by the fistful: they say they can eat three thousand and never get sick, although, truth to tell, a hundred of these apricots will give them the runs, locally known as Gilgit tummy. The cure for Gilgit tummy is more apricots—the kernels. Also, apricot kernels are squeezed for salad oil and hair tonic, or they're strung into necklaces for the kids, along with dried apricots. A hundred varieties of apricots are grown here, including the duck apricot, the first of which was found twenty years ago in the stomach of a duck, but most of them are round, firm, and fully packed, and in the Burushaski language, I was told, a pretty girl is called "a real apricot."

The day before I went to Punial, I was eating some of these apricots, catching up on the news from Monaco, and talking to some friends in Gilgit, the biggest town in these parts and the only one with an airport. With me were the Rah of Punial and the Dali-mustached Rah of Ishkuman, and they watched with amusement as I began nibbling on my fourth or fifth dozen. "If he doesn't get Gilgit tummy," the Rah of Punial said, strok-

PUNIAL

ing his red-dyed beard, "he's sure to dream of apricots tonight. Maybe he'll dream of them eating *him*."

I swallowed, smiled, and said, "I think I'll dream of that bridge I have to cross."

The Rah laughed. "Now, don't you worry," he said reassuringly. "We'll tell the fishermen downstream to keep an eye out, in case you fall in."

"What'll they use as bait?" asked the Rah of Ishkuman.

"Apricots, of course. He'll be sure to bite," the Rah of Punial said.

I went to Punial on a horse. (I might have gone in a jeep, but, as gasoline is carried in over the high passes in summer, it's selling at two dollars a gallon in spring, if it's selling at all.) Frankly, I'm no great shakes as a horseman—I have the fault, for one thing, of whipping my own behind and not the horse's—and, except for these stabs of pain and some rapids to be forded, I felt the journey was rather dull: the sun was hot, the mountains were dirty brown, the river alongside me was turbulent but turbid. The other travelers were few and far between; they said *"Salaam aleikum,"* a phrase apparently the same in Arabic, Pushtu, Tanawali, and Shina, and stared in wonder at the gringo. By late afternoon, as the sun was setting in the mountains dead ahead, I beheld the bridge at Sher Qila, and it was everything as dire as I'd been told—a hundred yards long, I estimated, and sagging a hundred feet in the middle, and made a hundred percent of vines. These, I saw as I drew closer, were woven into nine strands, of which three were tied together as a tightrope for the feet, and three were a railing for the right hand, and three for the left. At each end of the bridge, on a clifftop, the nine strands were wrapped around a log, and the log was buried in a rock pile, without cement. On the bridge itself, there were struts of wood to keep the handrails apart, and these, I gathered, had to be climbed over or crawled under by the would-be visitor, me.

The Rah of Punial's eldest son was waiting on the near side. His name is Jan Alam, he is properly called the Kaka, and he is

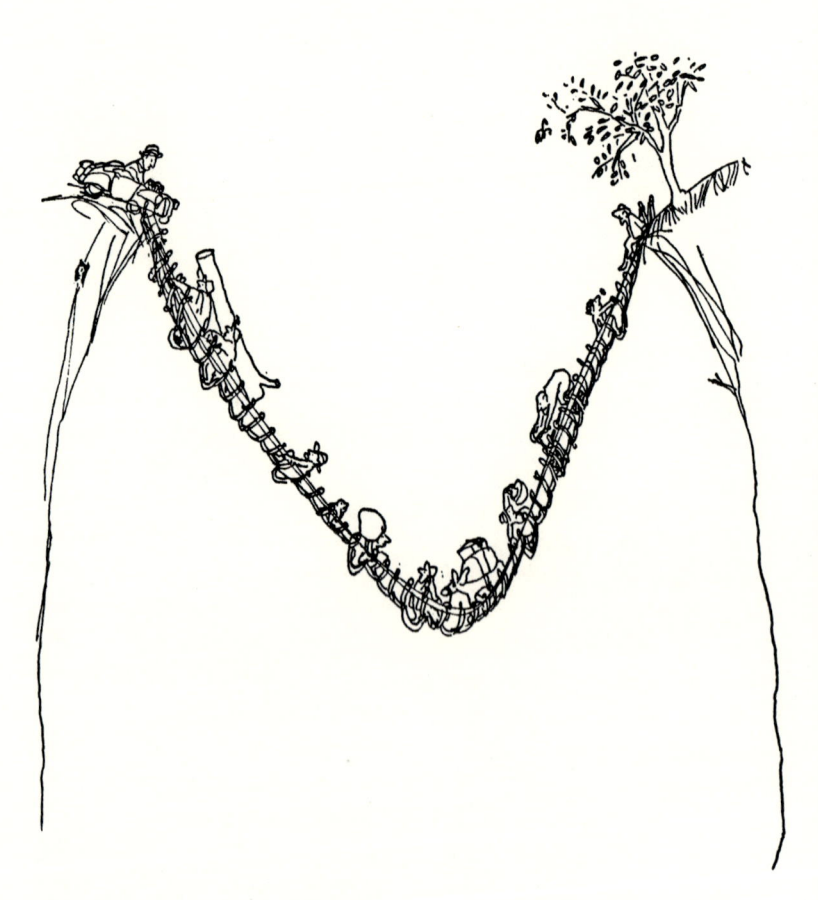

The Punialis think nothing of crossing the bridge.

a dark, mustachioed, healthy, good-humored man of thirty-five, who, in practice, is the real ruler of Punial, the Rah having high blood pressure and being more or less retired. With the Kaka behind me, shouting words of good cheer, and another man in front, I took my shoes off and started across the bridge. "My goodness, don't look down, sir," the Kaka said, but I couldn't

PUNIAL

help it, really, and I saw the river standing still and the bridge going upstream like a magic carpet; I lost the sensation of where I was; I simply put one foot ahead of the other, first downhill, then on the horizontal above the water, and then on the long, uphill climb. On the far side, a dozen or so Punialis were sitting and watching all this, and when I finally got there I shouted "Hooray!" and rather expected them to break into cheers. They didn't; they said "*Salaam aleikum*"; they were wondering, I suspect, why I didn't get the lead out of my pants. The Punialis think nothing of the bridge, crossing it in three or four minutes—three if sober, and four if drunk—with several sacks of wheat or even a live goat on their shoulders. (My own time was eleven minutes, twenty seconds, and when I was through, my legs were trembling and my hands were bloody from holding the rails too hard.) Indeed, there is a young boy in Sher Qila who gives his mother the willies by walking across on the handrails, all the while shouting, "*Aji chaki hati noosh*" —a bit of Shina that translates almost exactly as "Look, Mom, no hands!"

Later that evening, the Kaka and I sat on the porch of his guest house, and he told me something of how the bridge was built. The Kaka was wearing the native dress—white pyjamas, a plaid nightshirt, a floppy cap rather like Henry VIII's in Holbein's portrait, and a daisy tucked in the cap—and he was smoking Player's cigarettes, a habit he picked up in Srinagar, India, when he went to school there; and I was eating apricots, of course. The Kaka wasn't too adept at smoking; he made a deep, sucking sound like a boy on his first try or a Turk on a hubble-bubble. Between drafts, he said the bridge is in tiptop shape in spring, usually, but that it's breaking here and there in summer, and that in autumn it's pretty urgent to build a new one. This is done when the crops are in, and everybody lends a hand, the Yashkuns on their side of the river, the Shins on theirs, each of them bringing thirty vines or being fined the equivalent of twenty-one cents. In a single day, the vines are woven into strands, sailed across the river—it's slow enough at this season—

and carried to the clifftop, and a day or two later they're a bridge. Meanwhile, a good time is had by all. What with the harvest in, the Yashkuns are entering the wine-drinking season, which lasts all winter, and there is wine aplenty on the Yashkuns' side of the river; also there is singing and dancing well into the night, for the Yashkuns don't believe, as we do, that building bridges is necessarily a job for sober people. Mercifully, some sense of responsibility is inculcated in them by the village elders, who scurry from man to man explaining that if anything breaks, thereby plunging me or some other innocent pedestrian into the river, the whole community will be fined a cow. "Oh, you're going to lose that cow, I'll wager," the teetotaling Shins cry, from the other bank. Also they cry the Yashkuns aren't Mohammedans, to which the Yashkuns, waving their bottles angrily and staggering a bit, reply, "Allah has given us wine, so let's enjoy it!" For all their inebriety, or perhaps because of it, the Yashkuns usually turn out five strands, and the Shins only four, the Kaka told me. When the bridge is done, everybody rushes across to try it out. There haven't been any tragedies on these occasions or, for that matter, any other occasions in living memory; two people fell off in 1930, but both of them were fished from the river, safe and sound.

The Yashkuns' imbibing time, as I mentioned, starts at harvest time and stops at plowing time the following year. (There is nothing else to do.) Then the Yashkuns make merry, perpetrate their little practical jokes, and get pretty much of a bun on, until by February or March, in fact, they are so thoroughly blotto that they begin suffering from what, apparently, is a case of community DT's. They see *dains*. A dain, the Kaka explained to me with animation, is a vampire, and it's quite a danger thereabouts; it has a set of long, sharp teeth, it also takes the form of men, women, dogs, and horses, and every winter it's seen by a great many Yashkuns, though never by the abstemious Shins, a fact that struck the Kaka as being not without significance. It's death to be bitten by a dain, and the fact it doesn't exist isn't mitigating at all. Only a few years back, a Mr. Jafarro thought

PUNIAL

he saw a dain in Sher Qila; "It's got me!" he cried, and over he went, and a post-mortem didn't explain a thing. Also, the Kaka told me about a dain appearing as a woman, or so the Punialis think; a Mr. Nabillah saw it in 1954; he said it looked like a Mrs. Zabida; he struck it on the shoulder with an ax and went running to the Kaka. "And why," the Kaka asked him, "do you think it's a dain, and not Mrs. Zabida herself?," and Mr. Nabillah couldn't say. And indeed, an investigating party found a nasty wound on Mrs. Zabida's shoulder: she, however, said she had fallen on a rock, and she was still sticking to this a week later, when she died. To the Punialis, this was dramatic proof that the ways of dains are mysterious indeed, but I thought I saw a simpler explanation—a midnight tryst, a lovers' quarrel, a secret kept. I told my suspicions to the Kaka, and he nodded.

"I think so too," he said, "but who'd believe it?" The Kaka is a Sunni Mohammedan, doesn't drink, and thinks that dains are for the birds.

I want to explain right now that the Kaka may be a Sunni, but he certainly isn't a Shin, heaven forbid. He isn't a Yashkun, either; he's a Gushpur. This is the ruling family in the "political districts," and Gushpurs who aren't actively engaged in ruling feel—or used to feel, anyhow—that they shouldn't do anything at all. In the past, they loafed about the palace at Sher Qila, talking, falconing, scheming, demanding such rights as befitted royalty, like several men to wait on them, and acting, in general, like some of the royalty at the cocktail party in the Liechtenstein chapter, except there were more of them. In 1913, when the present rah took over, he learned he was saddled with four hundred of them, about five percent of the population, and all making a nuisance of themselves: so he told them to hit the road. Some of the Gushpurs went to India in a huff, joining the army, and some of them scandalized the family by becoming farmers. Some of them are still a nuisance, of course.

Historically, the present rah is the third, the first having been his grandfather, Isa Bagdur. Earlier, Punial, Yasin, Gupis, and

Ishkuman had been ruled by Gauhar Aman, a benevolent dictator who, though, died in the 1860's of an intestinal disorder—the symptoms are rather suspiciously like Gilgit tummy's—and was succeeded by Milk Aman, one of the worst dictators the area has known. (Not *the* worst; in ancient times it was run by a Hindu cannibal, Sri Badat, who frequently ate his subjects up.) Milk Aman's tragic flaw was women, and, walking in Sher Qila, he used to violate on the spot whichever of them particularly took his fancy, and frequently marry them, and when he insisted on taking all these lady friends into battle, giggling and swooning, he wasn't any match for Isa Bagdur, who quickly became the first rah. Isa Bagdur's son and rah number two was Akbar Khan, who murdered six or seven people he disrelished and got the British Empire so riled that, in 1913, it deposed him and installed his son, Anwar Khan, the present rah. Akbar Khan, the murderer, continued to grouch around the palace, telling his son he was doing everything wrong, and hinting, among other things, that certain individuals in Punial might wisely be disposed of. He died in 1935.

The present rah has certainly had a happy reign. Besides turning the Gushpurs out, cutting his household to sixty men, cutting his income to sixty tons of wheat, and getting to be called "Chhalo," he abolished the death penalty, and, for most infractions of the Puniali law, he established a few, easy-going fines. For assault and battery, it's $9.46, of which $3.15 goes to the victim, another $3.15 to the Rah, $1.47 to the jury, $1.16 to Mr. Johar Ali, the grand vizier—the spelling there is "wazir"—and 53¢ to Mr. Jamadar Miro, the fine collector. The fine for rape is $21, and $6.30 of it goes to the Rah, $6.30 to the girl's father, $2.10 to the Yashkuns, $2.10 to the Shins, $2.10 to Mr. Ali, $1.47 to the jury, and 63¢, this time, to Mr. Miro; the ravished girl doesn't get a red cent, I'm afraid. It's pretty expensive to run off with somebody else's wife: $63, all of which, but not the wife, goes to the cuckolded husband. (He'd only kill her.) Instead, the lady is sent to mother, and then, if she still cares to, can marry her abductor, though of course there would be some talk. Judg-

PUNIAL

ing all this is the principal duty of the Rah and the Kaka, and often they are woken up in the early hours of morning to do so. There is a jury, but the Rah has the last word: even if the jury says "Not guilty," the Rah can say "He is too." Nowadays, this doesn't happen much.

In his heyday, the Rah was the best polo player in all the countries, political districts, sub agencies, attached agencies, and tribal areas hereabouts, leading the Punialis to victory year after year. One evening, I saw the cups retired by Punial from the annual tournament at Gilgit, and the medals won by the Rah himself: he keeps them in a trophy room, in the palace. Outside is a polo field, and beyond it the farms of Sher Qila rise in golden terraces. Except for the palace itself, which isn't much, really, the polo field is the only thing of any size in Sher Qila—two hundred yards by thirty yards, I estimated, shorter and very much narrower than ones in America. At the midfield stripe it swerves a little; the Rah sits at the elbow there, I was told, commanding a view of both goals at once, and the players themselves don't mind. In Punial, anybody with a horse and a notion to have a go at it plays polo, from the commoners to the kakas, and only by fortuity are the two teams equal. The rules are thoroughly untrammeled: you can hook an opponent's mallet, you can horsewhip his pony, you can catch the ball, and you can be tackled. A significant thing is that polo games, in Punial, are never "scheduled"; they are "declared," like war.

In Punial they only play polo in the winter, so I wasn't able to see a game there, but in Gilgit, when I was back there, polo was declared, and a Puniali horseman stole the show. He was Number Four, a Mr. Mohammed Beg, I learned. His pony was sway-backed, so terribly slow it never really managed to overtake the ball, and Mr. Beg himself was dirty, ragged, and unkemptly bearded, the sorriest polo player I hope to see—a far cry from the others, quite nobby in white breeches, red helmets, and red waistcoats. Some Pakistani soldiers were on the sideline, and, as Mr. Beg went toddling by, they hooted, whistled, and teased him, until Mr. Beg, his color rising, couldn't take it any longer: he galloped by the soldiers swinging his mallet at their heads. What came next came thick and fast. A soldier pulled the mallet from Mr. Beg's hand; Mr. Beg jumped from his horse to retrieve it; another soldier jumped onto the field; and in a twinkling he and Mr. Beg were squared off, choking each other at arm's length. The game went on unabated. Polo balls, polo ponies, and polo players swirled about them as Mr. Beg and the soldier stood in the center of the field, turning purple, and nobody felt, apparently, that these goings-on infringed the rules of Puniali polo. After some minutes, the men were separated, and later, when the game was over, Mr. Beg was called to where I was sitting and given a severe chewing-out by the Rah of Punial. "If you *have* to play polo," said the Rah, testily, "get some breeches. Get a waistcoat. And get it *cleaned,* for heaven's sake. And clip your beard. Let's have no more of this in the future."

Mr. Beg salaamed, and shrank away. In Punial, where polo may have been invented, the king of games is still the game of kings.

"———"

—THE DEWAN OF SIKKIM.

SIKKIM

Sikkim, in the Eastern Himalayas, is a democracy now. Its first election was in 1953, and its first law in 1955, but, in these few years, the alert Sikkimis have learned not only the outward forms of democracy but many of the refinements, subtleties, and secrets that are, to us in the civilized world, almost its very soul—parties, platforms, partisan strife, mudslinging, muckraking, windbags, windfalls, major parties, minor parties, pull, plums, padded payrolls, stuffing, roughing, raucus caucuses, brass spittoons in smoke-filled rooms, bosses, losses, lobbies, gobbledegook, and gerrymandering, among others. True, some of these practices are not very widespread, but then again, neither is Sikkim itself, its area being two thousand seven hundred square miles, a bit more than Delaware's. Only a single case, respectively, of stuffing and roughing has been reported in Sikkim. On Election Day, 1953, a number of voters were roughed up in Psensang, and a ballot box was stuffed in Lhachen, not far away: it was quite inexpertly done, too, because when the ballot box was opened the ballots were in a wad, and it's clear that Sikkim has further to go in this particular art. On the credit side, the two major parties, the Nationalists and the Congress, have already struck the perfect attitude of mutual vilification, and the Sikkimi gerrymander puts even the New York State one to shame: the Nationalists, who only got a fifth as many votes as the Congress, have just as many seats in the legislature. As for lobbies, the most powerful are the landlords and the moneylenders, the moneylenders getting up to three hundred percent as interest and fearing encumbrances by the Sikkimi legislature, with some reason. The landlords, for their part, managed to hold up the Rent Control Bill in 1953, 1954, and most of 1955, but it got on the floor in 1955, and it went through. Sikkim's first law is a model of the democratic idiom. A random sentence is this one: "Where the landlord recovers possession of any premises from the tenant by virtue of a decree obtained under section (5) and the premises are not occupied by him or by the person for whose benefit the premises were acquired within two months of the date of vacation of the premises, or thorough overhauling is not commenced within one month of the date of vacation of the premises by the tenant, the Sikkim Durbar may let out the premises on a standard rent."

The Congress's symbol is a ladder, and the Nationalists' a swastika. Other than this, admittedly superficial at best, I couldn't find any differences between the two. After a few days

SIKKIM

in Sikkim, I got hold of the party platforms, but these, as I should have expected, were no help, for the Nationalists' one promised roads, bridges, hospitals, schools, and a fair rent, and implied that the Congress "stoop low and hurl abusive and vulgar languages," while the Congress, for its part, promised roads, bridges, hospitals, schools, and a fair rent, and saw little good in the Nationalists. Both of the platforms warned me of "the wrong views associated with a wrong candidate," or words to that effect. Having read all this, and being none the wiser, I went to the Sikkimi capitol and buttonholed the Chief Secretary, a sort of prime minister there, who said, "On the whole the parties are identical," but that I shouldn't noise it about. Down the hall, he suggested, I'd find the national chairmen of both, working in their office.

"In their offices?" I said.

"In their office," he said, and while he went back to his papers, I hurried down the hall and saw, indeed, that Mr. Sonam Tsering, of the Nationalists, and Mr. Kashiraj Pradhan, of the Congress, worked in the very same office, side by side. The office was cold, dark, and lackluster, and so, indeed, was Mr. Tsering: his clothes were shapeless and olive drab, and he might have passed for a yak driver in the nearby mountains of Tibet, while Mr. Pradhan, at the other desk, was dressed in chic orange jodhpurs and a white cutaway. All the while, a bunch of ward heelers and party hacks hurried in and out, whispering, of necessity, to Mr. Tsering and Mr. Pradhan, who kept busy, otherwise, by reading the morning mail and writing denunciations of one another; occasionally they stopped to gossip, or to offer the other a cup of tea. Really, this was a *fine* state of affairs, I thought, and yet, I also thought, it wasn't unlike the state of affairs in our country, at least in the State of New York. As a newspaperman, I used to cover the New York Senate, and there, too, I remembered, the Republican leader and the Democratic leader sat side by side, and seemed the very best of friends. Both of them were named Mr. Mahoney. When a critical bill was on the floor, Mr. Mahoney (R) would rant and rave, accusing the Democrats of all but rape and latrocinium, a favorite phrase of his being "Shame, I say unto you, shame!" Then, Mr. Mahoney (D) would stand up, revealing that the Republicans, in turn, were remorseless, treacherous, lecherous, kindless, etc. villains. This done, the Mr. Mahoneys would congratulate and slap each other on the back, saying it would look swell in the late editions. We newspapermen never wrote about these perorational embraces: it wasn't part of the game, and, I suppose, this is the first the voters know of it.

In Sikkim, too, the voters never know of the camaraderie of the Nationalists and the Congress; they are convinced that one is "high and noble . . . invariably," in the words of the party platforms, and the other a pack of thieves. Just which is which, is an easy matter: in Sikkim the Nepalis always vote for the Congress, and the Bhotias always vote for the Nationalists. The Bhotias are Buddhists, Mongolians, and speak a Far Eastern language that looks like this, ཇངས་འཇར་བ་མགོ་མིན་ཇངས་འཇར་བ་མགོ. The Nepalis are Hindus, also Mongolians, but speak an Indo-European language that looks like this, दोलोरेस दालय सीमोन दालय सीमोन. The Nepalis are immigrants, while the Bhotias, to their way of thinking, came over on the Mayflower.

Sikkim's minor parties are certainly an odd lot, but at least I know what they stand for. The Monastery Association stands for the monasteries, and the Scheduled Castes League is plumping for the untouchables; the Prajasameelan, which is the major minor party, and which, in 1953, got almost as many votes as the Nationalists but, because of the gerrymander, has no seats at all in the Sikkimi legislature, wants to unite with India. Right now, Sikkim is independent, with a maharajah the chief of state, but India runs its defenses, communications, and foreign affairs, and, at Sikkim's suggestion, has sent an Indian there as a kind of city manager—Mr. N. K. Rustomji, the Dewan of Sikkim. (Or you may call him the Divan of Sikkim, if that's your idea of fun.) While I was in Sikkim, I had the pleasure of meeting the Dewan, but I never met the Maharajah, an alcoholic who isn't shown to visitors. No head that wears the crown hangs heavier than that of His Highness Sir Tashi Namgyal, Knight Commander of the

SIKKIM

Star of India, Knight Commander of the Indian Empire, Maharajah of Sikkim. About twenty years ago, his wife took a vacation to Lhasa, Tibet, her home town, and there kept company with one of the lamas, a reincarnation of Buddha; she had a baby by him, and the Maharajah banished her to a palace in the suburbs. He hasn't seen her since. (The Maharajahs of Sikkim, like the Princes of Monaco, have seldom got along with the missis, I'm afraid. One of them married a lady so ugly that he fled the throne, the palace, and the country in disguise.) Then in World War II, the Maharajah's eldest son, the crown prince, died in a plane crash, and the Maharajah of Sikkim took to whiskey. Today his only joy is in painting, but he has the shakes, and his work is like Jackson Pollock's. The Sikkimis don't talk of him much.

Sir Tashi Namgyal, the Maharajah, played the part of King George III in Sikkim's democratization. A Mr. Tashi Tsering, no relation, was the George Washington of it, and, between the two, there was sort of a revolution, with five thousand Sikkimis marching on the Maharajah's palace. Someday, I suppose, the Sikkimis will have this as Independence Day, telling their children of Minutemen, Paul Reveres, and Patrick Henrys crying liberty or death, of Father Frommels and *Pfadfinderkorps,* or their Sikkimi counterparts—that for the history books, but for the present, alas! The revolution was in 1949, the memory is fresh, the truth is inglorious. The truth is that Mr. Tashi and his five thousand insurgents went to the palace one fine day, shouting, "Our demands must be met"; the Maharajah came to the window, and "Our demands must be met," they shouted again.

"*What* demands?" said the Maharajah, bewildered by it all.

"*Our* demands," said the people. "They must be met!" The awful fact is that none of them, except Mr. Tashi, had any idea what the demands were, or what the hell they were doing at the Maharajah's palace; it's just that everyone else was there, that's all. Presently, the Maharajah, trying his best to get on solid ground, sent his sons outside to talk with the revolutionaries. "What are your demands?" said the Maharaj Kumars, and were told, in no uncertain terms, "Our demands must be met!" The Maharaj Kumars hurried back to the Maharajah, and shrugged.

Well, things were getting ticklish now, but the Maharajah of Sikkim rose to the occasion. "My loyal people! I promise you," he cried from the window, as well as anybody remembers it, "that your demands *shall* be met! Oh, I promise you!" With a thousand hurrahs, the crowd broke up, and the Maharajah left the window, more certain than ever that the bottle was the only way. Later, though, he was visited by Mr. Tashi, who said the demands were land reform and free elections, and, rather wearily, the Maharajah of Sikkim acquiesced.

Since then, things have been buzzing. Sikkim got a dewan in 1949, its people got to vote in 1953, and a five-year plan got started on April 18, 1955—a day the Dewan said was "eventful" for lovers of freedom everywhere. ("In Bandung, the representatives of the Asio-African countries are, on this same day, commencing their deliberations, so that the forces of peace and order may be strengthened throughout the world. And it is today that His Highness is presenting to his people the Sikkim Development Plan.") The plan envisages a rosy future for Sikkim, with fertilized, chemicalized, non-insectiferous farms in every valley, with forest rangers gazing at acres of woods and fish-full lakes, with power dams on the Tista and Rangenokhu Rivers, and mills, wool presses, canneries, distilleries downstream, with coal, copper, graphite, gypsum rolling from the hillsides, and twice as many roads, and twice as many hospitals, and twice twice twice as many kids in school, taught, too, by teachers who went to school—a land of plenty, of happy people. The job has already begun (a badminton court for the government people). How the Sikkimis will take to this, however, is anybody's guess, for they can't even read the Rent Control Law, the first fruits of their democracy. The Sikkimis, afer all, are a simple folk, farmers and hill people, and it isn't easy to tell them, as the Rent Law does, that "any person contravening, attempting, or abetting the contravention of any of the provisions of this act shall be liable to a fine which may extend to Rs. 5,000/-, in default

SIKKIM

six months rigorous or simple imprisonment." Perhaps, when they hear enough of this gobbledegook, the Sikkimis will again rise up, marching to the Sikkimi legislature and shouting, "Our demands must be met!" (The ancient laws of Sikkim may have been harsh, but at least they were readable. They said the five crimes were matricide, patricide, lama-cide, making mischief among the lamas, and hurting good people, and added, "For the above offenses, punishments are inflicted, such as putting the eyes out, cutting the throat, having the tongue cut out, having the hands cut off, being thrown from a cliff, and being thrown into deep water.") On the other hand, the Sikkimis are rather used to mysticism, and many of their Buddhist rites—their prayer *om mani padme hum*, for instance—mean nothing at all to them. Perhaps, in the end, the Sikkimis will worship the Rent Law, too. Myself, I couldn't even guess.

The right pronunciation of Sikkim is "si*k*kim," as to a dog. It means "the new house." To the west of Sikkim is far-flung Nepal; to the north is Tibet, the Forbidden Land; and to the east is Bhutan, a country so hard to reach that Mr. George J. W. Goodman, who wrote a novel, *The Bubblemakers*, about an expedition there, couldn't get his expedition farther than St. Louis, Missouri. So far, Sikkim, in the middle of all this, apparently is the world's end, but south of it is India: and I, continuing east from Punial, was in a Pan American airplane one day, in Sikkim the next. From Darjeeling, India, to Gangtok, Sikkim, I went in a taxi, a wild and awe-inspiring ride. The taxi was always in the clouds; as it jigged across the Himalayas, fog and drizzle swirled about it, but I got a glimpse of the wet, green hillsides, terrace on terrace, of monkeys on the devious roadway, of Himalayan condors with ten-foot wings, and, occasionally, of that terrible white mountain of Kanchenjunga, the highest in Sikkim, the world's third. At a river, the taxi crossed the border, and then it clambered up to Gangtok, the country's capital, and to the Maharajah's red-and-gold palace on a skyline ridge. From there, I looked down, right and left, as from an airplane, at hundreds of green square miles of Sikkim—patches in the sunlight, patches in the rain.

The road I had gone on, a bridge at Hong Kong, and Panmunjom, Korea, are the only holes in Communist China's curtain. The road will be the one used if the Communists invade India; now it is trodden, and peaceably, by the tall, particolored Tibetans and their jingling mule trains, going south with yak wool—to be made into blankets, Santa Claus beards, and automobile floormats—and north again with Western things. In Sikkim, the Tibetans stop at caravansaries, where, at night, they sing of love and dance with their lady friends, gamble, and drink of such Tibetan delicacies as hot *socha* and *chang*—the socha being a popular non-alcoholic beverage of tea, salt, yak butter, and borax, and the chang a kind of fermented barley; the Japanese would call it *sake*. (As for socha, I think the Japanese would call it *socha*: it's their word for "bad tea.") Every Tibetan has fifty cups of socha a day, and he's sure to agree that it hits the spot. Otherwise, he is like a tourist anywhere, for he generally sells the yak wool and buys a Leica, and he roams the colorful parts of Gangtok taking shots of the natives—in Modern Tibetan there are words for "camera," "develop," and "print." Many things have changed in the Forbidden Land, in this twentieth century. Now a Tibetan who takes the desolate, age-old trail to Gangtok, Sikkim, needs a passport, and those who forget them, or think they're a kind of newfangled throw-away, are heavily fined; and now at the Sikkimi-Tibetan frontier, at fourteen thousand feet in the Himalayas, a customs agent, a photographer, and a fingerprint man shiver, blow on their knuckles, and wait.

The Maharajah of Sikkim is a Tibetan, but the common folk, as I've said, are Bhotias and Nepalis, and, as I've also said, there is some friction between the two. The Bhotias think of the Nepalis as being just off the banana boat; they hint darkly that the Nepalis are un-Sikkimi. Oh yeah? so are the Bhotias, say the Nepalis, inasmuch as *everybody* is un-Sikkimi except for the Lepchas, just as everybody is un-American except for the Indians.

SIKKIM

The comparison is well taken, I think, for the Lepchas are the Vanishing Sikkimis. A hundred years ago, the country was all theirs; a dozen years ago twenty-five thousand were left; and now there are fifteen thousand; and as for the future, the Sikkim Development Plan tosses them off by saying, "Their leisure hours could be usefully employed in making rugs, tweeds, and blankets." Like the Navahos.

Why the Lepchas aren't able to propagate themselves is something of a mystery, for they're certainly trying hard—this, at any rate, being the finding of a British anthropologist, Mr. John Morris, who went to Sikkim in 1937 and says the Lepchas are obsessed with sex. (The Lepchas say that Morris is obsessed with sex.) What's the matter, apparently, says Mr. Morris, is that the Lepchas get obsessed a little too early in life, and are all tuckered out when it's time for children. Among the Lepchas, he reports, a girl is used to losing her virtue at ten, an older man seducing her, and after that she may sleep—nay, she *must* sleep—with her older sisters' husbands' younger brothers, her older sisters' husbands' older brothers' sons, and, after she is married, her husband's or husbands' (the Lepchas are polyandrous) younger brothers and his or their older brothers' sons, which, in the close-knit communities of Sikkim, is half the people in town. On a journey, she may sleep with anyone at all—just the opposite, of course, of the custom in our country; the Lepchas are hard put to understand the Mann Act. By the time a Lepcha is married, she has known, and rather intimately, the lion's share of the wedding party, so there is a note of jollity at these affairs that is usually lacking in American ones. The bridegroom joins in the general mirth. "Now," he is told, as the bride is given away, "here is a little egg for you."

"Isn't this egg a bit stale?" he replies—not at all chivalrously, we would think.

"Well," one of the guests puts in, barely containing his merriment, "the fact is that I've carefully shelled the egg, so it'll be easier to eat."

When the guffaws die down, the groom retorts, if he's being

on his toes, "Quite so. But, it is clear the egg hasn't been freshly shelled." By now, everyone at the wedding is in stitches, and tears are rolling down their cheeks—except, of course, for the egg herself, who is hiding her head coyly, thinking, perhaps, of the tender nights in store with her brothers-in-law and nephews. There isn't any divorce among the Lepchas. As Mr. Morris says, it just wouldn't serve any purpose.

In Lepcha Land, the religion is Buddhism, but many other things are mixed in, including a dash of Christianity. The Lepchas are said to believe in the Flood, it raining for fifteen days (in the Himalayas a rainy day is like two or three of them anywhere else) and a Lepcha and his wife escaping, in an ark; there is also a Babel legend. Among the beliefs that are neither Buddhist nor Christian, fish nor fowl, are the satanic Mungs, the seraphic Rums, and the human Muns, who, by putting an egg to their foreheads, see the future, and one belief that *is* fish, fowl, and everything else under the sun is Go-sum, a salmagundic idol. A Go-sum is made of dough, but its navel is a turtle, its tail is a snake, and its sides are feathered with chicken feathers; there is butter in its hands, butter on its head, and a feed bag at its mouth, and round about are cups, cones, lamps, snakes, sausages, men, women, Mungs, Rums, and other gods, all of them made of dough, as well as raw meat, red sticks, bamboo slivers, tufts of wool, and wooden labels. All of this is sprinkled with blood, and then it's thrown to the dogs, who eat it, supposedly curing the sick. For childbirth, the Lepchas put an abracadabra on a piece of paper, roll it into a pill, coat it with butter, and give it to the expectant mother to swallow. In Nepal, the people use railway tickets for this, but the Industrial Revolution has yet to come to Sikkim.

Buddhism itself, as it's practiced by the Lepchas, Bhotias, Tibetans, and the Maharajah of Sikkim, is a religion of mysticism and mumbo-jumbo, the barest hint of whose profundity is seen in its idea of the universe—seven concentric whorls of golden hills intersticed by seven concentric oceans and environed by an iron wall that is 312.5 miles high and 3,602,625 miles long. At

SIKKIM

the heart of this religion, in day-to-day practice, are those enigmatic words *om mani padme hum,* which the Sikkimis murmur as they walk, as they work, as they tell the one hundred and eight beads of their rosaries; *om mani padme hum* is written on prayer wheels and flies to heaven, it is said, with every clockwise spin. In Sikkim, the prayer wheels abound, and lamas and laymen never miss a chance to spin them. While I was there, I shared a bungalow with such a lama, a certain Bhikshu Sangharakshita, of Kalimpong, India, who also was on a visit, and also knew English, and one afternoon I asked him to explain, if he would, just what *om mani padme hum* is all about. The lama was sitting at the foot of his bed, cross-legged, dark, and hollow-eyed, his yellow robes glimmering in a shaft of light; he began by saying that certain experiments, now being carried on in India and the United States, indicate the words *om mani padme hum* are vibrating 250,000 times per second—and that is where he lost me. The lama went on, however, to say that the universe, too, is vibrating, and that a person who says *"om mani padme hum"* again and again will, presently, vibrate in time with the universe. I listened to this patiently, and then I told the lama he was getting ahead of me, and would he simply translate the words? Of course, he said; *"mani"* means "the jewel," and *"padme"* is "in the lotus," and *"om"* and *"hum,"* which the dictionaries give as "oh" and "amen," really mean nothing at all, but are there because they vibrate. The jewel in the lotus, he said, is Buddha in the universe; or you can look at the universe as wisdom (jewel) and compassion (lotus), or, from another point of view, the absolute world is a jewel, and the relative world a lotus. That the jewel is *in* the lotus means the absolute world is a potentiality in the relative world, or that being a Buddha, an "enlightened one," is a potentiality in you and me. It really means a lot of things, the lama said, like the Chinese yin and yang. *Om mani padme hum* is a prayer popular with the laity—in fact, the only one it uses—but the lamas know quite a few others, including *om arapatsanadhi* and *om tare tutare mama ayur punyedsanyana pusphpita kuru swaha.* A

Sikkimi, in his lifetime, may say the *om* a hundred million times—yet never know what it means, for the words are in Sanskrit, a language as dead as Latin. This didn't seem to bother my friend the lama. It's the vibrations that count, he said.

In Sikkim, the Buddhist religion was unheard of until the seventeenth century, when it was brought there from Tibet, and by a Tibetan lama, Lha-tsun Ch'em-bo. "Lha-tsun Ch'em-bo" is really a title meaning the Great Reverend God; his given name was Kun-zan Num-gye, which means the Entirely Victorious Essence of Goodness, but then, too, he is properly called Lha-tsun Num Kha Jig-may, which means the Reverend God Who Fears Not the Sky, because he can fly; He-ru-ka-pa, which means the Naked One; Kusho Dsog-ch'en Ch'em-bo, which means the Great and Honorable Dsog-ch'en, which, in turn— enough of this. The important thing is that his name was mud in Tibet. In 1648, Lha-tsun showed up in Lhasa, demanded to see the Dalai Lama, and, having been ushered to the audience room of that divinity, proceeded to punch him in the nose and vomit on the floor. Lha-tsun insisted it was sort of a magic charm, but the rest of the court was rather upset, and I can't believe it was taken in. Anyhow, we find Lha-tsun in Sikkim soon afterwards. There, he preached a kind of Tibetan Buddhism—red-cap, as distinguished from yellow-cap—converted the Lepchas, founded a lamasery, and, last but certainly not least, founded Sikkim, for he gave the Lepchas a maharajah, their first. This person, too, was a Tibetan, Namgyal, and all the ensuing maharajahs, including Sir Tashi Namgyal, are his descendants, and all of them have married Tibetans to keep the blood pure.

Sikkim was my last stop. Then, having circumnavigated the least of all possible worlds, having traveled on thirty-five planes, twenty-three boats, fourteen trains, fifty-seven buses and "buses," automobiles, jeeps, tractors, paddle-wheelers, dhows, mules, horses, pedicabs, tongas, and the London tube, having spent two years in doing so, having still not seen the London

SIKKIM

Bridge, the Eiffel Tower, the Pyramids, or the Black Hole of Calcutta, but having seen such generally unappreciated tourist attractions as the King of Lundy, the Seneschal of Sark, the President of Andorra, the Prince of Monaco—well, almost—the Princess of Liechtenstein, *the* Princess of Liechtenstein, the Captains Regent of San Marino, the Chancellor of the Sovereign and Military Order of Saint John of Jerusalem, Rhodes, and Malta, the Protoepistatis of Athos, the Sheik of Sharja, the Wali of Swat, the Nawab of Amb and the Nawab Zada, the Rah of Punial and the Kaka, and the Dewan of Sikkim, and having talked to them, and their subjects, in English, Norman Patois, Spanish, Catalan, French, German, Italian, Greek, Russian, Bulgarian, Serbian, Latin, Arabic, Punjabi, Pushtu, Tanawali, Urdu, Shina, Burushaski, Bengali, Nepali, Bhotia, Sanskrit, and Lepcha, having had a wonderful time but, I'm afraid, having learned nothing of any importance, I went home. I don't know, really, what it's supposed to prove, but maybe there's something or other to be learned from my last evening in Gangtok, when Mr. Rustomji, the Dewan of Sikkim, asked me over for dinner. That was on June 1, when the monsoon was supposed to begin—and it did, with a vengeance. In a single hour, an unbelievable deal of rain lurched out of the sky, splashing into the bungalow where the lama and I were putting up, soaking the beds and floorboards. Outside, the Sikkimis put their umbrellas up, hurrying home. To me, there was something odd about an umbrella in the Himalayas: I'd rather expected the natives to use coveralls of yak wool, or nothing at all, perhaps, but the fact is that, in the monsoon season, they always go with umbrellas hanging over their arms, or from their collars in back of their necks. In a way, it is like Arabs who wear sunglasses, which many of them do.

Anyhow, I waited till the rain let up, and then I walked to the Dewan's home, up on the skyline ridge. There, I was received pretty much as Alice in Wonderland was, by the Mad Hatter. No one answered the door, and, after knocking and hallooing for a minute or so, opening it, and going inside, I

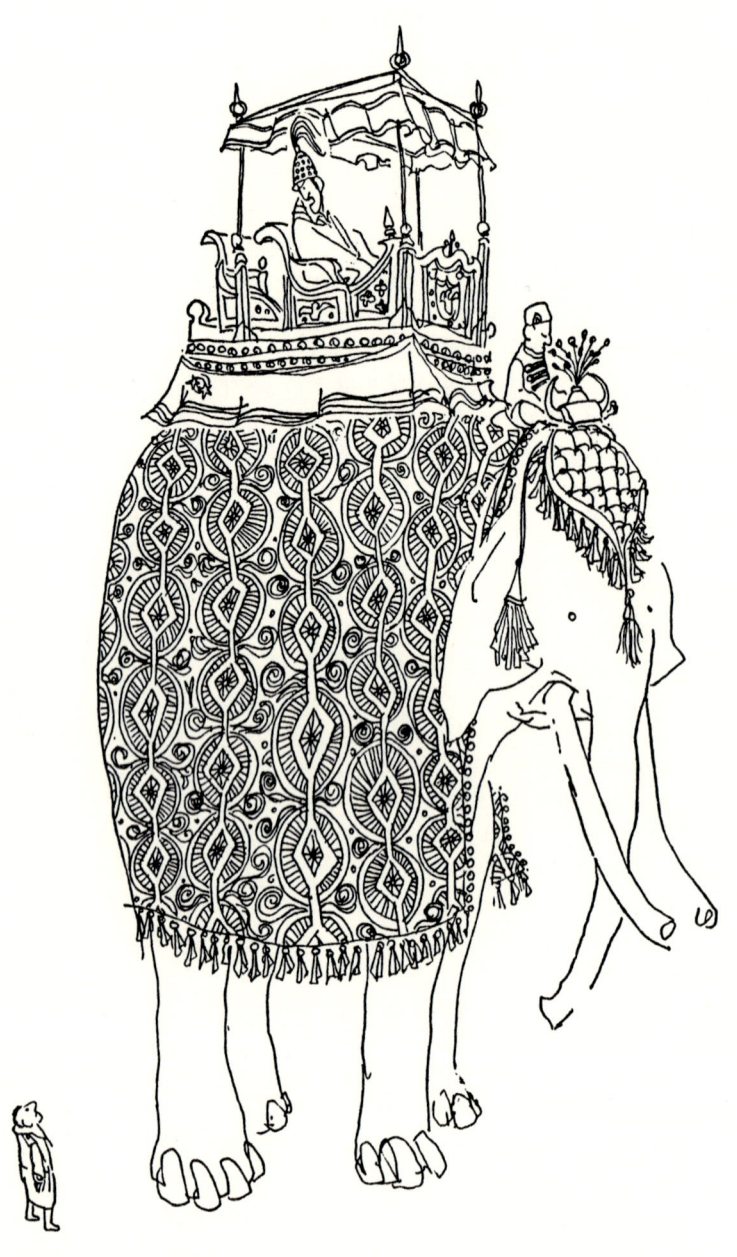

"*What if somebody called you the Gurgle of Sikkim?*"

SIKKIM

found the Dewan of Sikkim at tea, playing bridge with his mother, his sister, and a fourth party, a Sikkimi, and none of them saying a word to me. For a while, I sort of footled about, feeling like the man in Philadelphia who doesn't read the *Bulletin* but realizing, of course, that the Dewan of Sikkim didn't mean to be rude; it's just that bridge is bridge, even in Sikkim. After the hand had been played, and argued out, the Dewan said hello, introduced his family, and, pointing to the fourth, his partner, said, "You know the Maharaj Kumar, don't you?" I answered that I didn't, and the Maharaj Kumar and I shook hands. The Maharajah's younger son is tall, dark, and handsome, with hair like Senator Kennedy's; he wore a blue turtleneck sweater and a blue sport shirt hanging out, American-style, over corduroy pants; his English was perfect. He said he was graduated from Oxford in 1954.

After a few more bridge hands, and a few more arguments, the five of us adjourned to the living room, and we sipped brandy while the Dewan of Sikkim, an avid collector of things, showed us what he had picked up in Sikkim. Presently, he began to talk of Sikkim's history. In the distant past, he said, the maharajah wasn't called a maharajah but a *gurgle*, or pope, and, he added with tongue in cheek, "I was thinking of bringing the title back."

The Maharaj Kumar, who was sipping a brandy, just about gagged on it. "*What?*" he cried, a look of horror on his face.

"Sir Tashi Namgyal, the Gurgle of Sikkim," said the Dewan, trying the words on his tongue. He was enjoying himself hugely, although, to my way of thinking, the Dewan, or Divan, was hardly one to talk.

Desperately the Maharaj Kumar turned to me, and said, "What if somebody called *you* the Gurgle of Sikkim?"

"Frankly," I said, "I'd ask him to step outside."

"Precisely." The Maharaj Kumar glared at the Dewan, and then he saw it was all in fun. "Anyhow, *I* won't be a gurgle. It'll be my brother," he said.

"The *other* Maharaj Kumar," said the Dewan's mother.

The Maharajah's son looked at me impishly. Then he said, "My brother's a reincarnation, you know." He seemed to find this very amusing, which maybe it is.

"Oh?" I said. "Whom of?"

"Heaven knows. Of his late uncle, I suppose."

Here we were interrupted by the Dewan, who had been chuckling to himself up to now and muttering gurgle, gurgle. "*This* Maharaj Kumar is the Sikkim Development Commissioner," he said.

"Is that a political plum," I asked, "or are you really busy developing and commissioning?"

The Maharaj Kumar made as if he were shocked. "Oh, dear, if it weren't for my guiding hand," he said, "the country would fall apart."

"Yes," said the Dewan, smirking. "He works very, very hard."

"Work, work, work," sighed the Maharaj Kumar.

"He wakes," said the Dewan, "every morning at four o'clock, and, after the usual devotions, he falls diligently to." Then, the Dewan of Sikkim and the Maharaj Kumar laughed and laughed, until their laughter filled the room—two politicians, it seemed to me, playing their little game and having their little joke, but when you get down to it, after all, doing a dozen times more for the Sikkimis than a dozen dozen years of maharajahs.

AUTHORS GUILD BACKINPRINT.COM EDITIONS are fiction and nonfiction works that were originally brought to the reading public by established United States publishers but have fallen out of print. The economics of traditional publishing methods force tens of thousands of works out of print each year, eventually claiming many, if not most, award-winning and one-time best-selling titles. With improvements in print-on-demand technology, authors and their estates, in cooperation with the Authors Guild, are making some of these works available again to readers in quality paperback editions. Authors Guild Backinprint.com Editions may be found at nearly all online bookstores and are also available from traditional booksellers. For further information or to purchase any Backinprint.com title please visit www.backinprint.com.

Except as noted on their copyright pages, Authors Guild Backinprint.com Editions are presented in their original form. Some authors have chosen to revise or update their works with new information. The Authors Guild is not the editor or publisher of these works and is not responsible for any of the content of these editions.

THE AUTHORS GUILD is the nation's largest society of published book authors. Since 1912 it has been the leading writers' advocate for fair compensation, effective copyright protection, and free expression. Further information is available at www.authorsguild.org.

Please direct inquiries about the Authors Guild and Backinprint.com Editions to the Authors Guild offices in New York City, or e-mail staff@backinprint.com.